GRAVE UNDERTAKINGS

GRAVE UNDERTAKINGS

AN ARCHAEOLOGY OF
ROGER WILLIAMS AND THE
NARRAGANSETT INDIANS

Patricia E. Rubertone

Smithsonian Institution Press
Washington and London

EDITOR: Joanne Reams
PRODUCTION EDITOR: Ruth W. Spiegel
DESIGNER: Amber Frid-Jimenez

Library of Congress Cataloging-in-Publication Data

Rubertone, Patricia E.
    Grave undertakings: an archaeology of Roger Williams and
    the Narragansett Indians / Patricia E. Rubertone.
        p.   cm.
    Includes bibliographical references and index.
    ISBN 1-56098-975-0 (alk. paper)
        1. Narragansett Indians.   2. Williams, Roger, 1604?–1683.
    Key into the language of America.   I. Title.
    E99.N16 R83 2001
    974'.00497—dc21   00-045016

British Library Cataloguing-in-Publication Data available

Manufactured in the United States of America
07 06 05 04 03 02 01   5 4 3 2 1

    ⊗   The recycled paper used in this publication meets the
minimum requirements of the American National Standard for
Information Sciences—Permanence of Paper for Printed Library
Materials ANSI Z39.48-1984.

To my parents Pat and Virginia Rubertone

CONTENTS

ACKNOWLEDGMENTS

The book I have written is not the one I started, nor is it the one I could have written when I first became involved in what developed into a long-term project to excavate, conserve, and interpret the material record of a seventeenth-century Narragansett Indian burial ground. The invitation, stemming partly from the need for an institutional base for the research, provided me with an unexpected opportunity to pursue my interest in studying culture contact and colonialism in southern New England. The years that have accumulated since have been transforming. I have come to envision and practice archaeology differently than I had been taught and have learned many lessons.

I would like to thank, first of all, Ella Wilcox Sekatau, John Brown, and the Narragansett Indian Tribe for allowing me to examine and make sense of this record of their history and to share their experiences. Although I readily and willfully accepted the responsibility, I only later realized the full weight of my decision. For the conversations as I struggled to portray a far more complicated world both during and after the seventeenth century, I am profoundly grateful to Ella Sekatau, the ethnohistorian of the Narragansett Tribe. I also want to express my gratitude to Paul Robinson, with whom I shared this awesome task and who encouraged me to push ahead with my research.

In addition, there are those who offered different kinds of help at various stages in the research. Early on, the field team and the project consultants contributed their efforts and specialties. Later, when I became a regular, if not almost permanent, fixture at the Rhode Island Historical Society, members of the staff graciously guided me in my seemingly unending search. The librarians and curators at the British Museum, the Connecticut Historical Society, the John Carter Brown Library, the John Hay Library, and the Museum of Art, Rhode Island School of Design, as well provided expert assistance. For their suggestions, written comments, and technical and all sorts of indispensable advice, I thank Norman Fiering, Robert Goodby, Jeffrey Hantman, Ruth Herndon, Barry O'Connell, Daniel Odess, Robert Paynter, Ann Marie Plane, Neal Salisbury, Charlotte Taylor, Katharine Woodhouse-Beyer, and Desiree Zymroz. Throughout the research and writing, Russell Handsman offered close and perceptive readings, helping me think out ideas and sharing his own on related topics. For the intellectual challenges, unfailing support, and friendship, I owe him an enormous debt.

Brown University (including the Faculty Development Fund) and the Rhode Island Historical Preservation and Heritage Commission provided financial support without which the project would not have been feasible. The editors at the Smithsonian Institution Press have made the publishing end of the project a most pleasurable experience. I particularly want to thank Scott Mahler for his boundless enthusiasm, steadfast commitment, and good humor in seeing the final manuscript through from start to finish; and Joanne Reams for her sensitive copyediting.

Last but certainly not least, I thank my parents, Pat and Virginia Rubertone, to whom I owe everything and all that really matters. And to other members of my immediate and extended families, especially Aunt Marge, Uncle Vin, Kathi and Danny, Faila, and of course Brigs, and always Aunt Connie, you have my love for being there for me.

INTRODUCTION

"Key" is a synonym for dictionary . . . in this instance *key* is

a metaphorical term indicating the way in which the work

will use vocabulary as a means to a non-linguistic end.[1]

This book is about translation, not in a linguistic sense but in a cultural one, at the start of the new millennium. More specifically, it is about the difficulties of how to write about the lives of Native peoples who endured the history and consequences of colonialism. Writing about these peoples' lives, at least in a way that communicates the complexities, complications, and ambivalences, may be almost as challenging as having lived through the colonial experience and, often enough, continuing to survive within it. This statement is not in any way meant to diminish the harsh and very painful realities of colonial domination. Instead, it suggests that writing about this global enterprise is fraught with difficulties. The words used to explore colonialism must try to make clear its scope, intensity, and pervasiveness, as well as its successes; they must document its brutalities, displacements, and alienation; and they must call attention to accommodations and resistances and, in so doing, question claims about the enterprise's inevitable outcome.

As with any study of past lives, translation poses the dilemma of trying to reconstruct lived events with sources that are incomplete and filled with uncertainties. Written sources, even the most thorough and introspective, may be problematic. Often accounts of colonial encounters are intended to entice. Their messages about wealth, resources, and victories are meant to promote investment and recruit more colonizers and thus sustain the colonial enterprise. Other narrations may be penned in attempts to ascribe meaning. Instabilities, deceptions, and struggles in the colonial arena frequently generate indifference, doubt, and even a loss of confidence that demand words to justify the chaos or violence and make sense of them, words to make more acceptable a reality that may be difficult to comprehend and may even seem surreal. Once colonialism becomes entrenched, the words written about it may often take on new meanings. They become part of a legacy. Translated by later historians, they may be filtered and diluted, but nonetheless they are etched into the collective memory of subsequent generations. These are the stories of the way things were and, more significantly, of the way they are thought to happen. In sum, they are tales of inevitability, used to repeat and perpetuate colonialism's continuing contests over land, resources, and political allegiance.

Written accounts of colonialism such as these have been inscribed mostly by the colonists, rather than the colonized, who for the most part did not write and read. Sometimes these authors transcribed and even invented the voices of Native peoples, rendering their statements in halting, ambiguous, and often muffled tones. The colonists typically confirmed their particular views through these Native voices; few made any serious effort to detect in Native peoples' comments, asides, and omissions their different experiences and conflicts with colonialism. Although no amount of deconstruction or empathy can change the words that have been written about or attributed to Native peoples, a central claim of this book is that these texts are an essential part of the history of colonialism, and certainly one of its consequences. They cannot be ignored in an attempt to understand Native peoples' colonial experiences differently. Instead, these interpretations, occasionally spattered with Native peoples' own remarks, provide glimpses of their perseverance, as well as historical contingencies, invaluable to unraveling more complicated stories.

Some argue that archaeological evidence, as the material record of everyday life, can compensate for the gap created by indigenous nonliteracy, or what might be called a literal disadvantage, given the colonists' definition of writing.[2] Viewed through an anthropological lens, the archaeological record's things—broken and whole, "native" and "colonial"—reveal structures of daily routines that may provide access to otherwise unattainable information about Native peoples' lives in the colonial past.[3] Archaeology, then, presents an opportunity to hear Native sides of the story through material inscriptions that partially recall human actions, conflicts, and emotions that should be neither denied nor overlooked.

As with written sources, archaeological evidence presents problems of translation because of its partialities, intricacies, and ambiguities. Native artifact assemblages filled with, or dominated by, "colonial" goods can be and often have been interpreted as the entrapments of acculturation and assimilation. That they speak to contacts or sustained interactions between colonists and Native peoples may be indisputable; however, inferences about them as material signatures of asymmetries in cultural acquiescence and conversion cannot be assumed automatically. Instead, they must be tempered against what is known and, even more important, about what might have been possible. Thus, although the misinterpretations and past injustices advanced by those who wrote about Native peoples may be incontrovertible, their monopoly on meaning is not irreversible.

In addition to written texts and archaeology, memory is very much part of how the past is understood. But some insist that, like material remains, memory does not have the authority generally attributed to text. Unlike "faithfully recorded" (i.e., written) accounts, collective memory is thought to represent reconstructed or invented pasts intended to create illusions of social consensus. The inference is that text merits our trust, whereas memory does not. However, the distinction between written texts and collective memory may be invalid; recent anthropological and historical scholarship has suggested that the difference may not be in what is recalled, but how it is remembered. The recognition of this possibility has enormous implications for practice, in that it draws attention to "nontraditional" sources of evidence, notably a range of performative activities that ordinarily are not considered in scholarly studies of the past.

Memory, therefore, is something to be taken seriously. It is as complex and partial as textual and archaeological sources and as frequently riddled with paradoxes and contradictions. Within pluralistic colonial societies, memories (and also, ways of remembering) are not all the same; community memories may be entirely different from collective ones. Whether told in stories, songs, myths, or legends, or "forgotten," kept silent, or expressed in commemorative acts, these ways of remembering the past represent significant reservoirs of knowledge. How this knowledge is regulated or contained is crucial to comprehending Native peoples' colonial histories. What may propel them to speak openly or to be reticent about the past cannot be explained simply. Likely there are many reasons and complicating circumstances, including the probability that some things are not speakable. Thus, when cast in Native perspectives and sensibilities, memory recalls colonial experiences in ways that are distinct from other understandings but may be no less real or partial.[4]

In summary, each strand of evidence—text, archaeological sources, and memory—lends to the process of translating the lives of Native peoples. Each in a different way recalls a part of the story of their colonial experiences and offers a pathway to understanding. How these strands of knowledge may overlap and intersect with each other is rarely straightforward and always more complicated than supposed. Methodologies that recommend combining, toggling, or opposing do not exhaust the possibilities. Sometimes more than one creative approach is needed, because the ways that the different types of recall articulate with, diverge from, and trace over each other may be illuminating. Cultural translation, then, is a grave undertaking, and one that is especially challenging when the historical experiences being studied are part of an ongoing story of colonial relations.

The particular translation attempted here is of Narragansett Indians in seventeenth-century New England. Like that of other Native peoples along the eastern seaboard, their story has been told many times over. It tells of greatness, defeat, and eventual disappearance. In comparison with the Pequots, Mohegans, Wampanoags, Abenakis, and other Native groups in New England, the Narragansetts have been profiled as once the most populous, powerful, and industrious. Their fall from prominence came in December 1675 at their sheltered settlement at Great Swamp, near present-day South Kingstown, Rhode Island, in a battle with—or more accurately, a brutal attack by—English soldiers in the early days of King Philip's War. Subsequent histories depict them as a broken, defeated people who never quite recovered from the devastating insults of seventeenth-century colonialism. Portrayals of their lives after that time are always told in terms of contrasts. Later Narragansetts simply were not like their predecessors as described by Roger Williams in his 1643 book, *A Key Into the Language of America*. Although Williams was not the first European to write about them, his account is considered definitive. His *Key* became the standard by which subsequent generations of European Americans would come to know the Narragansetts.

An inquisitive man with a passion for languages, Williams recorded and attempted to make sense of what the Narragansetts said and did. Although he furnished English translations for their Algonkian words and phrases, *A Key* has been more widely used for its incidental information about the Narragansett people than for its linguistic contents. These insights have created an indelible impression of them, which time has not faded. Like the ink that flowed from Williams's quill, his words have bled through each line of text in the pages written about them by later authors. No amount of overwriting can obscure how he represented their lives, nor should it, because what he wrote about them is a crucial element of colonial history.

Nevertheless, his observations may be misleading. His firsthand involvement with the Narragansetts gave him opportunities to learn about their lives and how they might see things. Yet he did not notice, let alone fully comprehend, much of what influenced and sustained their way of life. These details would have been less visible to him, in part because they occurred largely outside of the settings where he engaged them. His social viewscape was limited to those with whom he interacted. These were in a sense public characters, almost entirely men, some (though certainly not all) self-appointed in their role to pronounce on particular topics, often solely by virtue of their availability or articulateness. They were the ones who provided Williams with partial entrée into Native communities. Their introductions and relationships defined his circle of contacts with other individuals like themselves, but rarely those of different genders, age groups, and more distant lines of descent.

If, as historians say, Williams's words decisively interpreted the Narragansetts even in later centuries, some recent archaeological scholarship has further extended their meaning. By applying them to the interpretation of the precolonial past, archaeologists' reliance on *A Key* has made the work foundational for deep and recent prehistory. By pushing the frontiers of meaning beyond Williams's ability to comprehend the Narragansetts in the first half of the seventeenth century, *A Key*'s monopoly on cultural translation has gained additional endorsement. Attributed with timelessness, Williams's dictums indicated how life was and had long been organized and thus defined the contexts of appropriate and meaningful interpretation for earlier generations of Narragansetts and other New England Native peoples.

If European Americans were and are convinced of Roger Williams's skill as cultural translator, then there are questions that need to be asked: What would seventeenth-century Narragansetts have thought of *A Key*, if they had read it? Would they have ever acknowledged that Williams, who "hath books and writings," knew more about them than they did about themselves?[5] What would they have thought about how he framed their words, phrases, and conversations? And especially, would they agree about what he said really mattered in their lives?

The questions raised concerning cultural translation and, more particularly, the canonical status of Roger Williams's *A Key* are not simply intellectual ones of special interest to scholars in the fields of history, archaeology, and anthropology who continue to write about seventeenth-century New England. These issues are not merely about people who died long ago or about things disconnected from the present. Rather, they are about past–present relations. More to the point, they concern the Narragansetts today, who, like many other New England Native peoples once declared extinct, continue to make their way into the twenty-first century. Underlying these concerns is the recognition that the past plays an active role in their lives and in their ongoing struggles over how their real story of survival, both then and now, has been told.

This book reopens a difficult chapter in their history. It does this by telling the stories of women, men, children, and elders buried on ancestral ground three or four decades after Roger Williams compiled *A Key*. The burial ground, partially exposed by accident in 1982, was for many reasons not just another Native American cemetery in southern New England. Many others have been unearthed either unintentionally or deliberately after their interments were made; some have been seriously studied.[6] What makes this one, known as RI-1000, different is how it is situated in colonial and Narragansett history.

During the time this burial ground was being used, Narragansett country, or at least the part Williams described, looked different from the way it had in the late 1630s and early 1640s. Although the houses, the planting fields, and the paths remained, and most people lived the same way as the generation he represented in *A Key*, much had also changed. Many Narragansetts had become more accustomed to English things. Some worked as laborers on nearby English farms; others continued to plant and harvest corn, though much less than Williams's descriptions suggested roughly thirty years before. Chronic illnesses and anxieties about persistent and mounting threats to their way of life prevailed, replacing their earlier fears of European disease. The graves at RI-1000, then, offered an unexpected but critically important strand of evidence for understanding the changes that were occurring by the late seventeenth century. Here was evidence of how they conducted their lives at a time when they had in many ways become much like their new English neighbors; when ancestral lands, not wampum and furs, had been exchanged by some of their sachems in deals made with the English for instant gratification and unfulfilled promises; and when other Indians prayed to the Christian god.

Shortly before the Narragansetts received federal recognition as an Indian tribe in April 1983, they consented to the excavation and study of the burial ground. Why did they agree? Did they think that an archaeological investigation would provide proof of an enduring presence in a former homeland and knowledge of traditions, and thus, cultural persistence when many non-Natives continued to question their identity? Could archaeology have offered the possibility of invoking memories and illuminating lives that would reveal more complicated and powerful stories than the ones ordinarily written about them? Would the archaeological record help others understand what it meant to live life as a Narragansett Indian in the late seventeenth century and since then as well?

The chapters to follow are organized into three parts. Those in Part 1, "From *Key* to Canon," trace Williams's life, how it was interpreted in written history and popular memory, and the connection between his reinvention as an iconic historical figure and *A Key*'s status as an authoritative text on Narragansett Indians. Part 2, "Rethinking *A Key*," begins by examining how the historical and particular contexts of Williams's interactions with Native peoples shaped what he saw, heard, and eventually wrote about them and ends by presenting a close reading of *A Key* itself to identify its partialities. The chapters in Part 3, "Beyond *A Key*," offer an interpretation of Narragansett peoples' lives through archaeology. The analysis contrasts the different experiences of individuals buried at RI-1000 and explores how they were remembered by later generations of Narragansetts, notably through commemorative acts that, when combined with textual accounts and community memory, tell a great deal about their struggles and perseverance since Roger Williams wrote *A Key*. The book concludes with an epilogue.

Because this study is about cultural translation, as a complex and historically contingent process and, more particularly, about Roger Williams's translations of Narragansett Indians in the seventeenth century, the text reproduces the original spelling, italicization, capitalization, and punctuation of words, passages, and dialogues from *A Key Into the Language of America*. Other statements by colonists and Natives, whether first written or spoken, are rendered as they appear in original sources with respect to the same conventions.

A BRIEF CHRONOLOGY OF ROGER WILLIAMS AND THE NARRAGANSETT INDIANS

	Roger Williams	The Narragansetts
1631	Arrives at Massachusetts	
1632	Writes against royal charters	
1634		Smallpox epidemic
1635	Banished from Massachusetts Bay	
1636	Settles at Providence	
1637		Ally with English against Pequots
1638	Acquires Prudence Island	Agree to terms of Hartford Treaty
1639	Establishes trading post	
1642		Miantonomi pleads for Indian unity
1643	A Key published in London	Miantonomi assassinated
1644	Obtains charter for Providence	
1647		Canonicus dies
1651	Sells trading post	
1654	Receives official approval not to coerce Narragansett conversions	Threaten war over grave robbing

	Roger Williams	*The Narragansetts*
1675		Great Swamp settlement attacked in King Philip's War
1676	House burned in King Philip's War	Matantuck killed
1677	Sells Indian captives into involuntary servitude	
1683	Dies at Providence	
1702	Dismissed as heretic	
1709		Reservation established by Rhode Island
1739	Praised for religious tolerance	
1740s		Some conversions to Christianity
1775		Some migrations to Brothertown, New York
1777	Lauded for ideas on civil liberty	
1779		Last hereditary sachem dies
1792		Tribal constitution approved by Rhode Island
1827	*A Key* reissued	
1832		King report suggests abolishment
1834	First full biography published	
1835	Authority of *A Key* established	
1840s		Some migrations to Brothertown, Wisconsin
1850s		Rhode Island considers detribalization
1859		File charges for a grave robbing in Charlestown
1860	Grave exhumed	
1866	*A Key* reissued	
1870	Statue placed in U.S. Capitol	
1877	First monument unveiled in Rhode Island	
1878		Rhode Island purchases "Indian Burial Hill"
1880		Rhode Island votes to detribalize

	Roger Williams	*The Narragansetts*
1883		Canonicus Memorial dedicated
1893	Proclaimed a martyr	
1910	Nominated to Hall of Fame	
1920	Elected to Hall of Fame	
1923		Join Indian Council of New England
1932	Remains moved and placed in vault at North Burial Ground, Providence	
1934	Renewed efforts for Providence memorial	Incorporate as nonprofit group
1935		Publish first issue of *Narragansett Dawn*
1936	*A Key* reissued	
1939	Remains reinterred in Providence memorial	
1973	*A Key* reissued	
1975		File federal suit to recover land lost in detribalization
1978		Receive 1,800 acres in settlement; apply for federal recognition
1982		Graves discovered (RI-1000)
1983		Gain federal recognition

PART ONE

From *Key* to Canon

1.

MAKING A LIFE

It has been estimated that more biographies have been written about Roger Williams than about any other figure in America born before Benjamin Franklin, yet most Americans know very little about him.[1] Simple facts such as the dates of his birth and death are not known with any certainty. Except for a thumbprint impressed into sealing wax, his physical attributes are a mystery.[2] Even those who actually knew him, either as friends or adversaries, remembered less about him than other notable English colonists in the seventeenth century.[3] Like the romantic images of him produced by later artists, he exists in the mind's eye as formal, distant, and benign. At best, he is vaguely familiar; at worst, generally indistinct. Yet his impact on New England history and interpretations of Narragansett Indians has been enormous.

Before analyzing this legacy, I want to offer a brief answer to the question, Who was Roger Williams? It is a direct question to which there are no simple answers. Deciding how to describe him and what is important about his life has been determined already by preserved documents and by historians who have relied on them to recapture what actually happened and really mattered in his life. These surviving documents seem to suggest that what is significant about Williams's life were his differences with the Puritans of Massachusetts and those within his own colony, rather than his relationships with Native peoples. Although the latter did receive attention in Williams's own writings, and to some extent have been commented on in the records of other colonial authors, these have generally not been

Figure 1. *Roger Williams*. Engraving by F. Halpin (ca. 1847). Seated at a table with his papers and books, Williams rests his right hand on the Bible and *A Key Into the Language of America*. (Courtesy of the Rhode Island Historical Society)

seriously studied by those who have attempted to represent his life. Perhaps this is because Native peoples' lives have been largely unstated or uncomprehended in written accounts of seventeenth-century New England, even by Williams, who wrote about them in more detail than most other English authors. It is tempting to say that they were "only" Indians and therefore did not warrant consideration equal to that of others whose lives intersected Williams's. Yet it seems that they were as instrumental in shaping the course of Williams's life in seventeenth-century New England as he was in representing them to later generations of European Americans.

Williams was born in London, probably about 1603, the third child of middle-class parents.[4] His father, James Williams, was a modest shopkeeper who belonged to the Merchant Taylor's Company. His mother, Alice Pemberton Williams, also came from a middle-class background, but the occasional titled person and officeholder in her pedigree suggest that her family was a bit better off than her husband could hope to be as a small, independent merchant in an age increasingly dominated by joint-stock companies formed to take advantage of distant markets. Beyond these thin facts of lineage, little is known about Roger Williams's family history. Three of his siblings, Sydrach, Catherine, and Robert, survived infancy with him. One could guess that Roger Williams's childhood was normal and even uneventful. Despite outbreaks of the "deadly plague" that threatened London repeatedly during the time he was growing up, Williams was spared.[5]

By his teens, he had received some formal education and had mastered the skill of shorthand. This form of writing enabled him to fulfill his classroom assignments, such as taking notes on Sunday sermons, but perhaps also prepared him for a career as a clerk, a scrivener, or, most unexpectedly, a recorder of Native American language and culture. It may have been Williams's intense scribbling that caught the attention of Sir Edward Coke, a prominent public figure and noted jurist. As with other chance acquaintances in history, the specific details of this encounter are uncertain, but regardless of the circumstances, Coke's patronage opened doors for Williams. He employed him as a note taker and was instrumental in securing his admittance to Charterhouse School, founded in 1611 for indigent students, even though Williams did not meet the admission criteria because of his age and his family's more-than-adequate income.[6] Nearly three centuries later, Roger Williams would be recalled as the earliest of the Charterhouse scholars to achieve fame.[7]

After completing two years of study, he was accepted to Cambridge in June 1623 and began his matriculation a year later as a scholarship student. As part of his university education, he studied logic, ethics, philosophy, metaphysics, literature, and rhetoric. These subjects emphasized the culture of the classical age and as such did not provide him with specific tools for studying Native societies. Imparting new knowledge about a much wider and more complicated world and recent scientific discoveries was not part of the curriculum. Despite these limitations, Williams's passion for learning, rhetorical style, and facility with languages were honed during his years at Cambridge, as was his interest in theology. During his undergraduate years, if not before, he developed an interest in Puritanism. He learned about the solemn and painstaking process of salvation along with the grim prospects for redemption. After earning his bachelor's degree in 1627, he remained at Cambridge to study theology and prepare for a career as a minister. A year and a half later, however, he quit without obtaining a degree. Although the reasons for his departure are unstated, it has been suggested that his leanings toward the more radical nonconformist strain of Puritanism known as Separatism, which demeaned the teachings and practices of the Church of England, may have made Cambridge's conservative environment seem a less-than-receptive place in which to explore to his ideas about church reform.[8]

From Cambridge, Williams went to Essex, where he was employed as a private chaplain on the estate of a nobleman, an appointment that would not have been uncommon for someone with his qualifications. In the Masham household, he tended to the household's spiritual needs, offered counsel, and counted among his contacts other reform-minded Puritans. Whether sympathetic to the Puritan cause or suspicious of it, many of his contacts were intrigued by the possibilities of colonizing ventures in America. Some were connected to the joint-stock companies sponsoring expeditions, including the Massachusetts Bay Company. One could reasonably suppose that Williams had heard many similar stories while growing up in bustling, commercial London, where talk about colonization was commonplace and news of overseas arrivals and departures almost as frequent. As a young, dissenting minister embarking on a career and presumably wanting a more permanent church appointment than that of a chaplaincy in a country estate, he must have found the possibilities posed by migration and the Puritan project in Massachusetts truly exciting.

Given these contingencies, Roger Williams's decision to leave the comfort of Essex and sail to America does not seem unusual. One could suppose that he acted on a childhood fantasy or on his own social ambitions and deep religious convictions. Perhaps even a broken heart, resulting from an early romantic infatuation, played into his decision.[9] Whatever the rationale, Williams and Mary Barnard, his wife of one year, with about twenty other passengers and two hundred tons of goods, boarded the *Lyon* at Bristol on December 1, 1630. On February 5, 1631, fifty-seven days later, they arrived at Nantasket, the entrance to Boston Harbor.[10] Like most accounts of early New England colonists told later by history writers, Roger Williams's story begins here. From this point, he was to embark on a personal odyssey that his contemporaries as well as later historians considered no less tumultuous than his North Atlantic crossing. In less than five years, his opinions would make him an unpopular figure in Massachusetts and lead to his banishment. To avoid deportation, Williams would flee to Narragansett Bay where, whether by force or perhaps partially by volition, he would live out the rest of his life.

As the New England chapter of his story opens, Roger and Mary Williams had made their way from Nantasket to the newly founded settlement at Boston, where the "godly minister" was asked to teach. In an act that was a portent of many to follow, he declined the invitation because of philosophical differences with the Boston Puritans. His refusal was an affront to the magistrates and to the ministers who had welcomed him wholeheartedly and had expected him to become one of them. It was then that his troubles in New England began. From Boston, the Williamses went to Salem. Although the Salem church was modeled on principles more suitable to his interests, the ministers withdrew an offer for Williams to assist the pastor, on the urging of Boston authorities who warned that his appointment would not bode well for the future of the colony.

By August 1631, the couple had moved to Plymouth, where they found security among seemingly like-minded individuals. Two years later, Mary Williams gave birth to their first child. Williams began to cultivate relationships with neighboring Wampanoag peoples and others who frequently visited the English plantation. This after all was still the Wampanoags' home, where they continued to fish and hunt and maintain connections despite the presence of the English. Williams, like other newcomers, would have used these occasions to barter his trading stock in exchange for furs, food, and the like and, as an added bonus, to gain some of their language. He also made excursions to their settlements, where he attempted to improve his knowledge of their Algonkian language by lodging in what he would later describe as "their filthy Smoakie holes to gaine their Toung etc."[11] Unlike most English colonists at Plymouth, who relied on Native interpreters like the famous Squanto to translate their words and phrases, Williams made a concerted effort to learn the local dialect. Through his initial apprenticeship, he acquired sufficient facility with their language and learned enough about their way of life to have the confidence to promote their interests.

Although Williams fulfilled his duties as the pastor's assistant with zeal and piety, there were soon signs of strain between him and the Separatist church at Plymouth. His concerns about the extent of the congregation's professed separation from the Church of England led to mounting discontent on his part and on that of other church members. Williams may have had other reasons for his departure, not least of which were his eagerness to live among Native people and his increasingly close friendships with some of them. These personal acquaintances may have influenced his questioning of the English colonists' right to appropriate Native land by royal charter and, more basically, by divine right. Before leaving Plymouth to return once again to Salem, he committed these controversial opinions to paper.[12]

Back at Salem, he preached without having an official church appointment, although it may have been an unwise decision to do so. He found support among a growing Separatist movement within the congregation, but as his popularity grew, so did his challenges to Massachusetts Bay authorities in Boston. He began to voice his arguments more vehemently against the use of royal patents in usurping Native land. From the perspective of the Massachusetts authorities, Williams's position was an indictment of the legitimacy of their colonial enterprise. He was challenging their right to hold title to Native lands by royal decree, rather than by purchase or gift, and thus implying that Native groups owned the lands currently occupied and claimed by English colonists. Although Williams's ideas about the illegitimacy of royal charters may have been encouraged by his associations with New England's Native peoples, a fundamental point of his argument was theological. He believed that English monarchs could not appropriate land in the name of Christendom because their claims about the existence of a truly Christian world were false. Unconvinced of their assumptions and professions of faith, Williams seriously questioned the rationale by which they had seized Native lands. [13]

By the end of December 1633, the General Court at Massachusetts met to consider Williams's treatise and what action it should take against him. The magistrates refuted his accusations and rebuked him for insulting the king. Williams appeared before the court, pledged his loyalty to the crown, and promised not to repeat his allegations in the future. This was not to happen. He continued to voice his dissident views and anger the authorities. They blamed his religious fervor and commitment to purify Puritanism for stirring up other troubles in their community. He broke his promise not to renounce the right of the English monarchs to claim territory in the name of Christendom and rejected arguments that English possession of Native land was preordained by the hand of God—which had conveniently swept away thousands of Natives in a deadly epidemic to prepare the way for their colonization. Repeatedly at odds with some in Massachusetts Bay Colony and a regular in the court, given the frequency of his appearances to answer charges, Williams continued to speak (and write) his mind.

In the summer of 1635 the congregation at Salem, in a reversal of an earlier decision, appointed Williams a teacher of the church. Ironically, the appointment came at a time when some members of the congregation had begun to question his wisdom and leadership. During the next few months, his persistent outspokenness led to still more court appearances and further admonitions. Authorities in Massachusetts Bay viewed him as increasingly dangerous; some even insisted that he should be removed from church office. Toward the end of the summer, Williams became ill and unable to preach to the congregation, but his illness did not prevent him from giving notice that he was about to break with the other churches in the colony. He threatened to leave the Salem church and sever connections if it did not follow his example. Although some members acquiesced rather than face the consequences of his ultimatum, the majority did not. As a result of these actions, Williams and his followers split from the congregation.

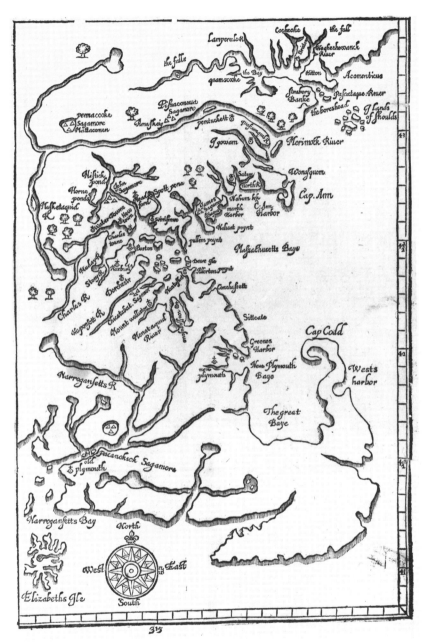

Figure 2. *The South part of New-England, as it is Planted this yeare, 1634*. Prepared for William Wood's *New England's Prospect*, the map's English and Indian place-names illustrate the closeness of English and Native American settlements during Williams's initial years in New England. (John Carter Brown Library at Brown University)

Figure 3. *Banishment of Roger Williams.* The oil painting by Peter Frederick Rothermel (ca. 1850) presents a romanticized image of Williams's escape from Massachusetts. The snow-covered, rocky terrain and gnarled tree trunks lend an impression of adversity, highlighting Williams's defiant stance and the books clutched in his left hand. (Courtesy of the Rhode Island Historical Society)

In October, the court summoned Williams and charged him with having written two offensive letters. In one, addressed to the churches in Massachusetts Bay, he had complained about the unjust and oppressive policies of the magistrates. In the other, he had called for the Salem church to separate from the other "anti-Christian" churches in the colony. He defended the contents of both letters and used the public forum as a venue in which to reassert his opinions, refusing to retract his statements or be persuaded by counterarguments. The colony's officials sentenced him to banishment for his views, which they considered slanderous and perilous, and ordered him to leave the jurisdiction of Massachusetts Bay Colony within six weeks.

Williams returned to Salem, presumably to prepare for his departure. During the next few weeks, he met privately with a few supporters. His wife gave birth to their second child, a girl he named "Freeborn," perhaps to capture the gist of his, if not her own, future. Yet despite the hope expressed in his daughter's name, Williams's health deteriorated. Although the exact nature of his ailment is unknown, his condition was allegedly serious enough to convince the General Court to postpone his banishment until spring. Williams claimed that his illness, which had brought him "neare unto death," had a positive spiritual effect, but its practical benefits cannot be diminished. The delay gave him time to mortgage his house and ten acres of land in exchange for supplies that he would need on his journey and in setting up a new home.[14] In addition, it gave him the time to contact Native leaders to negotiate for lands where he and his family could settle. In January 1636, informants told the magistrates that Williams and more than twenty persons were planning to build near Narragansett Bay, a place that John Winthrop, his friend and mentor, may have recommended to him.

Suspecting, and indeed rightfully so, that Williams was making plans for a renegade settlement that would further the spread of Separatism, the court at Boston issued a warrant for his deportation. Williams responded that he was unable to travel "without hazard to his life" because of his poor health. This time the authorities were not swayed and refused to grant him a stay of leniency. Instead, they sent Capt. John Underhill, whose name (like Williams's) is etched in the annals of events leading to the Pequot War (1637), to arrest him and bring him to Nantasket, where he would be placed on a ship bound for England. When Underhill arrived at Williams's house, he was already gone. He had left Salem three days earlier. No one knew, or could remember, where he had gone.[15]

Williams's solution was to run away, as he had done many times before. He had gone from Essex to America; from Boston to Salem and then to Plymouth; from there back to Salem; and now, to other parts of New England seemingly unknown. He was in many ways a Seeker, an idealist perhaps, striving to find spiritual perfection in a world that offered much less. His theological convictions aside, sev-

Figure 4. *Roger Williams Seeking Refuge among the Indians* (n.d.). Compared with Rothermel's painting, this engraving by an unknown artist depicts a less confident Williams. The direction of his head and outstretched hand gesture toward two Indians huddled near a campfire, suggesting that he sought their protection in a country he knew little about. (Courtesy of the Rhode Island Historical Society)

enteenth-century New England presented enough unknowns to make the possibility of exchanging one imperfect situation for another feasible.[16] Exiled from Massachusetts, which had become an increasingly unsuitable place for him, he sought companionship with Native peoples, some of whom he had presumably come to know through trade and his early linguistic apprenticeship. It is at about this point in the story that the fine-grained view of Williams's life as it has been told becomes a more wide-angled panorama, filled with fewer details about day-to-day events.

When he reached the headwaters of Narragansett Bay, local sachems offered him refuge.[17] Along with a few followers, he began to build a plantation on the eastern bank of the Seekonk River near Sowams, the home of Ousamaquin, or Massasoit, the chief sachem of the Pokanonket band of Wampanoags, whom written histories credit (and European American culture celebrates each Thanksgiving) with having aided the survival not of Roger Williams but of the Pilgrims. Ironically, Plymouth soon informed Williams that his new colony fell within its borders, rather than Ousamaquin's, and encouraged him to find sanctuary elsewhere. By the summer, Williams and his group had moved across the river to a point near the confluence of the Moshassuck and Woonasquatucket. His arrival at a place he called "New Providence" may not have been any more or less auspicious than the crossing of other notable watersheds in history.

Although incomplete records and conflicting accounts make it impossible to know when Williams's wife and two young children joined him, it seems likely that it was sometime before the next spring.[18] While he was consumed with the practical tasks of establishing a new home for his family, a new crisis was brewing right on his doorsteps. An impending war between the Massachusetts Bay Colony and the Pequots placed Williams in a precarious but also advantageous position. The possibility of an alliance between the Pequots and Narragansetts could destroy his plantation and that of other English colonists, or so he feared. But as someone who knew local Algonkian dialects and was situated with an ear to Indian country, Williams, the exile, came to play a pivotal role by furnishing intelligence to those who had expelled him. In retrospect, his escape to Narragansett Bay could not have happened at a more convenient time. Through some clever negotiating, he dissuaded the Narragansetts from siding with the Pequots in an anticolonial coalition. After the Narragansetts agreed, perhaps somewhat ambivalently, to join an alliance with the English instead, he translated some of the treaty's confusing terms that their sachems did not comprehend. Although Canonicus, the elder clan leader, and Miantonomi, the younger sachem, may have lost a chance to change the course of New England history, their decision may have rescued Williams and his small group of followers.[19]

Granted use rights to land in Narragansett country, Williams established a trading post at Cocumscussoc, near today's village of Wickford in North Kingstown, sometime in the late 1630s. For Williams, trade was a family occupation; he had dabbled in it before being expelled from Massachusetts and, in exile, could pursue it as a means of livelihood. Although his home was in Providence, he stayed at Cocumscussoc for months at a time tending to his business but also grasping at periodic lulls in activity to indulge his passions for spiritual introspection and learning.[20] A preacher without a formal congregation, he made his trading post a pulpit, a place where he could discuss matters of religion and spread his ideas on Christianity to Narragansetts who came to exchange their goods for his. More than simply an outpost of trade, Cocumscussoc provided Williams an unparalleled vantage point from which to observe Narragansett lifeways more closely.

The routine of his new life was interrupted in 1643 when, as the founding member of his settlement, he made a return visit to England. His purpose was to obtain a royal patent for Providence, as well as Newport and Portsmouth, the other English settlements of Narragansett Bay. His reason for seeking a charter was to ensure the political autonomy of Rhode Island's colonies against a series of internal and external threats posed by shifting allegiances among Native peoples and the English. Given the conditions of Williams's sentence of banishment from Massachusetts (at least partly a result of his disdain for royal charters), he left on his mission to London from New Amsterdam aboard a Dutch ship. During his ocean crossing, he wrote A Key Into the Language of America. Published soon after his arrival, his little phrase book and guide to Indian customs spread his reputation as a serious missionary. A few months later, Parliament voted to give him the charter of incorporation that he had sought. Before returning to home, he found time to write and attend to some family matters concerning his mother's estate. It was a productive though costly trip.[21]

Shouldering expenses that he had thought would be reimbursed by the colony and facing mounting debts from failed business ventures and the costs of raising six children, including a son born during his absence, Williams turned his energies to reviving his trade with the Narragansetts almost immediately upon his return from London.[22] His attention to business was soon curtailed, however, by his election in November 1644 to the position of chief officer of the newly incorporated Providence Plantations. He held this office for the next three years and then was chosen as deputy president. These were troubled times, which foretold difficulties to come. The Narragansetts, at war with the Mohegans, had grown more distrustful of the English. Among Williams's fellow colonists were contested land claims and accusations of deception. As the decade drew to a close, he removed himself from public affairs to devote more time to his trade. Although he did not often reveal his personal side, his correspondence with John Winthrop Jr. hints at an emerging friendship based on their shared interest in intellectual pursuits. Always the preacher, he continued to deliver his homilies but became more reticent about the goal of winning Indian converts.[23]

His withdrawal from public life was short-lived. In the fall of 1651, he reluctantly traveled to England again to obtain a confirmation of the 1644 patent, which had been violated by conflicting claims and incursions by other Puritan colonies.[24] To finance the trip, he sold his trading house, fenced fields, and grazing rights at Cocumscussoc to Richard Smith.[25] While the negotiations proceeded, he contacted old acquaintances, delivered some works to be printed, taught Dutch to John Milton, and conversed with Oliver Cromwell. After more than two years away from his wife and children, who had remained in Providence, Williams left London without a more definitive charter. But he did not depart entirely empty-handed. Cromwell and the Council of State gave him official approval for a petition that he presented on behalf of the Narragansett sachems, requesting that they not be coerced to abandon their beliefs in favor of Christianity.[26]

In 1654 he assumed the presidency of Providence Plantations, an office he would hold until 1657. Conflicts over land, religion, and politics continued, and rumors of an Indian war became more frequent. Williams, the civic leader, was the target of many complaints. The most serious attack came from William Harris, a Providence neighbor, who questioned the legitimacy of Williams's claims to land granted by the Narragansett sachems in 1636. His charge, a profit-driven maneuver intended to increase his and several associates' landholdings, was for Williams a personal assault, resulting in a bitter feud that lasted for almost two decades.

Despite his desire for solitude and his occasional retreats from public life, Williams could not ease quietly into old age. He continued to be drawn into the fray of local politics and quarrels with his fellow colonists. In the 1670s he became embroiled in a dispute with the Quakers. Although his criticisms of Quakerism were based mainly on religious principles, Williams also feared the Quakers' encouragement of "uncivilized behavior," which he considered to be as threatening and likely to undermine civil authority in the colony as the actions of land speculators. In 1672 he launched an unrestrained offensive in a series of debates in Newport and Providence. What he left unsaid in these debates he committed to print in what was his final publication, *George Fox Digg'd out of his Burrowes*. Judging from some of his letters and his "pamphlet debates" with John Cotton of Boston many years earlier, in which he had defended the positions that led to his banishment, the literary tactic was certainly not a new one.[27] Yet unlike his first published book, *A Key Into the Language of America*—which offered a youthful glance at New England and its Native peoples and may explain much of what Williams said and did in his adult life—his last tells about the other part of his existence, in Providence Plantations, and the colonists with whom he had worked out a way of life.[28] As the already complicated social landscapes of the seventeenth century became more confounding to him, he gradually withdrew into this other world.

When King Philip's War broke out in 1675, Williams was in his seventies. Although he was weary of fights over land and his community's political boundaries, this more serious battle demanded his attention and brought him back into that public world. Using his prestige as an elder statesman, he tried to persuade the Narragansett sachems to stay out of the war. When they joined the fighting, those he sometimes called "his Indian friends" became his enemies. In their raid on Providence in March 1676, they burned his house and property in retaliation for the colonists' attack on the Narragansett settlement at Great Swamp the previous December. His house destroyed, the Massachusetts court temporarily (and conditionally) lifted his sentence of banishment and offered him sanctuary in return for his years of service to English interests.[29] Williams declined; he had already accepted a commission as a captain in the local militia.

Some guess that, had he written about the war, his account might have been different from those of other English authors. Although their words were hardly neutral, his would have been most unforgiving and full of remorse about a war that he believed should never have happened.[30] From his perspective, it was a war waged directly against him and his idealism and in which he was badly defeated. At the war's end, he was instrumental in determining the fate of Indian war captives in Providence. Although the enslavement of Native peoples was prohibited in Rhode Island, Williams, as a member of the committee charged with their disposition, helped devise a plan for selling captives into "involuntary servitude" for periods of years. According to the provisions, each committee member, including Williams, was slated to receive a share in the profits from the sale of Indians both "great and small."

The subject of Williams's involvement in Indian enslavement has puzzled many of his biographers. Many have ignored it entirely; others have tried to explain and forgive it or have admitted their disappointment. Some have argued that his role in slavery was not atypical. Like other seventeenth-century Puritans, he may have thought that enslavement was just punishment for crime and a merciful alternative to execution. As a reasonable if not humane compromise, forced servitude was viewed to be an equitable retribution for the Indians' hand in obstructing the Puritans' mission to fulfill God's will on earth, and one that might provide them with a means to redeem their souls. Independent of how Williams's actions are rationalized, his participation in these transactions made him an accomplice in Indian enslavement, because the terms of servitude not only were unfair in themselves, they were also not binding beyond Rhode Island's borders, where anyone who purchased Indian servants was free to dispose them as they wished.[31]

Williams's conduct after the war implies his outrage, distress, and profound betrayal. The contrast to interpretations of his actions before the war is so perplexing that explanations of increasing frustration and bitterness seem almost too simple. Was his behavior following King Philip's War really so different from before? Were his approval of terms of involuntary servitude for Native war captives and his meek protestations against their sale into foreign slavery so unlike his mild disapproval years earlier about Pequot captives in the war of 1637?[32] After all, he had been known to strike back at those who disagreed with him; for all his admirable traits, he could be insistent, aggressive, and petulant. All this may be true; yet those who have heard or read about Roger Williams cannot help "but be surprised and sorry, to see [his] name . . . connected with such a transaction."[33]

In 1677 he declined an elective office because of failing health but agreed to serve on the town council for that year and the next three. Although he, like so many others, confronted homelessness and impoverishment as a result of the war, he also had continuing concerns about land claims around Providence, which, except for a brief hiatus during the eighteen months of fighting, had not disappeared. Old and infirm, Williams defended himself against those who questioned his integrity as well as his memory of earlier events. He continued to preach at Narragansett as he had before, but now only to a few scattered English families living there, rather than to Narragansett Indians who once might have listened to his clumsy pronunciations of their words and odd facts in the course of other business.

Having outlived many of his generation, he was in his own words "old and weake and bruised (with a Rupture and Collick) and lamenes on both my feete."[34] Death was something he chose not to ignore but had probably thought about steadily and often throughout his life. For him its cruel reality came sometime in the winter of 1683. Although the circumstances of his death are unknown, old age was undoubtedly a factor. Whatever the immediate cause, some commented that they hoped he had passed on peacefully. He was buried in his family's plot near the site of his Providence home, "with all the solemnity the colony was able to show."[35] Much later, a witness remembered a funeral with full military honors and, as the only monument, a show of musketry that left smoke temporarily hovering over his grave.[36]

2.

EULOGIZING A HERO

On the eve of the Civil War, few remembered Roger Williams's death or much about his funeral. Most had forgotten exactly where he was buried. Learned men like Ezra Stiles of Yale guessed that the grave was just two paces from the cellar hole he had seen on Williams's home lot. Usher Parsons, a professor of medicine with eclectic interests, including a taste for opening graves, ventured that Williams was buried behind the Sullivan Dorr residence in Providence in an old orchard that had once been a burying ground. A woman in her eighties remembered often visiting Williams's gravesite as a child. Another recalled being lowered into a grave at the age of ten to view Roger Williams's partially decayed coffin and moss-covered bones.[1] Someone even said that "a colored boy" was seen amusing himself by rolling small boulders down the hill in the direction of a gravestone in the Dorr orchard, with the purpose of knocking it over "like one of a set of ninepins." Shattered fragments of stone littered the site for years. Dorr, the proprietor of the orchard, eventually removed the portion of the gravestone still standing long after the boy's pranks and years of neglect.[2]

If anything was certain about Roger Williams's grave, it was that almost everyone knew something about it—much as they supposed they knew what had motivated him to leave England, or led him on a path toward banishment, or enabled him to endure his exile. Most of these questions have not been answered with certainty. Many details concerning how Williams lived his life or survived after being ostracized from Massachusetts Bay are simply unknown. His repeated references to his banishment in his polemical writings and letters reveal a preoccupation with his sentence and its effects on his life. In his later years, the memory of his ordeal, particularly his midwinter flight, the separation from his family, and the financial losses, remained especially vivid. Although he professed much pain and distress over his exile, his predicament was not unusual among those who were driven from or censored by Massachusetts Bay.

Despite his banishment and subsequent alienation, he continued to be a leader, albeit a minor one, in seventeenth-century New England.[3] Among those who condemned him, he was an object of scorn, best forgotten except by those who made his fanaticism an example. In 1702 Cotton Mather dismissed Williams as a hotheaded heretic whose crimes against the country more than justified the actions of his forebears, but at the time few were concerned about his notoriety in the old Puritan order.[4] Even in Providence and the colony of Rhode Island, Williams went virtually unnoticed. As a historical figure, his stock showed no appreciable gains until at least fifty years after his death.

Over the next two hundred years, he would be eulogized in sermons, books, and stone. How he is identified, and much of what is known about him, is the product of this eulogizing. It has impressed on popular memory indelible images of Roger Williams as a "pioneer of religious liberty," "an irrepressible democrat," "a friend of the Indians," and most vividly a folk hero in American mythology. It has placed him alongside Bradford, Winthrop, Penn, and Jefferson and compared him to Milton, Locke, and St. Paul. Regardless of whether these juxtapositions are grounded on reasonable analogies, they have placed Williams in impressive company and have served to transform him from a despised heretic into a hero. In this process, his words have taken on added import, and his thoughts have been imbued with greater astuteness than even he might have speculated at his most introspective and self-congratulatory moments. In this chapter, I trace the transformation of Williams as a historical figure before turning specifically to a consideration of *A Key* and its use as an authoritative source on Narragansett culture and history.

The first attempts at redeeming Williams's reputation occurred in Rhode Island. In a lengthy sermon on Rhode Island history delivered in 1738, the Reverend John Callender, a Baptist minister, offered what might be interpreted as a rejoinder to Mather's condemnation of Williams and his colony of religious exiles. He extolled the principle of religious tolerance and praised Williams for his role in establishing its foundations in Rhode Island. Callender's sermon, published as a pamphlet in 1739, influenced perceptions of Williams and his legacy, particularly among early history writers who relied on his account for about the next hundred years in championing Williams's contributions to religious liberty.[5]

In the hands of another Baptist minister, the Reverend Isaac Backus, Williams became the founder of the Baptist church and supporter of the first truly civil government. Backus's admiration was based on Williams's steadfast commitment to principle and liberty of conscience, rather than on shared religious tenets.[6] In the first volume of his major work, *A History of New England with Particular Reference to the Denomination of Christians Called Baptists* (1777), Backus aimed at delivering Williams from obscurity, especially outside of Rhode Island.[7] Writing at the time of the American Revolution, he emphasized Williams's ideas on liberty and their relevance to repudiating the past and, especially, the tyranny of tradition.

These sentiments were echoed by Stephen Hopkins. A governor of Rhode Island and a signer of the Declaration of Independence, Hopkins seized Williams as the colony's founding father and more. Drawing inspiration from Williams, he wrote a history of Providence and the colony of Rhode Island in his *Providence Gazette*, in which he stated that "Roger Williams justly claims the honor of having been the first legislator in the world; in its latter ages, that full and effectually provided for and established a free, full, and absolute liberty of conscience."[8] Hopkins made Williams a hero of revolution, if not the progenitor of principles that underwrote the American Revolution.

Aside from these few accolades, Williams remained a minor historical figure. As late as 1831, it was estimated that what was known about Williams would not fill more than half a dozen pages at best.[9] His papers, like so many other surviving records of public officeholders of the early colonial period, were scattered and in a miserable state.[10] In fact, most New Englanders really did not care about Williams. To this indifference they added a willful reticence about recalling the anxieties and hardships that pervaded life on the frontier, especially the difficulties that their ancestors had experienced in their relations with Native peoples. Attempts to "civilize" and subsequently convert the region's Native Americans to Christianity had been disappointing; the losses suffered in King Philip's War had been heavy (on a per capita basis, more than in any American war); and the postwar reconstruction had brought new struggles, causing more bloodshed and impoverishment. Roger Williams was part of this difficult episode between the English and the Indians. Despite allusions by supporters as well as critics to his efforts in advancing better relations with Native peoples, he was a reminder of difficult times that many wished to forget. So for a while he too was all but forgotten in the minds of most European Americans.

Despite this indifference and selective forgetfulness, some did care to remember. In the first half of the nineteenth century, some self-appointed "custodians" emerged who took an interest in tradition.[11] A modest number of tradition-oriented institutions were founded during this period, including the Rhode Island Historical Society. Organized in 1822 by a group of twelve men—two businessmen, three newspaper editors, and a majority of lawyers, who shared antiquarian interests—the society was formed with the purpose of "procuring and pre-

serving whatever relates to the topography, antiquities, and natural, civil and ecclesiastical history of this State."[12] The reasons for gathering these materials were
linked, at least in part, to the realization that knowledge of past events, even those
as recent as the American Revolution, relied more on fleeting memories than on
contemporary documents.[13] For the members of the Rhode Island Historical Society and similar institutions, history became an antidote to the present.

Much of the attention of the society's founders focused on promoting Roger
Williams's historical reputation and encouraging research into his life and writings. The first volume of the society's *Collections*, published in 1827, printed a copy
of Williams's *A Key Into the Language of America*, which had been procured by one
of its members, Zachariah Allen, from the Bodleian Library at Oxford. Allen had
originally planned to publish the work himself, but he agreed to oversee its printing in the *Collections* at the request of the society's secretary.[14] Also that year the
trustees mounted a serious campaign to search for Williams's manuscripts and
other documents associated with him. Although their efforts in locating and collecting historical materials of this favorite son were not very successful, the society
had a significant impact on the remembrance of Roger Williams and his place in
local history. Then, beginning in the 1840s, funding constraints and political rivalries among the society's officers initiated a period of inactivity in advancing
Williams's historical reputation, which, except for a few spurts of renewed interest, would last until after the Civil War.[15]

Difficulties in locating Williams's manuscripts contributed to the lull in the
mythmaking. Many would-be biographers were discouraged by their inability to
secure materials in addition to already published works, including Jeremy Belknap,
founder of the Massachusetts Historical Society. Unsuccessful in locating original sources, Belknap ultimately abandoned his bid to raise Roger Williams's name
to a rank only slightly below that of the two Winthrops, Bradford, and Penn.[16]
Those with less prosaic goals were undaunted, however. In 1832 the Honorable Job
Durfee made Williams the subject of an epic poem '*Whatcheer, Roger Williams in
Banishment,*' in which he was glorified for his heroic exploits in bringing religious
freedom to Rhode Island and the world:

> I sing the trials and the sufferings great,
>   Which FATHER WILLIAMS in his exile bore,
> That he the conscience-bound might liberate,
>   And her religious rights the soul restore;
> How, after flying persecution's hate,
>   And roving long by Narragansett's shore,
> In lone Mooshausick's vale at last he sate,
> And on *Religious Freedom* based our State.[17]

The task of writing a scholarly biography of Williams was eventually shouldered by the Reverend James D. Knowles, a Baptist minister on the faculty of Newton Theological Institution, who in 1834 published the first of many Williams biographies.[18] Knowles attempted nothing less than giving the "long misunderstood and misrepresented" Roger Williams "his appropriate place among the chief founders and benefactors of New England."[19] The full-length biography drew on Williams's writings to substantiate facts about his life and, in the hope that justice would prevail over prejudice, to evaluate conflicting claims about his place in history.[20] Knowles's efforts had unexpected dividends. His widely acclaimed biography became the most authoritative source on Williams in the nineteenth century; succeeding where others had failed, Knowles not only polished Williams's image but also spread his reputation beyond Rhode Island.

Knowles described Williams's actions and ideas as informed by an almost mystical notion of progress that benefited the whole of humankind.[21] This romanticism also colored the history written by George Bancroft, who in 1834, in the first volume of his popular *History of the United States*, portrayed Williams as an archetypical pre–Revolutionary American hero, whose sufferings and personal struggles laid the cornerstone of the Constitution and Jacksonian liberalism.[22] For Bancroft, Williams deserved a place not merely in regional or national history but in universal history, because of his notable contributions to moral and political science. Mythologized in the narrative histories of these authors and eulogized in epic poetry, Williams was well on his way to becoming more than a local hero.

The emerging idea of progress, which allowed these history writers to make Williams a contemporary rather than a figure of the seventeenth century, also gave his views on liberty and religious tolerance more importance than his relations with Native peoples. This assessment may have provided some resolution to the problem of reconciling the history of conflicts between colonists and Native Americans with the memory of Williams. Ironically, it also may have served more pressing concerns about the place of Native peoples in the new American Republic by diverting attention away from any suggestion that Williams's philosophy of noninterference provided an alternative to Andrew Jackson's policy of forced removal. By casting Williams in the role of a religious as well as civil hero, his relations with Native Americans were downplayed and made to seem of little consequence in the more complicated business of nation building; at the least, it placed his dealings with Native peoples, along with his other exploits, in a category that seemed to be beyond reproach.

As the nation moved toward Civil War, scholarly and popular interest in Williams intensified. The search for his papers and other information pertaining to his life continued, but now there were those who were anxious to do more about preserving his memory. Some lamented that no memorial had been raised in his honor or monument placed at his gravesite. In 1859, Stephen Randall, a Williams descendant, mounted a noble effort to memorialize his illustrious ancestor. His purpose was as much to exonerate the character of Williams's relatives, and the state of Rhode Island for its oversight, as it was to celebrate the memory of this founding father.

Randall's pangs of ancestor worship were not the first to be felt. Almost ninety years earlier, some incipient stirrings had led the town of Providence to appoint a special committee to ascertain where Williams was buried and draft an inscription for a monument to be placed "over the grave of the Founder of this Town and Colony." The impending Revolution had interrupted the committee's work, and the search for Williams's grave was left a matter of unfinished business. Those who debated Williams's burial place surmised that his grave was located in one of three known Williams family burial grounds: at the rear of Sullivan Dorr's residence in Providence, near the junction of the old and new portions of the Stonington Rail Road (now the New Haven branch of Conrail) in Cranston, or possibly just a short distance west from there.[23] The Providence location was the most logical spot because of its proximity to the original Williams homestead. Described as a "greensward," this grassy, seemingly nondescript space was, in fact, a field of remembrance that evoked stunning, if not ghoulish, memories of Williams and his mortal remains.

On March 22, 1860, the grave believed to be that of Roger Williams was exhumed at the site of the abandoned Williams family burial ground in the Sullivan Dorr orchard by "two old sextons, whose services were put in requisition for this special occasion."[24] Although suitable boxes were prepared to receive the exhumed remains, Zachariah Allen, who supervised the disinterment in the presence of several witnesses, noted in his diary:

> The utmost care was taken in scraping away the earth and excavating the bottom
> of the grave of Roger Williams. Not a vestige of any bone was discoverable; nor
> even of the lime dust which usually remains after the gelatinous part of the bone is
> decomposed.[25]

What was discovered instead was the root of an apple tree, which had pushed its way into the grave, entering near where Williams's skull would have been and then following "the direction of the back bone to the hips, and thence divided into two branches, each following a leg bone to the heel, where they both turned upwards towards the extremities of the toes of the skeleton."[26] Upon seeing this curiously shaped root resembling Williams's skeleton, one of those present accused the proprietor of the orchard of having eaten Roger Williams. The accused admitted that appearances were against him but suggested that his father, who had planted the tree in the first place, was the one who had eaten most of the fruit. If these accu-

Figure 5. Apple Tree Root. Uncovered during the exhumation of Williams's grave on March 22, 1860, the apple tree root allegedly conformed to the shape of his torso and limbs by following the outline of his disintegrating bones in the soil. The Rhode Island Historical Society first mounted the curious root on this coffin-shaped backing for exhibition in 1924. No longer displayed, the root remains part of the society's research collections and may be viewed by appointment. (Courtesy of the Rhode Island Historical Society)

sations of cannibalism were accurate, then would it not be true that father and son alike might indeed be part of Roger Williams, relived?[27] In addition to the skeleton-shaped root, the only human relic recovered in the excavations was a braided lock of hair, found in an adjacent grave and believed to be that of Williams's wife, Mary.

There was, of course, a legend to be made from this and lessons to be learned. In an address delivered to the Rhode Island Historical Society on the evening of May 18, 1860, Zachariah Allen expounded on Williams's decomposition:

These researches for the discovery of the grave of Roger Williams have led to . . . several interesting facts, showing the actual transmutations of the organic matter constituting the human body. The incorporation of the lifeless elements of organic matter into the bodies, the grains, and the fruits of plants, and the re-incorporation of the latter in the form of food into the bodies of living animals, is unceasingly going on, thus continually reviving and quickening dead organic matter under the control of ever-renewed life and intelligence. Under this view, the entire disappearance of every vestige of the mortal remains of Roger Williams, teaches after his death an impressive lesson of actual physical resurrection of them by ever-acting natural causes into re-newed states of existence constituting a physical victory over the grave, as his precepts and example before his death, have taught the greater moral victory of the christian faith over worldly oppression.[28]

Williams was gone, his bones disintegrated, but his spirit lived on. He was well on his way to becoming both the subject of popular science and the stuff of legend.[29]

In 1860 the Rhode Island General Assembly took a step in the direction of constructing a fitting memorial, by granting a charter of incorporation to the "Roger Williams Monument Association of the State of Rhode Island and Providence Plantations." Disagreements about the design of the memorial, a shortage of funds, and simple inertia delayed the project. Fearing that interest in the Williams memorial had waned irretrievably because of the Civil War, Stephen Randall deposited a thousand dollars in Providence's Peoples Savings Bank in trust for the monument he hoped would be built "at an early day to promote that end, and to give citizens of Rhode Island an opportunity to manifest by their acts, their veneration for the memory of the distinguished founder of our State."[30]

The Williams monument that Randall hoped to see built, whether through voluntary subscriptions or interest accrued on his donation, was to be constructed of granite and "not less than 170 feet [52 meters] in height," excluding the addition of an ornamental cupola of any suitable material, and placed on the summit of Prospect Hill in Providence. The design of the monument would satisfy those who had emphasized the need for building a memorial with high visibility, one that might even be seen from Boston by the Puritans of Massachusetts as a symbol "to their ever-lasting reproach for having banished Williams."[31] The original declaration of 1865 also specified that bronze statues of Canonicus and Miantonomi were to be placed in the memorial and paid for out of the trust fund. Marble statues of Williams and other first citizens of Providence were to be furnished by their descendants and situated on the lower floor of the monument.[32] Until sufficient funds accumulated to execute the plans for the monument, all earthly substances that could possibly have formed any portion of Williams's mortal body or that of his wife were given a temporary haven in Stephen Randall's family mausoleum at Providence's North Burial Ground.

In the meantime, Rueben A. Guild, the librarian of Brown University, called for another kind of memorial to Williams: the publication of a comprehensive volume "of the Life, Works and correspondence of Roger Williams," to serve as "a 'Monument' worthy of the genius and character of the man who was founder of Rhode Island, the founder of the Baptist denomination in America, and the great advocate of civil and religious liberty."[33] In 1865, a Providence-based group responded to Guild's call. They formed an organization, known as the Narragansett Club, for the purpose of reprinting "the various scarce and rare volumes of Roger Williams's publications."[34] Between 1866 and 1874, the club published six volumes of Williams's writings.[35]

The Narragansett Club's series was only a partial solution to the need of an appropriate memorial to Williams, however. In the next decade, he would finally get the monument that many believed he deserved, but it would not be the one that Randall and others had envisioned. In the 1860s, plans for the Williams memorial had included artistic representations of Canonicus and Miantonomi, who were considered to be part of a different, more harmonious era in Indian–European relations, unbeset by struggles over sovereignty. At a time when the nation was plagued by bigotry and deeply divided over the question of slavery, the inclusion of statues representing the sachems in the Williams memorial symbolized the friendship possible between whites and peoples of color, but in the 1870s, the Narragansetts were not to be part of the monuments executed to commemorate Williams.

This generation was to give Williams a different persona. He was praised as someone who upheld the right of individual conscience for the nation and for all of humankind, rather than as one recognized for his place in the annals of local history and in the early struggles between Native peoples and colonists. Now heralded as a national symbol, Williams was given a monument in Washington, D.C. It was one of two full-length marble statues of illustrious citizens furnished by Rhode Island at the request of the Thirty-eighth Congress in 1864 for a place of honor in the newly renovated Capitol. In presenting the statue to the Congress in 1872, the Honorable Henry B. Anthony, senator from Rhode Island, stated that the dedication was more than idle ceremonial gesture. The ritual placed Williams in the company of other famous Americans who had founded or defended the nation's greatness and whose statues were or soon would be included in this impressive assembly of silent effigies. Williams deserved this place of honor because he "did not merely lay the foundation of religious freedom, he constructed the

Figure 6. Statue of Roger Williams, given by Rhode Island to the National Statuary Hall at the U.S. Capitol. Like all artistic depictions of Williams, this sculpture is an idealized image rather than an authentic likeness. Williams would have disapproved of the shoulder-length hair, a fashion he condemned as a symbol of spiritual degeneration, especially when worn by the English. (Courtesy of the Rhode Island Historical Society)

whole edifice, in all its impregnable strength" and made it the cornerstone of civilized government.[36]

The statue of Williams placed in the Capitol's "Pantheon of America" was strictly a product of an artist's imagination. In that era of glorifying national heroes, an individual's form and features, even if known, often failed to inhibit the more important transformation from subject to symbol. Qualities of strength and patriotism prevailed and permitted a fair degree of artistic license, even when the evidence was contradictory. This point was moot in the case of Roger Williams, because there was no authentic likeness of him to reproduce. In the absence of surviving portraits or sketches, or even descriptions of his physical attributes, his ideas, along with the profile of America's national character, provided more than sufficient inspiration for artistic interpretation. The shape of his jaw, the gaze of his eyes, and even his stature and dress could all be captured to suit the mood of the times.

A 7.5-foot (2-meter) bronze statue, replicating the one in the U.S. Capitol, became the crowning element of the first monument that Rhode Island erected to honor Williams. Until this memorial was unveiled by the city of Providence on October 16, 1877, in a new park bearing his name, the Rhode Island founder's name was attached to just about everything except an enduring local monument. As public art, the 27-foot (8-meter)-high monument was a massive work that intertwined classical and allegorical imagery, portraying Williams's arrival in Rhode Island as the inevitable triumph of history and the human spirit. Beneath the statue's pedestal was a sculpture depicting Clio, the muse of history, inscribing the words "Roger Williams, 1636" on a granite tablet. To the right of the muse were bronze emblems—a scroll, book, laurel wreath, and shield—inscribed with an anchor, the Rhode Island state symbol.[37] Whether or not the messages encoded in this mix of metaphors were received by those who gazed upon the memorial, these small bronze symbols eventually disappeared. But lost symbolism aside, the Roger Williams monument was highly praised by sculptors, civic leaders, and the public, who gathered twenty-thousand strong to attend the dedication ceremonies and witness this hero's formal entry into the rolls of history.[38]

By the end of the nineteenth century, Williams's historical reputation had undergone a radical transformation. A full battery of devices—biography, poetry, parody, monumental art, ceremony and pageantry, and even exhumation—had been employed to save him from obscurity and promote his legacy. He had reached or at least neared the apex of his fame as a historical figure. Despite the public adulation and scholarly acclaim, however, some opinions about him differed.

His more vocal critics were not as easily dismissed as those who remained silent and uncommitted to text. For more than a century, Williams had served as the battlefield on which filiopietistic historians from Massachusetts and Rhode Island waged an unrelenting struggle. Those in Massachusetts studied him to vindicate their forebears from any wrongdoing in banishing him, whereas those in Rhode Island countered by treating him with even greater reverence. But the growing awareness that the pursuit of the past was a "quest for moral truths that could be known with assurance," rather than a simple question of provincial loyalties, resulted in a crisis for Puritanism and for the traditions associated with it in American society.[39]

Figure 7. Unveiling of the Roger Williams statue in Roger Williams Park. This photograph, taken during the 1878 dedication exercises, shows the large crowd gathered for the ceremonies on land that Betsey Williams bequeathed to the city of Providence for a new park on the condition that a memorial be built for her illustrious ancestor. (Courtesy of the Rhode Island Historical Society)

Brooks and Charles Francis Adams Jr., scions of a prominent Boston family with deep New England roots, were among those who launched the assault on Puritanism. In 1887 Brooks Adams published a full-scale attack on Puritanism's legacy, in which he questioned the integrity and piety of the Puritan leaders and disputed what had been accepted throughout the nineteenth century as the official creed concerning their purging of individual dissent. His brother, Charles Francis Adams Jr., also denounced writers who felt constrained by filial duty and class to excuse the actions of their Puritan ancestors. In his book, *Massachusetts: Its Historians and Its History: An Object Lesson*, Charles Francis Adams Jr. accused them of failing to apply the rules and canons of historical criticism evenhandedly to all situations and all characters. The matter of Roger Williams and his banishment from Massachusetts served as a case in point.[40]

Not surprisingly, Adams's statements did not go unnoticed in Rhode Island. In 1893, his book was singled out by the president of the Rhode Island Historical

Society in his annual address as being one of the most valuable and remarkable publications of the year. Adams was commended for drawing comparisons between Williams and other notable seventeenth-century figures who defied conventional understanding. He imputed that John Winthrop and John Cotton, possessing less turbulent dispositions than Williams, conformed at least outwardly to tenets in which they did not wholly believe. Principled beyond a fault, Williams would not and could not be suppressed. Adams's verdict was that Williams's life course could be compared to that of a martyr, because he "bore fearless evidence regardless of consequences whether imprisonment, exile or death." Williams's courage to testify to the truth never failed him, even in his later years, when most men would opt for the comforts of a noncontroversial life. In the search for suitable ancestors, nothing better recommended Williams to posterity.[41]

Although many Rhode Islanders needed little encouragement in their filiopietistic loyalties, it is tempting to suggest that Charles Francis Adams Jr. struck a chord when he referred to Roger Williams as a martyr. No other appellation evokes sentiments as intense as those reserved for individuals given this designation. Around the turn of the century, when ancestor worship was rampant, this response was especially profound. Organizations like the D.A.R., the Colonial Dames of America, the Society of Colonial Wars, and others were formed specifically for the purpose of cultivating lineage. For members of these organizations, bloodlines mattered; for many other Americans, however, blood was a less important link to the past than kinship reckoned through heroic ancestors. Places and things associated with these ancestors became increasingly important, particularly those associated with individuals whose trials and sacrifices made them martyrs for a cause—like Roger Williams.

The transformation of places and things associated with Williams into sacred ground and precious relics began as early as the 1870s and continued over the next three decades. The first place to be sanctified was the site where Roger Williams landed in 1636. In 1872 some members of the Rhode Island Historical Society expressed concern that, unless preventive steps were taken, the slate rock believed to mark the spot would soon be obliterated. Alteration of the Providence waterfront in 1828 had left the rock buried in a 20-foot (6-meter) hollow filled with sand and gravel, roughly 200 feet (61 meters) from the original shoreline of the Seekonk River. People living in the adjacent area, known colloquially as the "What Cheer" tract, had proposed to the Providence City Council the possibility of deeding certain lands for an open square. Although their one stipulation was that the council take measures "to preserve in some manner, that venerated portion of Rhode Island soil," the motives of the property owners were suspected as having more to do with enhancing land values by creating waterfront lots than with memorializing Williams's landing site.[42] Ironically, much of the rock was destroyed in 1877 by a dynamite charge intended to salvage it from the depths of invisibility and historical forgetfulness. The portion of the slate that survived the blast was enclosed by an iron fence. Fragments of this time-honored rock (or stones carved to resemble it) were sold in downtown Providence for years thereafter. Other remaining pieces were acquired by the Rhode Island Historical Society, the First Baptist Church, and Central Baptist Church where they were displayed for public viewing. In 1906 the Providence Association of Mechanics and Manufacturers erected a commemorative monument at the traditional landing site, now called Slate Rock.[43]

That was only one of the sites associated with Williams to be venerated as a sacred place. For those seeking to trace the route of his life and times, as well as his journey around India and Fox Points and up the Moshassuck River to the spot where he eventually settled, this was but one stop on the pilgrimage. In 1906 the house site and the historic spring from which he drank also were enshrined; near his Providence home, two commemorative bronze tablets were placed that read:

A FEW RODS EAST OF

THIS SPOT STOOD THE

HOUSE

OF ROGER WILLIAMS

FOUNDER OF PROVIDENCE

1636

. . . .

UNDER THIS HOUSE

STILL FLOWS

THE

ROGER WILLIAMS

SPRING

In connection with the placing of these two tablets, Norman M. Isham, an architect as well as an antiquarian, and George F. Weston conducted excavations that brought to light what they "confidently believed to be the remains of the fireplace and hearth of Roger Williams's house."[44] The one station in the Williams legend left unmarked was the site of his original plantation in Seekonk, which he built or had begun to build before being advised to move to the other side of the river. According to local tradition, the site of Williams's crude shelter—nothing more than a hole in the ground—was not built upon by subsequent owners of the property, who considered it a sacred place. However ephemeral the evidence might be, though perhaps not any less so than that authenticating other places linked to Williams, this too was consecrated ground, not to be overlooked by those intent on keeping his memory alive and by sojourners seeking to retrace his footsteps following his banishment.[45]

Among early-twentieth-century scholars, Roger Williams remained an important, if not untarnished, historical figure. Many who wrote about him continued to build his reputation as an American hero. As the anti-Puritan movement reached its zenith in the 1920s, the value of his stock as a historical figure rose to new highs. Although a Puritan, Williams was not considered representative of the Puritan social values that underscored the more pernicious features of capitalist culture. Though he was criticized and even banished by the Puritan leadership, his allegiance to the ethics of the Puritan legacy were seen as tenuous. At a time when conflicts were increasing between an old order, based on conservative values inherited from Puritanism, and a newly emerging counterculture of liberation and individual expression, Williams came to be linked to the latter, regardless of historical accuracy or continuity.[46] By the end of the decade, Vernon L. Parrington pronounced Puritanism essentially foreign, elitist, and antidemocratic, but he proclaimed Williams a visionary who "lived and dreamed in a future" of American democracy that he did not live not to see.[47]

It was in this climate that Roger Williams was elected to the Hall of Fame, an institution established at New York University in 1900 for furthering patriotic and educational aims. He was recognized as a pioneer of religious liberty and democracy, who proclaimed "a true and absolute soul freedom to all the people of the land impartially so that no person be forced to pray nor pay otherwise than as his soul believeth and consenteth."[48] But his journey to this shrine to famous Americans was perhaps no less arduous than some notable trips he had taken during his lifetime. When the Hall of Fame was first established, no foreign-born person like Williams was eligible for election. Four years later the trustees decided to establish a separate Hall of Fame for foreign-born Americans. With his eligibility assured, Williams was elected to the illustrious group in 1910 as a foreign-born American. The trustees amended the constitution governing the institution again in 1914 to abolish the separate quota systems for membership because they were discriminatory. Fairness now demanded that the names of foreign-born members be resubmitted for election along with native-born nominees. Williams's name was thrown in the ring, but he failed to win a majority of votes in the first round of the competition. In 1920 he finally won the approval of the electors.[49] So despite mounting assessments that Puritanism, being an import from England, was actually foreign, the Hall of Fame acknowledged that denying admission to immigrants was unwise, because that policy would have excluded many early ancestors of those who considered themselves American nativists. In 1921 a bronze bust of Williams, modeled on the features of his descendants and representing his own passionate convictions about democracy, finally was unveiled in this hallowed colonnade. Here the conflicts being fought in America, even at the hall's very portals, among native and immigrant, rich and poor, and racial and ethnic populations, were temporarily suspended.[50]

In the 1930s Williams was praised even more vigorously for his contributions to democracy, the acclaim now coming from writers without any animus toward the Puritans or their apologists. On the eve of the tercentennial of Roger Williams's arrival in Rhode Island, the conflicts and contradictions that plagued American democracy were acerbated by insecurities resulting from the Great Depression and the rising tide of fascist dictatorships in Europe. Glorifying the past and its cultural heroes was important in confronting these concerns and, especially, in defending free institutions that were increasingly under attack. Given the growing need for a crusade for democracy, the tercentennial could not have come at a better time. Williams was given a new image by civic leaders. He was refurbished as a humanitarian and inspirational figure, a common man who had overcome adversity, rather than the political philosopher portrayed by scholars in the halls of academia. He came to represent someone whose vision, experiences, and compassion offered hope to people in the face of crisis.

It was in this spirit that the celebrations for the Roger Williams tercentenary began. *A Key Into the Language of America* was reissued in a one-thousand-copy edition printed in a type similar to that used in the original publication.[51] Williams's sentence of banishment was revoked by the Commonwealth of Massachusetts without any serious objection from Boston's Brahmin families.[52] Pageants were staged, public lectures were delivered, and plaques were raised in his honor. The site of Roger Williams's spring was purchased and presented to the city of Providence by Judge J. J. Hahn in memory of his father, the first citizen of the Jewish faith to hold elective office in Providence. Even the site of Williams's crude shelter in East Providence was procured, landscaped, and dedicated.[53] And after being in "temporary" repose for about seventy years, the "bones" of Roger Williams, which had almost been forgotten, finally were laid to rest in a proper memorial.

Despite a few attempts in the intervening decades to reactivate the idea of enshrining Williams's remains, including a proposal to transfer the trust fund established in 1865 to the custody of the Colonial Dames, the project languished. In fact, until some concerned individuals went to the Randall tomb in North Burial Ground in the early 1930s to ascertain the condition of the box containing traces of material evidence recovered in the 1860 exhumation, no one could be sure that they were still there. Assured that all that remained of Roger Williams was intact, they transferred the contents of the box into a steel container, which would stay in the receiving vault at North Burial Ground for a few more years.[54] In 1934 the Rhode Island General Assembly incorporated a new Rhode Island Roger Williams Memorial Association for the purpose of carrying out the wishes of Stephen Randall to raise a monument to Williams at (or at least near) his grave. With $45,000 accrued in the trust, a $21,000 contribution from the state, and $19,000 raised by the Rhode Island and Providence Plantations Tercentenary Committee, the association was able to build what they hoped would be "the ultimate memorial."[55]

In soliciting designs in an open competition, the association asked the architects to meet only two requirements stipulated by Stephen Randall: to design a monument of sufficient height so that it would be visible from a distance and to situate it on Prospect Terrace, a promontory overlooking Providence. Although it was Randall's intention to have statues of Canonicus and Miantonomi in the monument, the association did not specify this in requesting proposals. The original design selected for the memorial in the competition had statues of Williams and the two sachems. Williams was to be perched on a pedestal at the edge of Prospect Hill, and the sachems were to be placed on a lower terrace to one side of a reflecting pool. The statues of the sachems were eventually eliminated from the design because they were not required in the request for proposals. The overriding sentiment expressed by those involved in the memorial was to project an image of Williams "as a practical statesman." Ostensibly, design elements could convey this idea more effectively than by having Williams flanked by statues of Indians. A stylistic interpretation of the metaphor of "a ship at sea," often used by Williams in his writings, was chosen as the theme of the redesigned memorial. In this reincarnation, Williams was depicted standing serenely in the bow of a canoe with water lapping at his feet and his hands extended over the city of Providence.

As the 14-foot (4-meter)-high granite statue of Williams neared completion, Williams's remains were transported to the Rhode Island Historical Society, where they stayed for about a year before being transferred to the association by one of Stephen Randall's descendants for final burial in the Prospect Terrace memorial. At the dedication ceremonies on June 29, 1939, the bronze box containing Williams's remains was deposited in a recess of the monument by a Williams family member, while an honor guard comprising a delegation of Narragansett Indians and four men in colonial military uniform stood by and watched. Samuel H. Brockunier, one of Williams's biographers, delivered the key address, in which he proclaimed Roger Williams "a folk hero of the American people." Brockunier was aware that this public celebration served a greater purpose than simply honoring Williams's memory by enshrining the specks of dust, rusted nails, and fragments of wood that constituted the only tangible traces of his mortal remains.

Brockunier's rhetoric was reserved for the inspirational role that Williams played in sustaining and furthering the concept of democracy. Like ordinary Americans in the 1930s, Williams had lived in troubled times. But this "irrepressible democrat," as Brockunier would call him in the title of his 1940 biography, was someone "who recoiled from the oppressions, the scourgings, the banishments,

Figure 8. Roger Williams's remains being carried to the Roger Williams Monument. Following their disinterment, Williams's remains reposed in a shallow wooden soapbox labeled "RW" inside a tomb at Providence's North Burial Ground for more than seventy years before being reburied. Cropped versions of this photograph appearing in the *Providence Journal* and the *Providence Evening Bulletin* on June 30, 1939, did not show the Narragansetts who were part of the honor guard. (*The Providence Journal*)

the purgings, the heresy-hunting of a world where force held sway and reason was unfree" by his persistent belief in the democratic faith.[56] Alluding to deepening economic insecurities, the "fear of an enemy within the gate," as well as the growing specter of extremism abroad, Brockunier characterized Williams as someone having profound insight into the essence of modern democracy. His speech was not a simple pitch to a dead hero but an appeal to reason, in which Williams and his experiences reaffirmed the past as firm ground and offered assurances in the midst of crisis.[57]

With the construction of this memorial, Roger Williams's stature as a historical figure had reached new heights. His stately statue now cast an imposing and permanent shadow on the cultural landscape for present and future generations. A record box placed in the crypt of the monument during the dedication exercises held written materials that provided an authoritative commentary on Williams as a historical figure and on the campaign to memorialize him. Among the memorabilia was Knowles's *Memoir of Roger Williams* (1834), considered seminal in transforming Williams's image for posterity. All aspects of the memorial—the scale of the monument, the crypt for Williams's remains, and the dedicatory cache of his-

Figure 9. The unveiled statue of Roger Williams at the dedication of the Roger Williams Monument. The photograph shows the full honor guard of Narragansett Indians, members of the Williams family, and colonial militia standing at attention. (*The Providence Journal*)

torical materials—offered enduring testimony to the status he attained long after his death.

As the century progressed, however, historians gradually began to temper Williams's exaggerated reputation. Rather than inflating his contributions, they focused on a particular aspect of his life or his ideas. Compared with earlier treatments, those that appeared in the middle decades of the twentieth century asserted that Williams was a man neither for all times nor for our times, but one whose actions and ideas could be best understood in the context of his own times—the seventeenth century. With a new wave of interest in Puritanism following the Second World War, Williams was portrayed as an heir of Calvin, rather than as the intellectual progenitor of Jefferson or Jackson, as had been claimed by those who, after the spread of the enlightenment, saluted him as an almost forgotten prophet of themselves.[58] Historians like Perry Miller stated unequivocally that Williams's slant was theological and not political.[59] He was, pure and simple, a Puritan; but compared to earlier discussions of Williams and Puritanism, this time around he was not a partisan for a cause, and his fate could not be tied to partisan interests.

The story of "Master Roger Williams," as Ola Winslow wrote, could better be told as he lived it, rather than as it has been portrayed in myth and romantic legend. He was "not ahead of his day, not an inch," but only an ordinary man who lived his everyday life in what were uncommon times.[60] In writing his biography, she gave much attention to Williams's early years, compared with the last two decades of his life, and implied that if it were not for the critical timing of his birth, he might have gone unnoticed. This ordinary, individual life, as Ola Winslow interpreted it, was lived with feet planted "very firmly on the Narragansett earth" and with more practical "weekday wisdom than his posterity has allowed him," a life enriched by a vision of possibility that sprang from knowing the pulse of the community and meeting the challenges of the times.[61] Her characterization of Roger Williams as a simple man, who saw that "he had to do a very simple thing," and did it simply, is perhaps as romantic and inaccurate in its own way as the more obviously flagrant claims about his legacy. The irony is that the call to interpret Williams in the context of his own times offered no guarantees that he would be understood any better. Debunked as a patriotic icon, he was singled out for his integrity, nonconformity, and bold commitment to liberty of conscience. He became the symbol of freedom and pluralism, a voice of reason in a field crowded with invincible, larger-than-life heroes.

Williams's capital as a subject of scholarly discourse and popular interest has continued to soar. More anniversaries have been celebrated; other historic landings reenacted. An ever-growing number of tourists flock to the city that Williams founded, where they can visit landmarks committed to his memory. At the bottom of the hill where the "serene grey giant" stands, the National Park Service maintains a tiny parcel of land, known as the Roger Williams National Memorial, as a greenspace.[62] Here anyone can pause for a moment's respite from the clamor of urban life (and a weary visitor from a frenzied tour of the major attractions), much as Roger Williams must have done when stopping to drink from the spring that serves as the park's only tangible link to his memory.[63] The more adventurous can visit Smith's Castle (a.k.a. Cocumscussoc), the elusive site of Williams's trading post, and soon, if those peddling Rhode Island's heritage industry have their way, no one will be able to travel to any part of the state without finding something attributed to him.

Among scholars, Williams is no longer just prime subject matter for historians (and theologians). He has captured the attention of scholars in a variety of different disciplines, who have made him the focus of innumerable articles, books, and doctoral dissertations.[64] Linguists, sociologists, and literary scholars now also lay claim to Williams. They are busily at work analyzing his speeches, his actions, and his verse. These recent interpretations of Roger Williams hint at a growing appreciation not only of the complexity of his life and ideas, but also of the difficulties posed by the task of disengaging the man from the myths. Although he "belongs to that sparse category of those for whom no generation speaks the last word," the eulogies made to him by each passing generation have made lasting impressions.[65] Although no single image of Roger Williams—the favorite son, the hero of the Revolution, the statesman of the Republic, the man of impeccable character to American Anglophiles, the ordinary person, the democratic visionary, and the leader in the cause of freedom—stands out, he endures. Withstanding this process of reinvention is a folk hero, who has been endowed with an uncanny ability to understand not only his own society and culture but also that of the Narragansett Indians.

3.

ACCLAIMING A CANON

The transformation of Roger Williams in the centuries after his death did more than alter his reputation as a historical figure. In the process, his writings became heroic messages filled with deep and multiple layers of meaning.[1] They were, in Williams's own words, "as thick and over busie as the Muskeetoes."[2] Considered insightful and not uncomplicated, his writings, like the writer himself, have come to be extolled. Liberally quoted, frequently cited, and often retold for the edification of later generations, Williams's words have become in many instances common knowledge. They made his story possible, sometimes subjecting him to scorn, placing him in peril, jeopardizing his livelihood, but also opening doors for him.

The small treatise he composed at Plymouth sometime in 1632, in which he questioned the English colonists' right to appropriate Native land under the aegis of a royal patent, became a matter of serious public concern. Massachusetts Bay officials refuted its most offensive passages and demanded a retraction, fearing that Williams's statements might fall into the hands of those in Parliament eager to revoke their charter. Although Williams was not officially censured, the provocative treatise added to his mounting troubles in the colony and placed him on the road to banishment. Oddly enough, the work, later described as a *"large Book in Quarto,"* has not survived. The circumstances surrounding its disappearance are a mystery, but the treatise apparently provided sufficient justification for Williams's fellow colonists to want it destroyed.[3]

But as troublesome as this treatise was for its author, it paled in comparsion to

his *The Bloudy Tenent of Persecution, for cause of Conscience*. In this impassioned defense of religious liberty and the separation of church and state, Williams rolled
out the heavy artillery in what would be a bitter contest of words against John
Cotton, the churches of Salem and Boston, and Parliament. Although the book
was published anonymously, few doubted the identity of the author, given the
topic and the harsh phrases directed toward the persecutors. Williams's words
provoked a vindictive counteroffensive. In August 1644, Parliament ordered *The
Bloudy Tenent* to be publicly burned by a hangman, just one month after its printing. Within five years of its publication, the book (apparently still in limited circulation among its detractors) was viciously condemned in approximately one
hundred pamphlets.[4]

Compared with these works, Williams's book on Narragansett Indians, *A Key
Into the Language of America*, was uncontroversial. Williams was neither reprimanded nor censured because of it. Although it could be argued that it represented
a different genre of writing than that of his polemical tracts, *A Key*'s apparent immunity to criticism demands a better explanation.[5] Whether it was considered incidental or accepted as matter-of-fact remains uncertain. Scant reference to it in
the years following its initial publication rendered it virtually invisible and disguised
whatever effects it may have had on perceptions of Narragansett Indians. Only
after the third decade of the nineteenth century, roughly two hundred years after
it rolled off the printing press, was *A Key* recognized as an unquestionable authority
on the Narragansetts from the standpoint of the dominant culture. Because the
Narragansetts, like other New England Indians, did not record their history in written words, at least not in the seventeenth century, Williams's *A Key* told their story
for them. In the ensuing decades, his version of their story has maintained its
canonical status, informing scholars' understandings of Narragansett culture and
history. In this chapter, I ask how *A Key* came to be acclaimed as an authoritative
text on the Narragansetts and, perhaps even more important, how it has shaped
European Americans' perceptions of them.

A Key was not only the first extensive book on Native American language published in English; it was also Roger Williams's only one on Indians.[6] It was written
during his return voyage to England in 1643, and soon after his arrival in London
it was delivered to the printing press of Gregory Dexter. The finished product was
a small, moderately well-printed book of 224 pages.[7] Independent of minor typographical errors, Williams's *A Key* was not simply a collection of hastily written
notes and scrawled observations thrown together during the course of a few
seaborne hours.[8] It is a complex work composed of intertwined elements of linguistics, manners and customs, accounts of personal experiences, and commentary.

In naming *A Key*, Williams selected his words carefully. As with all words, he believed they both expressed and embodied one's thoughts and beliefs. His under-

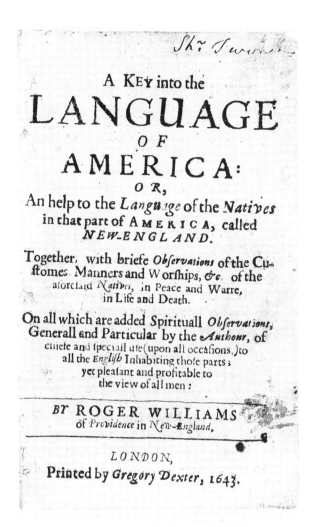

Figure 10. Title page of the first edition of *A Key Into the Language of America* (London, 1643). (John Carter Brown Library at Brown University)

standing of the centrality of language became the means by which he, like other literate New England Puritans, revealed his quest for spiritual piety, devotion to principle, and commitment to virtue.[9] The language of his titles proclaimed his particular vision. They were sometimes contentious (e.g., *The Bloudy Tenent, for cause of Conscience*), but always telling.[10] *A Key Into the Language of America* was no exception. Its title heralded its uniqueness among early texts on America's Native peoples by announcing that America did not begin with the English.[11] America already had its own language, the Algonkian dialects spoken by New England Native Americans, and learning it would help the English understand Native culture. It was the metaphorical "key" that could open doors.[12] "This *Key*," Williams said, "respects the *Native Language* of it, and happily may unlocke some *Rarities* concerning the *Natives* themselves, not yet discovered."[13]

As implied in the title, Williams intended that his book—comprising a title page, a preface (or epistle) to the reader, directions for use of the language, thirty-two chapters, and a table of contents—would "bring that mighty *Continent* of *America* to light" to those who would read and listen to what he had learned about its Native people.[14] The practical and basic knowledge he offered about words, phrases, and manners would help his *"Deare and Welbeloved* Friends *and* Countrey-men, *in old and new* ENGLAND" navigate the social and cultural landscapes of Native America.[15] If his words served him (and presumably others) well, they would accomplish even more: they would contribute to personal and spiritual growth and provide an instrument for winning future Native converts. Regarding the possibility of Indian conversions, he alluded to "a brief additional discourse concerning this great point," which he would soon present.[16] In the interim, he offered *A Key* to those who wished or needed to converse with Indians, even if imperfectly. But more than this, he gave them a tool for carving a path through America as he knew it.

A Key's chapters, forming the main body of the text, are each organized in three parts. Williams first presents words and phrases of the Narragansett language, which he organized as "implicit dialogues" so that they assume the pattern of a conversation, presumably between a Native person and himself. He then interjects general observations in which he comments on a specific word or on the subject of the vocabulary by offering an anecdotal or spiritual insight. Williams concludes each chapter with a "more particular" observation, in the form of a poem in which he contemplates the question of cultural differences between Native Americans and the English, apropos the loftier matter of salvation.

Although various scholars have attempted to discern a narrative structure in *A Key*, the text—like its author—defies simple categorization.[17] Rather than following a birth-to-death cycle or mirroring the drama of a moral allegory, the chapters steer the reader on a pragmatic course by providing rudimentary skills for getting acquainted and only gradually introducing more detailed information on Narragansett culture. For example, the first few chapters, which focus on salutations, eating and entertaining, sleeping and lodging, numbers, kinship, home and family, person and body parts, and discourse and news, furnish the reader with terms of address and phrases for making introductions and general inquiries. They trace what seems to be a protocol for establishing relations with Native people.

The next chapters provide a description of the geography and natural history of Narragansett country. Here Williams presents the reader with terms for the time of day and seasons of the year, sun, moon, and stars, weather and winds, flora and fauna, and travel. In contrast to this literary invitation to explore the land and its natural resources, *A Key*'s remaining chapters offer an account of Native cultural institutions and various other domains of daily life. By touching briefly on "nakednesse and clothing," religion, government, marriage, currency and trade, hunting, sports and gaming, war, sickness, and death and burial, Williams, in his own words, truly hoped "to bring some short *Observations* and *Applications* home to *Europe* from *America*."[18]

Appended to Williams's words are those penned by John Langley. He was a licenser of the press, who had the job of giving official government endorsement to manuscripts. At the time of *A Key*, a license entered into the Register's Book at Stationers' Hall, London, served as a form of censorship, intended to prevent the printing of seditious, libelous, and otherwise offensive material. In the history of the printed word, licensing not only ascertained whether a particular manuscript was acceptable and printable but also protected the interests of printers who were given rights to published works as assurance against infringement. In the licensing process, manuscripts were categorized into one of nine different classes, based on their subject matter, and assigned to an appropriate review committee for critical readings.[19] Langley was one of three members on the panel reviewing works on philosophy, history, poetry, morality, and art. He endorsed *A Key* with the words: "I *Have read over these thirty Chapters of the* American Language, *to me wholly unknowne, and the* Observations, *these I conceive inoffensive; and that the Worke may conduce to the happy end intended by the* Author." In vouching that *A Key* was printable, he indeed was the first to give it official authorization.[20]

At the time of its publication, *A Key* received a warm reception from Londoners who yearned for news about America, and especially about its Native people. *A Key* joined a small but growing list of printed works that satisfied readers by offering more than a passing glimpse at Native New Englanders. It provided them with seemingly meticulous evidence about the region's First Peoples, with verbal assurances that the Puritan mission "to reduce and convert" them could be achieved. In 1645, Sir Robert Baillie wrote that of all the Puritans who had crossed the Atlantic "I have read none of them that seem to have minded of this matter: onely Williams in the time of his banishment from among them, did assay what could be done with those desolate souls, and by little experience quickly did finde a wonderful great facility to gain thousands of them."[21] If *A Key* was an instrument to "civility" and conversion, it also was a means for Williams to enhance his prestige and perhaps influence among those who would eventually vote on a charter for Providence Plantations. Although *A Key* was not intended as mere propaganda, Williams did leave London in August 1644 with a document of incorporation for his colony and a letter addressed to Massachusetts Bay officials citing approval of his labors among the Indians.

Although *A Key* fascinated its inquisitive London audience and caught the attention of readers in continental Europe having a general curiosity about Indian life or a more serious, scholarly interest in philology, history, and the origins of the races, its reception among New England colonists is shrouded in uncertainties.[22] Some knew of *A Key*. Several seventeenth-century authors mentioned it or quoted from it in their writings. Others seem to have had at least a general awareness of Williams's efforts in acquiring the rudiments of Native language. Nine years before *A Key* was published, William Wood remarked that "one of the English preachers, in a special good intent of doing good to their souls, hath spent much time in attaining to their language, wherein he is so good a proficient that he can speak to their understanding and they to us."[23] Given the date of Wood's observation (1634), he could have been referring to none other than Roger Williams. Praise was also forthcoming from John Winthrop, who was well aware of Williams's "great industry and travail *in his printed Indian labours*." Even Cotton Mather, who had few good things to say about Williams, mentioned, if somewhat wryly, the "little relation of his observations, wherein (Mr Williams) *spiritualizes* the *curiosities* with two and thirty chapters" and borrowed freely from it in his own writings.[24] Yet beyond these few examples, it is unknown how many copies of *A Key* actually made their way into the hands of literate New Englanders in the years immediately following its original printing or later in the seventeenth century. Books were rarities. Even one like *A Key,* which might have furnished the literate colonist with useful information about New England's Native peoples, would have had limited availability.

Existing colonial records and texts make little reference to *A Key* until the nineteenth century. In 1794 and 1798, the Massachusetts Historical Society printed two series of excerpts from a copy of *A Key* thought to be the only one extant in America. The first series contained passages on Indian customs, and the later, sections of the vocabulary. Without Roger Williams's observations and poems, sections of *A Key* in which he sometimes commented on the relative merits of Native American and English culture, the Massachusetts Historical Society versions simply presented a straightforward list of terms and cultural traits pertaining to Narragansett Indians. For more than thirty years, this "truncated, neutralized form" of *A Key* remained the only edition published in America.[25]

In 1827 the Rhode Island Historical Society reprinted *A Key* in its entirety in the first volume of its *Collections*.[26] The road leading to this reprinting was not without its mishaps and delays. About forty pages of the manuscript and proof sheets were lost in a fire that consumed the printing office, including the type used in setting the letters of Williams's text for this new edition of *A Key*. The committee in charge of publication later detected errors in the entries of some Indian words after the first pages had been reset. To correct these omissions and redo the pages of the text destroyed in the fire, the publication committee had no alternative than to ask the Massachusetts Historical Society for the loan of their original edition of *A Key*.[27]

Of the thousand copies finally printed, some were offered by subscription at seventy-five cents per copy, and 334 subscriptions were sold at the outset. Other copies were distributed to literary and antiquarian societies. The Massachusetts Historical Society, for example, received a copy as a favor in kind for its loan of *A Key* at a time when Rhode Island's reprint seemed anything but a foregone conclusion. Although the trustees of the Rhode Island Historical Society anticipated that the remaining copies "would find a ready sale in other states," sales failed to meet expectations.[28] In July 1829 they were obliged to draw $110 from the society's treasury to defray the costs of publication.[29]

Reciprocal agreements established between the Rhode Island Historical Society and other newly founded historical societies to facilitate the exchange of publications made *A Key* available throughout the eastern United States and, in some cases, well beyond its continental borders. Copies were given to the American Antiquarian Society in Worcester, the American Philosophical Society in Philadelphia, and the Essex Institute in Salem, which became important repositories for documents pertaining to colonial New England. Outside of North America, the Rhode Island Historical Society exchanged publications with the Royal Society of Northern Antiquaries in Copenhagen and the Royal Academy of Sciences at Lisbon. Still more copies of *A Key* made their way into the hands of individuals who were designated honorary members of the society. Included among them were the Honorable George Bancroft, the prolific historian, and Henry Rowe Schoolcraft, a respected ethnologist. The society presumed that this "sketch of the language of one of the principal aboriginal nations, as it existed at the first settlement of this country by the whites would not be unacceptable" to Schoolcraft, who had more than a passing interest in "the welfare of the remnant nations."[30] In his letter of acknowledgment to the society, Schoolcraft called *A Key* nothing less than a "valuable monument of one of the principal languages spoken in New England on its first settlement, and its publication, at this time, is a service rendered to the reading public, which can be properly appreciated by those only, who have directed some share of their attention as [to] the curious philosophical principles displayed by the Indian languages."[31]

Although the 1827 reprinting made *A Key* more widely available than it had been previously, its appeal, as Schoolcraft (and others) indicated, was still limited to a specialized audience of antiquarians and scholars. For these individuals, some of whom were beginning to write the histories of New England, *A Key* became an important source of information on Narragansett Indians at the time of early colonization and, ever increasingly, a point of departure in their characterizations of the nineteenth-century Narragansetts, whom they considered remnants of the former nation. Many compared statements in *A Key* with those written by Williams years later, suggesting that the degeneration of Narragansett culture was inevitable. In their estimation, the lesson learned by Williams, at great personal cost, was that the decline of the Narragansetts was attributable more to flaws inherent in the nature of Indian people than to contact with Europeans.

One of the first local historians to make extensive use of *A Key* as a source of information on Narragansett culture and history was Elisha R. Potter. A Harvard graduate with a strong taste for historical pursuits, he wrote *The Early History of Narragansett* in 1835 when he was just twenty-four years old. In gathering "the scattered and perishing memorials of the early settlement of the ancient King's Province," he eyed *A Key* as an important work on the region's indigenous peoples.[32] According to Potter, Williams's statements in *A Key* gave abundant testimony to Narragansett generosity, hospitality, and general integrity, which he had no reason to doubt. His faith in Williams's knowledge of Narragansett cultural and moral attributes rested on the length of time that Williams had lived among them (i.e., five or six years), and the close and intimate acquaintances he had developed with them. Potter claimed that the bonds of friendship established between Williams and the Narragansetts in the years before *A Key*'s publication sustained the severest trials. In the war of 1676, when the Narragansetts were "exasperated against the English and driven almost to madness by the repeated insults and injuries they had suffered from them; the friend of the Indians [Roger Williams] found their friendship for him still as strong as ever."[33]

Potter's history, published as the third volume of the Rhode Island Historical Society's *Collections*, apparently took some liberties in representing the loyalties of the Narragansetts at the time of King Philip's War, and by implication, perhaps, even those of Roger Williams. The Narragansetts' sentiments toward Williams are not easily captured in words. They did not write about Williams, as he did about them. But their opinions were sometimes transcribed into the printed record; they were, after all, not speechless. For example, Williams described how a group of Indians, including "John Wall Maker" (a.k.a. Stonewall John), a Narragansett, said to him: "You have driven us out of our own Countrie and then pursued us to our Great Miserie, and Your own, and we are forced to live upon you."[34] The statement, made during an attack on Providence in March 1676, did not mince words. Stonewall John's and the other Indians' opinion of Williams is not lost in his transcription. Having failed to negotiate a peace and seeing much of Providence, including his own house, burned in the raid, Williams could hardly have felt that "their friendship for him was as strong as ever." If anything, he in turn felt betrayed. Although Potter may have miscalculated the sentiments of the Narragansetts toward Williams (and other English colonists) in the late seventeenth century, his use of *A Key* as a principal source of information gave the work a strong vote of confidence, which had a lasting effect on those who would continue to write histories of New England.[35] Organized more as a "form of annals than digested historical narrative," Potter's history identified for the first time important historical materials for interpreting the early history of Narragansetts, but most especially, it recognized Williams's *A Key* as an essential book on its original inhabitants.[36]

In the second third of the nineteenth century, few history writers doubted the decline of the Narragansetts. The issue to be resolved was just how much they had fallen from prominence and to what extent their numbers had dwindled. In making these determinations, history writers played a numbers game in which *A Key* became a critical source of evidence. Using Williams's statement that "in Nariganset Countrey (which is the chief people in the Land:) a man shall come to many Townes, some bigger, some lesser, it may be a dozen in 20 miles [32 kilometers] Travell," they garnered support for their argument that the once-populous Narragansetts were vastly reduced in number and fading into obscurity.[37] Williams's description of the social landscape served as a vivid contrast to Narragansett country as it existed in the nineteenth century. With its acreage shrunk, its geographical boundaries circumscribed, and its settlements reduced in size and number, Narragansett land, a reserved area of less than 64 square miles (166 square kilometers) in Charlestown, scarcely resembled the ancestral territory depicted by Williams. It was reasoned that what had happened to Narragansett ancestral land—its gradual reduction and transformation by colonists—must have happened inevitably to its Native people. They too dwindled and became acculturated, then assimilated, and soon would become extinct. Thus, *A Key* came to validate the decline of the Narragansetts and confirm European Americans' expectations about their eventual disappearance.

Additional confirmation of the dwindling visibility of the Narragansetts was provided by John De Forest in his *History of the Indians of Connecticut from the Earliest Known Period to 1850*.[38] Based on an extensive study of written sources contained in local historical collections, colonial archives, and volumes in the Yale College library, his book demeaned the enduring presence of Native peoples not only in Connecticut but in other parts of southern New England as well. Neither an apologist for the losses nor one to lament the Indians' passing, De Forest confronted what he perceived to be the facts about the colonial history of New England Native Americans with scholarly and scientific assurance.[39] His assessment of "the great tribe of Narragansetts" was that they were not once as populous as many had supposed. Although De Forest deferred to the authority of Roger Williams on most things and drew heavily from *A Key* in sketching his historical account of the "ancient appearance" of the region's peoples, customs, language, and institutions, he seriously doubted the demographic projections that relied, at least partially, on Williams's observation concerning Narragansett country.[40] Arguing that initial appraisals of Native population were invariably inflated, he revised earlier estimates on the Narragansetts downward.[41] Although he had a valid point, the argument made the Narragansetts' rate of population decline on official rolls more palatable (and perhaps more morally acceptable) and cast a disparaging shadow on their former greatness.[42]

De Forest did more than play a numbers game, however. He had a theory about the "remnant" state of the Narragansetts. It was based on an account found in the manuscripts of Ezra Stiles about Narragansett mothers' abandoning their infants. Written almost eighty years after King Philip's War, the story was told to Stiles by John Paul, a Narragansett, while Stiles was traveling in Rhode Island.[43] Unwilling to interpret the practice of infant abandonment within the broader context of Native culture, De Forest took the account of "Bastard Rocks" as evidence that "the morals of Indians were very corrupt before the arrival of the English."[44] He concluded "that, although a strong prejudice against illegitimate births existed, it did not prevent prostitution, and only produced abortion and infanticide; and that these last customs being broken up by the influence of the whites, all reserve was thrown aside and the Indians became openly and shamelessly licentious."[45]

Excesses in "the form of vice here mentioned"—that is, what De Forest and presumably other nineteenth-century Puritan descendants viewed as inappropriate sexual conduct—were thought to produce both sterility and disease. Here then was the cause of the decline. Posing a rhetorical question, the answer to which was never in doubt, De Forest asked himself (and his readers): "Is it wonderful that communities so licentious, and added to this, so indolent and drunken, should not increase? that they should even rapidly decline?"[46]

The histories of the Narragansett people, as they were being written in the second third of the nineteenth century, constructed a narrative that has become the dominant one. The narrative borrowed heavily from *A Key* to describe the "original Narragansetts." Befriended by Williams, these Indians—brave, populous, powerful, generous, hospitable, mannered, and civil—in turn professed their friendship to the early English settlers. Then, according to the story, they came to resent the settlers' encroachments on their lands and the erosion of their autonomy. In 1675 they allied with other New England Indians and fought a desperate war. Nearly exterminated in a military battle at Great Swamp, in present-day South Kingstown, Rhode Island, they were no more by the summer of 1676. Those who called themselves Narragansett after this date, and certainly in the nineteenth century, had lost the admirable traits of their ancestors. They were Narragansett in name only.[47]

The Narragansetts' story as told in these histories was laden with myths and legends that even today have refused to die. The narrative was short and matter-of-fact; however, its brevity and assuredness left much unsaid. It made no mention of the importance of family, the bonds of kinship, and the ties to community and place that shaped the Narragansetts' everyday lives and social relations, nor of how these were sustained through the seventeenth and later centuries. It did not tell how family, kinship, and community helped the Narragansetts in ongoing struggles over their identity and history. Glossing over the years after 1676, the narrative made invisible the gradual dispossession, forced indentures, and cycles of debt and poverty that rendered the lives of many Narragansetts economically marginal, and it overlooked their efforts to regain ancestral land, secure the welfare of their children, and, in general, survive.[48]

Not surprisingly, these histories became important references for individuals attempting to redefine the relationship between the state of Rhode Island and the tribe.[49] Included among these histories was Elisha Potter's, the first comprehensive account of the Narragansetts to identify *A Key* as a primary source of information. A report proposing the abolishment of the Narragansetts appeared as early as 1832. It was vigorously challenged by the Narragansetts and, ironically, by Potter himself, who dismissed the report as "a rather shabby document."[50] Although no action was taken on the recommendation, the notion to abolish the Narragansetts resurfaced several times again in the 1850s. In 1858 the state commissioner of the Narragansett Tribe of Indians wrote to the general assembly, providing reasons why the Narragansetts should become Rhode Island citizens. By granting Indians the right to act as individuals within European American society, citizenship aimed at the destruction of tribal organization. In making a case for putting tribal members "on equal footing with other citizens of the State," the report told of their early history, citing Potter (1835) as a primary source, and described the deplorable condition of Narragansetts then living in Charlestown.[51] Although the report recommended detribalization, the matter remained unresolved for the next two decades. During this period, the story of the seventeenth-century Narragansetts and their decline would be spread to a wider readership and become ever more familiar to a European American audience.

In part, the dissemination of the history of the Narragansetts was facilitated through the efforts of the Narragansett Club. Like similar literary associations founded in the nineteenth century, the Narragansett Club was acutely aware of the "intrinsic value" of the early works such as those relating to the history of Rhode Island and New England. More importantly, it realized that many of these works were not widely available and existed only in great public libraries and in private collections. The rare editions available for sale commanded exorbitant prices that placed them entirely beyond the reach of the ordinary collector (or reader).[52] Of these, Roger Williams's writings were among the scarcest and most costly. The last copy of the original 1643 edition of *A Key*, in fact, was reportedly sold at a London auction for twelve guineas—the equivalent of about sixty dollars in gold.[53]

It was in an attempt to make these early writings more available that the Narragansett Club drafted its plan to reissue the rare works of Roger Williams and other early authors, which appeared between 1866 and 1874. Each volume was to be an exact reprint of the first edition. The "style of type, the same quaint orthography, the same illustrated initial letters"—all were to replicate the original. Even the paper was to be modeled "after the old style of manufacture." On the recommendation of the club's secretary, it was decided to issue the volumes as a limited-edition series: two hundred copies were to be offered to subscribers and an additional fifty to the members. The latter were to be known as "club copies," which none of the eight members was authorized to sell.[54] To announce the series and promote publication of the first volume containing *A Key* and other works by Roger Williams, the association sent a circular to potential clients, printed with words inspired by Williams's Narragansett vocabulary. Addressed to *Netop*, the Algonkian term for "friend," the advertisement was sent from the "Narragansett Club Wigwam, Mooshaussick, Paponakeeswush [the winter month], 1865." At five dollars, the club's asking price for the first volume was well below that supposedly commanded for the last original edition of the Williams's book on the Narragansetts.[55]

The editors of the volume were Rueben A. Guild and James Hammond Trumbull. Guild contributed the biographical sketch of Williams, and Trumbull, a respected expert on Indian languages, edited and annotated *A Key*.[56] Trumbull praised it as a "trustworthy, or tolerably full" vocabulary and excellent phrase book, but one that was deficient as a grammar. Although he analyzed *A Key* as a linguistic work, he acknowledged that to many readers, the "briefe observations of the customs, manners and worships, etc., of the natives" are the most "pleasant and profitable" portions of Williams's book. These, in his opinion, were of great value for the information they supplied "respecting the manners and customs, the conduct and character, of the Indians of New England, 'in peace and warre, in life and death.'" He added that Williams's observations on Native life "have been so often and so largely drawn upon by later writers, that our obligations to their author are almost lost sight of, and they are held, as if by prescription, the common property of historians."[57]

Although *A Key* may have been rare and costly, and not widely read by a popu-

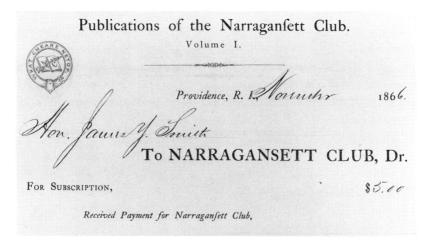

Figure 11. Subscription form for volume 1 of the Narragansett Club publications, which the club offered to the public as a limited-edition series. *A Key Into the Language of America* was reprinted in the first volume. (Courtesy of the Rhode Island Historical Society).

lar audience, it was foundational in the works of scholars who were writing the histories of the Narragansetts, other Native Americans, and New England. Through the publication of their works, information contained in *A Key* on Native life was disseminated to those who might not otherwise have been aware of Williams's book on Indians. The curious reader who had come across references to *A Key* in other accounts could now examine it firsthand, reprinted in the Narragansett Club's series. The response to the club's circular was enthusiastic. Indeed, inquisitive minds longed to read Williams's work for themselves. Orders were steady and reviews positive.[58] Even the Rhode Island Historical Society, which had been criticized by the Narragansett Club for inactivity, offered congratulations. The society indicated that Trumbull's notes were "peculiarly valuable, and leave little to be desired" and added, perhaps somewhat sardonically, that the club's publication would greatly enhance the value of their own edition published as the first volume of their *Collections* in 1827.[59] Given the aggressive promotional campaign and the high accolades, *A Key* was well on its way to becoming common knowledge about Narragansett Indians, rather than privileged information known only to a handful of scholars.

But popularity had its drawbacks. *A Key*'s increasing availability and widening acclaim inspired imitations. One such work appeared in 1867— *A Summer's Ramble through Ten Kingdoms*, a collection of letters written by John Dunton, a London bookseller, publisher, and voluminous writer who had visited New England in 1686.[60] During his six-month stay, Dunton made a profit selling books, conducted a full social life, and simply "couldn't stop scribbling."[61] As an indication of his extreme scribaciousness, he managed in the first three weeks to keep a lengthy diary of his activities and send off innumerable letters to his friends and relatives in England, including two or three each day to his wife. Among his letters, the one written to "Mr. John Woolhurst at his house in Clare Market London," contained an account of the customs and ideas of Indians, which Dunton claimed were told to him "personally, from time to time, by an occasional fellow-traveler, during a few months residence in New England in 1686."[62]

His companion and source of information could not have been any other than *A Key*, as Williams himself had died three years earlier. Dunton copied liberally from *A Key*, rearranging chapters and verse to suit his purposes. He presented the secondhand information in the form of conversations he allegedly had during his travels in New England:

> The Captain told us that there were a sort of People in the Countrey call'd Mihtuk-mecha, that is, Tree-eaters; these People live between three and four hundred miles [480–640 kilometers] West within the Land: They set no Corn, but live on the Bark of Chestnuts and Walnuts, and other fine trees: They dry and eat this Bark with the fat of Beasts, and sometimes of Men; from whence they are also called Men-Eaters; they are a Strong People, and the Terrour of those Indians that live near them.[63]

The account appears in *A Key's* chapter "Of *Eating* and *Entertainment*," in which Williams describes:

> *Tree-eaters.* A people so called (living between three and foure hundred miles West into the land) from their eating only *Mihtúchquash,* that is, Trees: They are *Men-eaters,* they set no corne, but live on the *bark* of *Chestnut* and *Walnut,* and other fine trees: They dry and eat this *bark* with the fat of Beasts, and sometimes of men: This people are the *terrour* of the neighbour *Natives.*[64]

Dunton's other nine rambles borrow just as freely from Williams's *A Key*. Although the volume's editor, W. H. Whitmore, acknowledges Dunton's great debt to Williams, he stops short of accusing him of intentional plagiarism, on the pretense that the letter was not published while Dunton was alive. He supposes that if this had happened, Dunton might have admitted his indebtedness. Perhaps, but not necessarily. Leaving the sticky issue of plagiarism aside, he commends Dunton for doing a good service. In writing about his rambles through New England, John Dunton "republished information which had been out of reach for nearly forty years, and which he always confesses he had 'from a friend.'"[65] After all, Williams's *A Key* had been off the printing press for slightly more than four decades at the time Dunton wrote his letter to Woolhurst about his travels through New England. (Actually, his travels involved just a few short jaunts from Boston to Medford and back, to Chelsea, Saugus, Salem, Weymouth, Dorchester, and Roxbury.) Whitmore went on to say that "although the book by Williams has been twice reprinted, once in 1827, and again in 1866, very few persons, comparatively have access to it."[66] He expressed the hope that this version, which presented the information contained in *A Key* in a "much more readable form," would remedy the situation.[67]

Not everyone agreed with Whitmore's assessment of Dunton's *Rambles*, however. His plagiarism drew fire from a critic for the *North American Review*. In praising the initial volumes published in the Narragansett Club's series (including Williams's *A Key*), the reviewer called Dunton, known as being eccentric and, in his later years, partially insane, an "unconscionable liar, and otherwise absurd person" who had the audacity to say that the information he presented on the manners and customs of the Indians of New England was imparted to him personally.[68]

Others who borrowed from *A Key* could hardly be accused of such vulgar plagiarism. Although they used its contents freely and selectively, their aim was not to take poetic license. Rather, it was to use *A Key* to forward, if not confirm, opinions of the Narragansetts' fall into oblivion and thus increase public pressure to push ahead with detribalization. In 1879 the state of Rhode Island appointed a committee to conduct public hearings on the matter. The official report made by the Committee of Investigation in January 1880 to the Rhode Island House of Representatives contained transcripts of three public hearings, allegedly complete, along with a historical sketch of the Narragansett Indian tribe that was included in an appendix because of "the gravity of the subject under consideration, and the interests at stake."[69]

In preparing the historical sketch, the committee made "copious extracts" from a number of nineteenth-century histories that used *A Key*. The list included: *Westerly and Its Witnesses*, by the Reverend Frederic Denison; *A Historical Sketch of Charlestown*, by William F. Tucker; and John De Forest's *History of the Indians of Connecticut*. In addition, the committee consulted the first volume of Samuel Greene Arnold's *History of Rhode Island* and referred the curious reader to Potter's *Early History of Narragansett* and Updike's *History of the Narragansett Church*.[70] The selections leave little doubt that the committee had chosen its sources wisely. All were unanimous in expressing the opinion that the Narragansetts were an expiring tribe. They confirmed arguments made by officials and many others in attendance at the Indian Meeting House in Charlestown and at Card's Hall in Cross Mills, where the public hearings were held, urging resolution on the matter of the Narragansetts' legal abolition.

Although the historical sketch contained few direct citations from Williams and none from *A Key* itself, the authors whose works were used in preparing the document had relied on *A Key* in their own writings. Samuel Arnold, for example, derived much of his information on the seventeenth-century Narragansetts from *A*

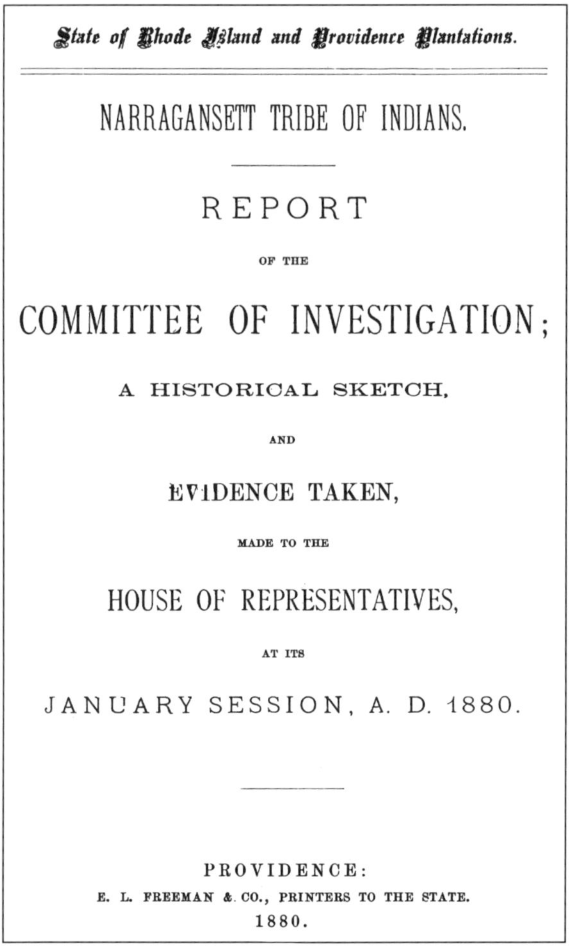

State of Rhode Island and Providence Plantations.

NARRAGANSETT TRIBE OF INDIANS.

REPORT

OF THE

COMMITTEE OF INVESTIGATION;

A HISTORICAL SKETCH,

AND

EVIDENCE TAKEN,

MADE TO THE

HOUSE OF REPRESENTATIVES,

AT ITS

JANUARY SESSION, A. D. 1880.

PROVIDENCE:
E. L. FREEMAN & CO., PRINTERS TO THE STATE.
1880.

Figure 12. Title page of *Report of the Committee of Investigation; A Historical Sketch, and Evidence Taken, Made to the House of Representatives, at its January Session, A.D. 1880.* Providence, 1880. (Courtesy of the Rhode Island Historical Society)

Key, but he used few direct quotations and mentioned Williams sparingly. His account of the Narragansetts conveys to the reader a sense of the already known— a narrative so familiar, so well understood, and so authoritative that there was no need to ground its points in a sustained argument or in a weighty presentation of evidence. Here was a people once the most numerous and powerful of all the New England tribes, now on the verge of extinction. At one time, one could meet "a dozen of their towns in the course of 20 miles [32 kilometers] travel." Although they were annihilated in the War of 1676, Arnold reasoned that destiny, perhaps more than the war itself, had sealed their fate.[71]

Writing boldly, Arnold commented not only on the disappearance of "the Narragansett empire" described by Williams but also on the prospects for its survivors. He predicted that "the same path to death" followed by the Narragansett Nation (and before them the Pequots) would be the course taken by other Native groups, however powerful or warlike. "All history," he stated, "points to an inevitable law controlling the occupancy of the earth."[72] The law of inevitability to which he alluded spoke of the progress and the advance of "civilization" but reeked of racism. Adhering to this logic, Arnold surmised that the remaining Narragansetts (and other Native Americans) would completely vanish within the century and leave no "proof upon the earth that they have existed."[73]

Both Denison and Tucker presented the Committee of Investigation with historical accounts of the two Rhode Island towns having the densest concentrations of Narragansett Indians in the nineteenth century. These also were places where local citizens had a vested interest in the Narragansetts' detribalization, and especially in ancestral land that would then be made available to them. In writing about Westerly, and specifically its Native peoples, Denison stated that the "real condition of Indian life was truly deplorable," an interpretation he based largely on his rather peculiar reading of Williams's *A Key*.[74] In Denison's view, "The men were only hunters and warriors; the females were only overtasked slaves. They together made up only precarious hordes, scarcely superior to the wild beasts with which they disputed the possession of the forests."[75] He went on to suggest that even their "best works of art, their dwellings and canoes, were fit types of their national life, temporary and decaying."[76] Neither persuasion nor incitements of civilization could save them from the depravity they exhibited as a people. Not even Roger Williams.

If Denison's assessment of the real condition of Indian life did not offer sufficient cause for the Committee of Investigation to declare the Narragansetts extinct as a people, then his statements about their claim to land in southwestern Rhode Island surely must have. Relying on familiar words and phrases, Denison undermined the Narragansetts' ties to the Charlestown reservation. "This famous tribe, anciently holding jurisdiction over most of the present State of Rhode Island, able, in their palmy days, under Canonicus and Miantonimo, to call to the field about four thousand warriors," he stated, "had rule over Misquamicut [that is, Westerly and the neighboring towns of Hopkington, Charlestown, and Richmond] only through their allies or confederates, the Niantics."[77] With their jurisdiction broken in King Philip's War (and their numbers reduced), remnants of the Narragansett tribe consolidated with the Niantics and lived with them on Niantic land. By italicizing the printed words, the committee gave added weight to Denison's statement that Narragansetts living on reserved land in Charlestown were dwelling on Niantic soil. This insinuation—along with assumptions about racial purity, forecasts about Indian extinction, and an inability to grasp the phenomenally complicated issues of Native American survival in New England, including attachments to familiar places and clan homes—provided the committee with added justification for recommending the legal abolition of these "last vestiges of the sons of the forest."[78]

Tucker's history of Charlestown, like Denison's *Westerly*, had little to say about Roger Williams or *A Key* specifically. He was utterly convinced that nineteenth-century Narragansetts were not real Narragansetts. In his opinion, they were "the Ninigret tribe," pretenders who had defamed the name of the ancient Narragansetts by having assumed it. Referring to the course of accommodation steered by Ninigret, the seventeenth-century Niantic sachem, in King Philip's War, in which he allied himself to the English, Tucker declared that "not one drop of the blood of Canonicus, Mantonimo, or Canonchet, ever coursed in the veins of a sachem who could sit neuter in his wigwam and hear the guns and see the conflagration ascending from the fortress that was exterminating their nation forever."[79] His words provided reinforcement for those who wished to believe that the Narragansetts had not only become "few and feeble" but had ceased to exist. In his view, the seventeenth-century Narragansett sachems known to Williams had no connection to those who later claimed them as ancestors. Narragansett blood had not merely become diluted: it had completely evaporated.

The Committee of Investigation concluded its historical sketch of the Narragansett tribe with a verse taken from a poem inscribed by Denison in which he reflected on the passing of the Narragansetts:

> We children of a favored day,
> Inheriting their homes,
> Would guard their history from decay,
> And mark their mouldering tombs.[80]

Denison's poetry captured the mood of those seeking to abolish the tribe. Although tinged with a just a hint of nostalgia, the words of this romanticized cant expressed unequivocally the opinion that the Narragansetts—the ones described by Williams in *A Key*—had largely disappeared. With their homes and history possessed by European Americans, they existed only in the past. Soon after the Committee of Investigation submitted its report, the Rhode Island legislature voted to abolish the Narragansetts' tribal status and thus declared them "extinct." The action terminated formal relations between the state of Rhode Island and the Narragansett tribe and granted citizenship to those who continued to call themselves

Narragansett. As it was used in lamenting the passage of the Narragansett tribe, *A Key* was not a mere footnote, but a very powerful tool in the protracted struggle over Narragansett identity and history taking place in nineteenth-century New England.

Under the terms of their detribalization, the Narragansetts agreed to sell all land held in common except for a 2-acre (1-hectare) parcel of reserved land. The tribal council had agreed to the sale in a closed and undocumented meeting held at the office of one of the commissioners.[81] The outcome of the meeting came after the issue of land had been debated at length in the public meetings. At these hearings, many Narragansetts expressed strong attachments to the reservation where they and their parents had been born and their ancestral remains were buried, and they wished to avoid selling it. Some tentatively acquiesced to selling the reserved land but first wanted to receive financial compensation for ancestral lands acquired earlier by Rhode Island. With the official transcripts indicating that the Narragansetts were unwavering in their concerns about the disposition of the reservation, and knowing well the consequences of dispossession for keeping the community intact, the tribal council's reversal on the question of selling common land seems abrupt and even puzzling. However, it is perhaps no less understandable than the commissioners' reasons for removing the issue from public discussion and negotiating with the Narragansetts behind closed doors.

The proceeds from the sale of approximately 922 acres (369 hectares) were divvied up among those who claimed Narragansett ancestry, but only after the state of Rhode Island conducted a lengthy and tedious inquiry into tribal genealogy. The division of property—a total of five thousand dollars from the sale—finalized the Narragansetts' detribalization. In 1883 the Commission on the Affairs on the Narragansett Indians sought to explain the appropriation of tribal lands by inferring that Rhode Island was founded on the principle that the soil belonged absolutely to the Narragansett tribe of Indians "and could only be taken by strangers upon such terms and conditions as the Indians chose to part with it."[82] This principle was credited to none other than Roger Williams, who, prior to his banishment, had attacked the validity of Massachusetts Bay's patent and questioned "the right of King James to send his subjects in to the Kingdom of Massasoit uninvited."[83] It was with the Narragansetts' free will, then, that the people of Rhode Island formed a colony, assumed the status of their protectors after the murder of Miantonomi and the death of Canonicus left the tribe "less united under one chief," and, most important, became the beneficiaries in the sale of what remained of the Narragansetts' homelands.[84]

With detribalization completed, the Narragansetts existed only in myth and memory for most European Americans and were known from "the imperfect and only data remaining," namely, the stone implements, ancient shell heaps, and burial places of Narragansett ancestors. These were things to be salvaged and places

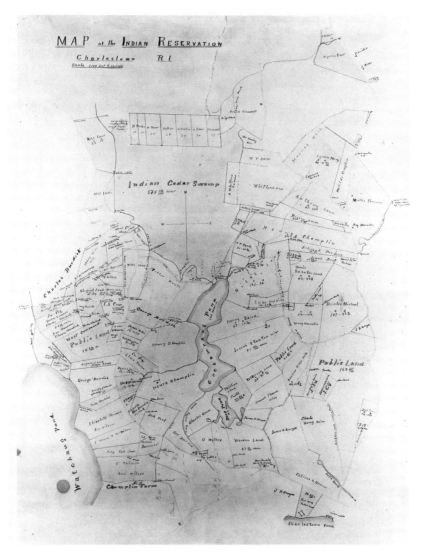

Figure 13. Map of the Indian Reservation, Charlestown, Rhode Island, 1878. (Courtesy of the Rhode Island Historical Society)

to be memorialized of "an old Indian empire." In the absence of writing, codes of law, arts, and real estate, these could serve to broaden and deepen a reverence of the past among those "who sat in darkness" because their predecessors neglected to transmit "knowledge to the centuries following them."[85] Perhaps inspired by the sentiments echoed in Denison's verse, some local history writers (including Denison himself) became involved in the movement not only to mark sites but also to excavate them, in order to gather empirical evidence for what was developing as an increasingly artifact-centered antiquarianism. Their "cabinets," the early forerunners of museum collections, came to be filled with eclectic objects that served as keys for explicating the customs and character of the ancient inhabitants of Narragansett Bay.[86]

For others, however, the Narragansetts existed more perfectly in Williams's *A Key* than in antiquities. For the steadfast defenders of *A Key,* the reprinting in 1886 of Potter's *Early History of Narragansett,* in an expanded version containing notes and primary source material, must have seemed an auspicious event. The same timeliness also applied to the publication one year earlier of Henry C. Dorr's long essay, *The Narragansetts,* in which he reasoned that *A Key* not only provided ample information about these Native people but also addressed topics more "grave and urgent" than could be explored through ruins and other material evidence.[87] In offering praise, Dorr announced that the writings of Roger Williams alone offered abundant material for studying Narragansett Indians. Of Williams's writings, *A Key* was the standard. "By this book, they have been estimated in subsequent generations," Dorr claimed. Few, even today, could rebut his point. He attributed *A Key*'s importance to good timing—Williams observed the Narragansetts before they had become corrupted by trade and alcohol—but more significant, he argued, was the fact that Roger Williams came to the Narragansetts "not as an explorer or an archaeologist," but as a missionary believing that they were ready to welcome Christianity and civilization.[88] Dorr's statement was as much a direct volley against collectors, preservationists, and others promoting the study of Narragansett Indian history through local antiquities, as it was a tribute to *A Key*. In Dorr's opinion, Williams sketched in *A Key* "a vigorous outline of the last generation of the Narragansetts," at least those who had any semblance of national life.[89]

Dorr's assessment of *A Key* was echoed by other local history writers in the early twentieth century. Even those who questioned Dorr's accuracy as a historian agreed with him about the enduring value of *A Key*. Among them was Dorr's most vigorous critic, Sidney S. Rider.[90] A staunch admirer of Williams, Rider relied almost wholly on *A Key* in describing Narragansett Indians in his account, *The Lands of Rhode Island as They Were Known to Caunounicus and Miantunnomu When Roger Williams Came in 1636*. Forthright in his opinions, he proclaimed that Williams knew the Narragansetts "more thoroughly than any other man."[91] Coming from Rider, this was a strong endorsement. Not known to suffer fools lightly, and overly pedantic for some tastes, he was one of Roger Williams's most devoted fans.

In his *Book Notes*, an eight-page pamphlet of literary and historical criticism that he published fortnightly between 1883 and 1916, Rider repeatedly indicted Williams's detractors. He championed the "little book published by him in 1643," calling it nothing less than a classic piece of "prose literature."[92] A Key had been called many things, but never before had it been included in the category of literature or represented as the best that Rhode Island had to offer in the realm of literary texts. This was, after all, a book on Indian language to be used as a dictionary, a phrase book, or a guidebook. It offered interesting and even useful information on the customs and manners of Narragansett Indians, but A Key was typically read or reported on annalistically. To Rider, A Key was an important scholarly contribution on the Narragansetts, which should be appreciated for its form and content. He encouraged readers to look at it firsthand and in its entirety. No digested, abridged, or annotated version would do Williams's "little book" justice.

How many readers took Rider's recommendations seriously is, unfortunately, mere speculation. Most had come to know A Key as condensed, secondhand information released through the works of history writers in the nineteenth century. Thomas Bicknell, an amateur historian with romantic notions about Narragansett Indians and their past, decided to take a close look at A Key Into the Language of America for himself. In his multivolume history of Rhode Island, published in 1920, he stated that A Key was perhaps the most valuable contribution from the pen of Roger Williams and the only one intelligible to modern readers.[93] Given Bicknell's fascination with the past of New England's Native Americans, A Key held enormous appeal. Based on notes of what Williams saw, heard, and experienced that were "put in print as soon as made, after his contact with the natives," A Key must have given Bicknell the kind of communion with seventeenth-century Narragansetts for which he yearned and which most historians, amateur or professional, are denied. As if to confirm Williams's accuracy and authority, if not recapture what had been dead for so long, Bicknell chose to do "a double service to the reader by quoting liberally from Mr. Williams' own pen the results of his studies and observations."[94]

Soon after publication of his volumes on Rhode Island history, Bicknell began to engineer the dedication of monuments celebrating the Narragansetts' past. He came to learn somewhat indirectly that New England's Native peoples would prefer living memorials, rather than stone markers commemorating their past.[95] The informant, a young Mohegan woman named Gladys Tantaquidgeon, was no fool; she understood that memorial acts implied termination. Yet she, the Narragansetts, and other New England Native Americans were not dead. They were very much alive. Seeing the error of his ways, Bicknell responded by forming the Indian Council of New England, an organization of Natives and non-Natives dedicated to cultural revitalization through the "preservation of Indian language, folklore, traditions, history, and the record of achievement of great chiefs and tribesmen" and public events.[96] The tall, aristocratic, white-bearded Bicknell granted himself the title of Paleface Honorary Sachem, a position he shared with another honorary sachem. In assuming the title, Bicknell solved the seemingly insoluble quandary of living in the Narragansett world of his imagination, a world whose people he once thought were as dead as the Indian language transcribed into *A Key*.

For members of the Indian Council of New England, including Bicknell, *A Key* took on significance as an important educational tool that would aid in restoring and preserving lost aspects of Narragansett culture. Although Narragansett had ceased to be a spoken language by around 1810, the version put into print by Roger Williams along with English translations illustrated the nature of Native American thought and expression, even if layers of meaning were unstated or misrepresented by equivalent English terms. The vocabulary also provided testimony that some Narragansett words had become Anglicized. Like ancestral lands, terms like "wampum, sachem, squaw, samp, pappose, hawk, tautog" had been taken by the English and made their own.[97] Rather than showing the extent to which Narragansett and English cultures had become blurred, the adopted words recalled the complicated world of seventeenth-century New England, a place that Indian and English people once thought could accommodate both cultures. Bicknell idealized this world, a middle ground between two cultures; in writing a constitution for the Indian Council of New England, he indicated that among the council's purposes was that of promoting acquaintance and friendship among Native and non-Native people. This renewed relationship would be reinforced by the structure of council offices, which included two honorary sachems—one white (assumed by Bicknell) and the other Native. In furnishing evidence of the kindness, generosity, and other admirable traits that were said to be part of the Indian character, Williams's *A Key* offered more than hints about the meanings or corruption of Narragansett words. It provided the very basis for a fraternal association such as the Indian Council of New England.

Yet despite the activities of the Indian Council in the 1920s and the publication a decade later of a popular magazine, *Narragansett Dawn*, chronicling the Narragansetts' rebirth, most European Americans were convinced that the Narragansetts had vanished. Neither public events like powwows and dedication ceremonies, with regalia and other visual displays of "Indiannness," nor a monthly magazine filled with articles written by Narragansetts on their history, sacred traditions, recipes, and lessons in their native tongue (derived from *A Key* and from words and phrases that continued to be used after Narragansett ceased to be a spoken language) altered this perception.[98] Moreover, those who still called themselves Narragansett carried the stigma of mixed ancestry. As with other Native American groups in southeastern New England and throughout the east coast, some Indians had intermarried with persons of African descent and also with those of European background. Intermarriage was part of their colonial adjustment, part of their very survival, but it had tainted them. As a result, some Narragansetts were darker or paler than the hue perceived by European Americans as connoting racial purity for Indians. Their ancestral bloodlines showed, but so too did their composite zeal and the fortitude built in reaction to indifference and discrimination.

But the Narragansetts' transformation into a people of "mixed blood" (and the stigma attached to that term) was at least as much a product of official misrecognition that served to confirm their disappearance as it was simple genetic admixture. According to written records, their indigenous blood began wasting away around the middle of the eighteenth century, when children born to Narragansett mothers and non-Indian fathers were described by Rhode Island officials as "Mustee," rather than "Narragansett" or "Indian."[99] By the end of the century, Narragansetts who were racially mixed by half of their blood or some other fraction, or were thought to be so, were labeled "Negroes" or some roughly analogous appellation like "black" or "colored." Given the prevailing attitudes about race and class in the dominant society, diluted blood meant that Narragansetts were "simply Negroes," who deserved little attention and commanded the lowest esteem when compared with recent immigrants and "real Indians."[100] "Real Indians" were icons: idealized images that emerged from white New Englanders' understanding of A Key. In their view, true Narragansetts could only be those who fit Williams's description in the pages of A Key.

In the twentieth century, the passing of these Narragansetts was not lamented as it had been by earlier history writers. Although their degeneration and decline were accepted matter-of-factly, seventeenth-century Narragansetts continued to enthrall those who wrote (and presumably read) about southern New England Indians. Hallmarks of their greatness, such as the institution of the sachemship, were celebrated. Howard M. Chapin, energetic author of numerous studies of the early history and antiquities of Rhode Island, for example, published his Sachems of the Narragansetts in 1931.[101] Chapin, who critics said "was never much interested in anything after 1800," used information from Williams's A Key to comment on Narragansett leadership and reconstructed from slim threads found in his other writings the genealogy of ruling Narragansett families.[102] Citing Williams, he acknowledged the existence of a monarchical government in which authority was divided between an elder and a younger sachem, but he noted that the dual sachemship had gradually weakened. Limping along into the eighteenth century, a mere shadow of its former greatness, the institution came to an end around 1779 with the death of George II, the last hereditary Narragansett sachem, when a tree accidentally fell on him just when he was about to enlist in the Revolution on the side of the Americans.[103]

The irony of George II's untimely death is that most white New Englanders found it difficult, if not impossible, to reconcile "Indianness" with being an American, either at the time of the Revolution or in the 1930s. The recruitment of Narragansetts in the Revolutionary War arguably sapped the strength of adult male members of the tribe who enlisted as soldiers and, in this time of crisis, suddenly became visible to colonial officials.[104] Yet what may be portrayed as their pro-American stance reaped few benefits for their community.[105] In reasserting their "Indianness" a century and a half later, the Narragansetts sought to rid themselves of identification as "Negroes" or "coloreds" once and for all, but at the same time they shunned any insinuation that their concern about their Indian heritage was in any way "un-American," which in the climate of the 1930s would have imposed on them an additional liability. They after all had been soldiers, sailors, and even whalers. Others were skilled craftspeople, such as carpenters and stonemasons, or day laborers, farmers, or household domestics. Some had lived and died among non-Natives and in some cases even married them. They had jobs, some of them odd, seasonal, and part-time, not at all unlike other poor Americans faced with economic necessity and lacking formal education and training in the emerging industrial trades. They had proclaimed their Indian identity and renewed their commitment to preserve the integrity of their community by retribalizing as a non-profit corporation, but they also wanted a share in the American dream.[106] Some had gained employment as secretaries, railroad and factory workers, and musicians. Others practiced law, taught, and published. And like other Americans during the 1930s, many were unemployed. In the opinion of most white New Englanders, however, "life as an American meant death as an Indian."[107] Narragansetts could be assimilated and "American" or separate and "Indian"—one or the other, but certainly not both.

Almost without exception, these New Englanders perceived that real Narragansett Indians existed in a remote past that was much farther away than the arm's length that separated the reader from the printed pages of Williams's text. *A Key*, reissued in 1936 by the Rhode Island and Providence Plantations Tercentenary Committee, contributed to maintaining this distance and sustaining the illusion of what real Narragansetts should be like. Published as a facsimile of the original text with only a few minor changes to accommodate the modern alphabet and no lengthy editorial notes, this became the populist edition of *A Key* through which more non-Natives could learn about Narragansett life and culture. More to the point, they could learn about the manners and customs of local Indians who "formerly lived in and ruled the district that is now the State of Rhode Island."[108] *A Key*'s Narragansetts, whose lives bore little resemblance to persons calling themselves by that name and living in 1930s Rhode Island, were the only true Narragansetts.

A Key had therefore become a form of entrapment. By freezing Narragansetts in time and fixing them rigidly in place, it was used to deny the existence of actual Narragansett people and their complicated histories of conquest, resistance, and

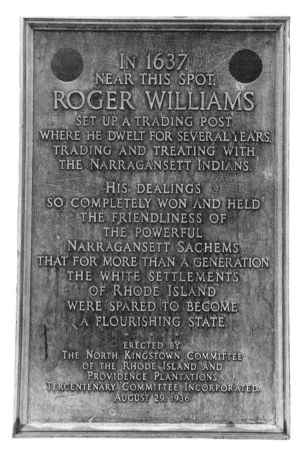

Figure 14. The Roger Williams plaque, North Kingstown, Rhode Island. It was one of many public memorials erected to Williams in the 1930s as part of Rhode Island's tercentenary celebration. (Photo by Patricia E. Rubertone)

survival into the present. This narrow definition left them outside of the forces that shaped American society. As some Narragansetts had anticipated, the citizenship granted to them at the time of their detribalization in the nineteenth century did not give them a full voice in American democracy. In the 1930s, their voices were as mute as ever. To Americans who chose not to listen, the Narragansetts' stories—alternative versions about their history and their struggles to keep their identity as a people intact—remained as silent as the paper on which *A Key* was printed. Even in the atmosphere of Rhode Island's tercentenary, in which ceremony and pageantry celebrated pluralism and democracy, Narragansett Indians remained provisional participants in the American way.

In the later twentieth century, *A Key* continued to be revered as a canonical text by those writing histories of the Narragansetts. Among these authors are archaeologists who have joined the chorus in praising the book. Although *A Key*'s pages provide neither ready answers to archaeological problems nor a material vocabulary to supplement its Narragansett–English dictionary, archaeologists have heeded Roger Williams's observations about seventeenth-century Narragansett lifeways and adopted them as a model for Narragansett culture. But they have also extended *A Key*'s applicability as an interpretive tool by applying it in the study of Narragansetts and other southern New England Native peoples in the centuries before European contact.

To most archaeologists, *A Key* is relevant and unproblematic in interpreting seventeenth-century material evidence, which to date has come largely from Narragansett graves. The anthropologist William Simmons, for example, combed *A Key* for information on Narragansett cosmology, beliefs about death and an afterlife, and mourning and burial to aid in interpreting burials from Conanicut Island whose meanings were cloudy with ambiguity.[109] As if learning a new language, Simmons mastered *A Key*'s words and phrases, pulling words apart to learn their roots and gain familiarity with subtleties in meaning, at least to the extent that these were preserved in Williams's translations. He found clues in *A Key* that unlocked meanings in archaeological evidence pertaining to Narragansett sacred traditions. Leaving the door ajar, Simmons left to others the task of revealing additional meanings in Narragansett sacred traditions than are implied by Williams's translation of their culture.

Despite archaeologists' enthusiasm for Williams as a source of analogs, *A Key*'s fit to archaeological evidence has not always been this good, especially where Williams's observations have been appropriated for use in contexts different from their reported ones. Such misappropriation has imbued Williams's statements with greater insight into Narragansett culture than he ever assumed. Williams was thoughtful, perhaps more so than other English observers of Native life in seventeenth-century New England, but *A Key* is no Rosetta stone; for archaeologists it has not always been illuminating. For example, *A Key* has sometimes been used to demean and misrepresent testimony for Narragansett sacred traditions by serving as corroboration for social inequalities and increasing personal wealth in seventeenth-century burials. Read as signatures of confusion and decay, these interpretations condemn Narragansett communities to a sentence of eventual and inevitable extinction as much as the pronouncements of other writers who forecasted the Narragansetts' disappearance.[110]

In a similar vein, *A Key* has informed the assumption that prehistoric coastal settlement in southern New England was seasonal.[111] Although recent archaeological research suggests that Williams's observations may not be an apt description of Native lifeways before *A Key*, the implications of the model are profound and complex.[112] By locking Native peoples into a mobile lifestyle, the model has inhibited and perhaps even prevented the exploration of Native peoples' attachments to place.[113] Assumptions about Native mobility, as many historical analysts have noted, helped the English lay claim to Native land and justify its dispossession.[114] But it also contributed to expectations about village-based life that, for the most part, are not born out by archaeological evidence. The absence of evidence can be a powerful indictment, and, as in the case of residential mobility, may be used to make Native peoples invisible. Without denigrating continuing traditions, *A Key* is no more an appropriate model for later generations of Narragansetts than it is for those who lived centuries before European contact. To assume that it is reinforces the negative stereotype that Narragansett and other Native cultures in New England, like those throughout North America, remained unchanged throughout "prehistory."[115] The denial of cultural change implies that they were, in effect, a people without history, except, of course, for that imparted to them through scholars' readings of *A Key*.

In sum, much of what European Americans know about Narragansett Indians—in the seventeenth century, or after or before it—comes from words penned by Roger Williams in *A Key*. Although there is the chance that other documents might be discovered that could prove more thorough or revealing in their documentation of Narragansett culture, many scholars, if asked, would probably question whether these could provide much more than Williams's *A Key* has. To suppose that there could be more veers close to posing an ideological challenge, because it raises the possibility that *A Key* might be surpassed, its veracity undermined, and the histories of extinction spawned from it reversed. Without a doubt, *A Key* has become a "great book" for those who have written, and continue to write, the histories of the Narragansetts. Like other texts considered classics, it has endured and enjoyed immense popularity. But neither appeal to its intrinsic or socially authorized value nor its durability and popularity are sufficient criteria upon to which to evaluate or hinge understandings of Narragansett culture and history. *A Key*, like other classics, warrants closer scrutiny.

PART TWO

Rethinking *A Key*

4.

CASTING *A KEY*

Imagining Roger Williams's experience with the Narragansetts in the years preceding *A Key* brings to mind an anthropological "primal scene," filled with situations and experiences inspired by archetypes like the Garden before the Fall,
Rousseau's Natural State, and Columbus's first encounter with the New World.
The plot as imagined is a familiar one: traveling across the sea or into the wilderness to encounter an untouched people, there to be stripped of the defensive trap-
pings of civilization and reborn in the study of a "simpler" culture, and returning
with new knowledge and a vision of alternative possibilities.[2]

With Williams cast in the lead role, the epic begins with an arduous sea voyage,
but this is merely a prelude to the story that commences when he chooses exile
in "an Indian wilderness" over deportation. Leaving behind the life he knew in
Salem and Plymouth, he embarks on a journey into a territory most English
colonists consider vast and untamed, a "space of bewilderment," full of unknowns, dangers, and heathens.[3] For fourteen weeks, he steers his way through
winter snow whose cold chilled his bones even thirty-five years later.[4] He arrives
at a place called Narragansett Bay, where he encounters a "shaggy world of
primeval forests, red men, and freedom," which becomes his home and remains
so by choice.[5] This place extends his perspective, making the universe seem larger
and more diverse, but it also teaches him about ideas sharply different from his
own.[6] In learning about others, he gains knowledge about himself.

Many of the details of this imaginary anthropological encounter share little in

Figure 15. *Landing of Roger Williams* (1857), oil painting by Alonzo Chappel. The rocky
shoreline and Native American onlookers are standard conventions in iconic renderings
of early colonial encounters. Notable here is the vitality of the Narragansetts, who are
shown offering gifts and assurances of peace to Williams and his party. (Museum of Art,
Rhode Island School of Design, Museum Works of Art Fund)

common with the actual circumstances surrounding Williams's Narragansett experience in the years before *A Key*. The territory beyond the fringe of the English
plantations was not an untamed space inhabited only by roaming bands of "savages."[7] During his journey, when he allegedly knew neither bread nor bed, he
crossed many well-ordered Native communities where he was extended the hospitality of important clan leaders, as he had been when he lived at Salem and Plymouth.[8] Upon reaching Narragansett Bay, he first settled on the eastern bank of the
Seekonk River, where he had purchased land years earlier from Ousamaquin, the
Pokanoket sachem. The real estate he had secured sight unseen, if this was indeed
the case, was not to be his haven because it was claimed by the English as well as
the Pokanokets. He crossed the river to Moshassuck, where Canonicus, the Narragansett sachem, welcomed his arrival. If legend serves correctly, a group of two
or three (or perhaps as many as five or six) Natives huddled on the shore and

greeted Williams by shouting "What cheare Netop," a salutation part English, part Algonkian, a hybrid phrase revealing that a connection had already been made.

Despite what is implied by the apparent transparency of language, Roger Williams came to the Narragansetts at a time that many early-twentieth-century practitioners of the modern fieldwork tradition in anthropology considered favorable for observing Native peoples. Arriving more than ten years after initial colonization, he observed them when conditions were considered ripe for conducting such work: long enough to have brought them under the mollifying influence of colonialism, which would have ensured for him a "friendly reception and peaceful surroundings," but "not long enough to have allowed any serious impairment" of their culture, or the passing of a generation who had participated in any "rites and practices" that might have "disappeared or suffered change."[9] Following the logic of this reasoning, the 1630s and early 1640s were the ideal period in which to observe the Narragansetts.

Whether viewed through a mythic or pragmatic lens, however, Williams's Narragansett experience did not occur at a "right time." Neither romantic illusion nor some acknowledgment of the enabling circumstances of colonialism guaranteed that he would capture a "pure" Narragansett culture or be better equipped to describe it. It would be a mistake to pretend that an appropriately timed ethnographic encounter, either pristine or conducted relatively early in the colonial process, held such promises. In the years preceding *A Key*, Williams simply had an opportunity to observe the Narragansetts at a particular point in time and a particular moment in their history.[10]

This chapter will situate Williams's experiences with the Narragansetts in the context of colonial relations. I begin by tracing the history of these encounters, from the time of the first recorded landfall in Narragansett Bay to the date of the book's publication in 1643, in order to explore how the events illuminate, with few uncertainties, the expectations that came to permeate these interactions. For the English colonists, the anticipated outcome was settlement and the establishment of a new society; for the Narragansetts and other Native peoples, the hope was survival in a much-altered world. This complicated story of conquest and survival, which defies reduction into a primal scene, provides the backdrop for examining Williams's ethnographic encounters and, ultimately, his representation of the Narragansetts in *A Key*. I argue that his role as interpreter (or transcriber) of their culture cannot be obscured, but neither can it be simply accepted—minus overarching cultural and ideological assumptions—without first considering the specific contexts in which he encountered the Narragansetts, who were not merely products of textualization but who existed independent of *A Key*.

When Roger Williams arrived at Narragansett Bay in 1636, the apprehension that had accompanied initial sightings and the tentativeness associated with early encounters were long gone. More than a century earlier, the Florentine explorer Giovanni da Verrazzano had entered the bay. According to written accounts, Verrazzano and his crew were the first Europeans the Narragansetts had ever seen. They cautiously approached his ship, *La Dauphine,* eyeing the vessel and its sailors with curiosity and uttering cries the meanings of which can only be guessed. To assure them that it was safe to come closer, the crew tossed them a few little bells, mirrors, and other trinkets in a gesture that would establish a protocol for trade in furs, fish, and other commodities. Some who had neared the ship eventually came on board. They were taller than the Europeans, with well-proportioned physiques, bronze-colored skin, and sculpted faces pierced by black eyes. Two appeared to be kings. Each was bare headed and naked except for a richly decorated deerskin mantle and a necklace of multicolored beads. Convinced that he had won their confidence, Verrazzano stayed for two weeks and a day. With *La Dauphine* anchored in a sheltered harbor near Newport, the Europeans ventured into the interior for a distance of 5–6 leagues (about 15–18 miles or 24–29 kilometers), where they observed Native wigwams, cultivated fields, and open woodland rich with game.

Although Verrazzano was unable to speak their language, he concluded that the Native people of Narragansett Bay were willing to give away all that they had— except for their women. Described as "just as shapely and beautiful" as the men were virile and handsome, they were coveted by the Europeans and carefully guarded by the Narragansett men. Despite numerous appeals and various enticements, the Europeans failed to persuade them to bring the women aboard ship. As a precaution, women who were part of visiting entourages waited at a distance in boats ready to carry them to safety at the slightest provocation.[11] The Narragansetts' vigilant protection of their women suggests that this was not a first encounter and that the sailors were viewed as merely lecherous humans rather than powerful, otherworldly beings. Regardless of the interpretation imposed on this event, it soon became clear that Europeans would be accommodated into the Narragansetts' lives and wider mythology, as they in turn would become part of the Europeans' worldview.[12]

In the decades to follow, Europeans made other brief, and perhaps chance, sojourns into Narragansett Bay. The occasional fisherman making landfall and the navigator exploring the bay's shoreline have left little material evidence of their contacts. Although written history is virtually silent about these sporadic encounters, these visitors' faces would have been vaguely familiar and their wares recognizable. In spite of friendly receptions and prospects for regular trade, rumors of abduction, murder, and disease tainted these casual contacts with mutual uncertainties. Such apprehensions often led to an abrupt breakdown of relations, which temporarily stalled commercial and colonizing ventures.[13]

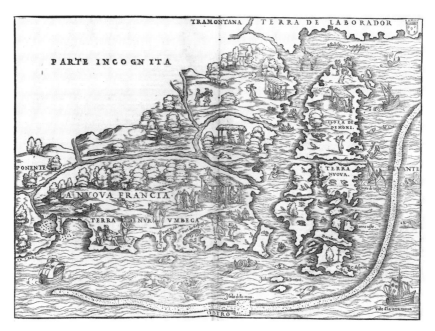

Figure 16. *La Nuova Francia* by Gracomo Gastaldi (1566). The early cartographic image shows the location of Narragansett Bay ("Port du Refuge") on the lower coastline. (John Carter Brown Library at Brown University)

These setbacks aside, the Dutch had established a routine trade with the Native peoples of Narragansett Bay by the early part of the seventeenth century. This trade was facilitated through a network of rendezvous points along the southern New England coast, which involved neither the founding of permanent colonies nor investment in military outposts to maintain a commercial presence. The English, who were relative latecomers to the region, had made several attempts to set up frontier outposts under the pretext of trade, but these were unmitigated failures.

English settlement finally took root in New England in 1620. Those who landed at Plymouth in December of that year included adventurers, employees of English overseas enterprises, servants bound by the terms of indenture, and some families seeking to relocate permanently "for sundry weighty and solid reasons" of religion and economics. They brought with them goats, pigs, poultry, dogs, and possibly a few sheep; feed grains and garden seeds, hoes, shovels, and pitchforks; axes, saws, muskets, shot, a few pots and pans, trenchers, and bedding; and a small amount of goods for trading.[14] Unlike many who had come before them, they had come more or less provisioned to establish new homes and not just to trade from shallops or makeshift stations meant to accommodate occasional commerce with Native people.

The Narragansetts made their first recorded contact with the English at Plymouth in January 1622. A year had passed since the latter's arrival, with little indication that they would soon depart. Perceiving the potential threat lurking in English colonization, the Narragansetts sent the authorities a gift of several arrows wrapped in a snakeskin. It was an unusual offering, quite unlike the pelts of fur that typically were presented as an overture in establishing relations with Europeans. The English surmised that the gift was a gesture of hostility and returned the skin filled with powder and shot to the chief sachem, Canonicus. He refused to accept it, as did other sachems. Like a chain letter, it was sent from place to place until it made its way back to Plymouth, whole and carrying multiple, albeit unwritten, messages.[15] The Narragansetts had no need to receive it or inspect its contents; their suspicions about the English had been confirmed. Unlike those who had come before, the English at Plymouth had no intention of leaving.

Between 1629 and 1641, they were joined by thousands of new immigrants, who crossed the North Atlantic in what has become known as the "Great Puritan Migration." Although estimates vary, the best figures place the number of emigrants at about twenty-one thousand.[16] Not all survived the trans-Atlantic journey, the rigors of frontier life, or the pangs of homesickness, but enough did to plant yet another English foothold in Massachusetts.[17] More than many of their predecessors, the Puritan colonists had come better prepared, educated, and financed to build new homes, in a place where the prospects for economic prosperity and religious freedom seemed much more favorable than in England. By 1630 one or perhaps two thousand people had settled at Salem, Boston, and Plymouth or had scattered farther north.[18] Their numbers doubled by 1634 and continued to increase at a rate of about one to two thousand per year until the end of the decade. By the mid-1630s, satellite communities had been formed around the original English settlements at Massachusetts Bay and Plymouth, and others had been implanted along the Connecticut River and at Narragansett Bay, including Williams's plantation of Providence.

Despite the influx of colonists, they were fewer than the Natives, at least until the latter began to succumb to the devastating effects of imported diseases. Many Native groups living along the coast between Cape Cod and the Penobscot River died between 1616 and 1619 from a "plague" attributed to French sailors shipwrecked in Massachusetts Bay.[19] Others had experienced bouts of strange new "fluxes and fevers" brought about by foreign pathogens, but the suffering from these diseases paled in comparison to that which resulted from a smallpox epidemic that struck in 1633.

For most of the colonists who came to New England in the 1630s, smallpox was a fact of life: it was part of their ancestral record and their personal histories. Those who boarded an advance party of ships that arrived at Salem in 1629 were probably not surprised that smallpox had come with them, infecting two children in the course of the voyage, but New England's Native peoples were unfamiliar with the disease, both immunologically and psychologically.[20] They were confounded by the intensity of its symptoms, the disfigurement of its survivors, and the astounding number of deaths it claimed along the coast from the Long Island Sound to the Gulf of Maine, and in the interior as far west as the St. Lawrence–Great Lakes area. In some cases, entire communities were ravaged by the disease, with nearly everyone—those in the prime of life, the old, and the young—becoming sick, often at the same time.

By the winter of 1634, the death toll among the Narragansetts reached seven hundred. The meaning of this loss in terms of a mortality rate is difficult to gauge, because estimates of the pre-epidemic Narragansett population vary widely.[21] A conservative estimate places the figure at about 4,000, whereas more generous projections suggest a pre-epidemic population as high as 35,000–40,000.[22] Regardless of which pre-epidemic figure one uses, the death rate was relatively low compared with the reduction factors estimated for the initial outset of smallpox elsewhere in New England.[23] Although one may conclude that the Narragansetts escaped the worst of the infection, these gross estimates can be misleading, for they fail to assess how individual villages or families might have been affected. Considered at this scale, the death of seven hundred people takes on a different magnitude of significance.

A highly contagious disease, smallpox could spread rapidly among immediate kin living within the confines of a single house or settlement. With the pathogen's incubation period of ten to fourteen days, an unsuspecting carrier could introduce the disease to friends and neighboring kindred in whose communities the entire process might repeat itself.[24] Beyond the epidemiology and mortality of the disease would be lost opportunities: seed unplanted, fields untended, or crops left unharvested. Hunting, collecting, and fishing might be temporarily curtailed.[25] Hypothetically, the birth rate might decline as a consequence of the epidemic's compounded effects on the lives of Native people, especially women in their peak reproductive years.[26]

Although smallpox took its toll on the Narragansetts and caused human suffering far exceeding its clinical description, there is little written documentation to suggest that its effects were catastrophic.[27] Existing networks of kinship and authority remained intact, with little concrete evidence to suggest that spiritual beliefs and religious practices were undermined. Doubts were mounting about the English, however, whom the Narragansetts would eventually blame for the smallpox and other problems they faced in the 1630s and early 1640s.[28]

For despite the disease's profound impact, smallpox was but one of many factors contributing to the increasing tensions between the Narragansetts and the
English colonists. Another was expansion of trading and colonizing interests after
the epidemic had subsided. Struggles for preeminence in trade among different
colonial groups, the Pequots, and the Narragansetts heightened mutual suspicions
and led to increased incidents of violence. The murders of a Pequot sachem and
an English trader in 1634, and that of another trader on Block Island two years later,
provoked punitive reprisals. Although the circumstances surrounding the execution of John Oldham on Block Island are not entirely clear, the Narragansetts, who
had protested their innocence in the assault, were implicated along with the Pequots.[29] In August 1636 the Massachusetts Bay Colony retaliated by sending a military expedition led by John Endicott to Block Island. Unable to kill and enslave
the Native people as ordered, the expedition instead burned their wigwams and
stores of corn from the summer's harvest. Departing Block Island, Endicott and
his troops proceeded to Connecticut, where they demanded from the Pequots
large amounts of wampum, hostages, and the identities of the traders' killers.
When the Pequots failed to comply, the English party raided their villages and
destroyed their supplies of corn and caches of goods. Over the next few months,
tensions mounted, rivalries flared, and rumors flew. With war imminent, the Pequots and the English each attempted to enlist the Narragansetts as allies. Although the Narragansetts were dissuaded from joining an anti-English alliance
with the Pequots, largely through the intervention of Roger Williams, who had
recently settled at Narragansett Bay, the precise terms of the treaty they entered
into with the English are unknown.

War was officially declared in May 1637. In the predawn hours of May 26, English forces, assisted by the Narragansetts and other Native groups, attacked a for-
tified Pequot settlement at Mystic. Under the direction of Captains John Mason
and John Underhill, the invading forces divided and charged the fort's two en-
trances. They set fire to the wigwams, killing perhaps as many as seven hundred
Pequots, including women, children, and old men, as well as some warriors. Those
who did not perish in the blaze were slaughtered by English soldiers, who had surrounded the fort so that any Pequots fleeing the burning village would first face
their waiting swords and guns, rather than the army's Native allies. This was not
the kind of war the Narragansetts had expected. Some were killed or wounded in
the melee outside of the fort, but even more unsettling was the havoc that occurred inside the palisade, especially because the Narragansetts had been assured
just weeks earlier that women and children would not be harmed. The massacre
created a scene of incredible carnage, unmatched even by the smallpox epidemic.

For the Narragansetts and other Native groups, the massacre at Mystic exposed
the English as untrustworthy and ruthless and only heightened any resentment

Figure 17. *Roger Williams Opposing the Pequot Emissaries* (n.d.). The engraving by an unknown artist depicts Williams in his role as a cultural mediator and translator in seventeenth-century Native politics. (Courtesy of the Rhode Island Historical Society)

they harbored against them. For the leaders of the English colonies, the Pequot War brought the realization that they could instill fear into their enemies and conquer them at will, though even this did not give the colonists any real sense of security. Armed with these hard-won revelations, the Indians and the English got on with their lives and the business of dealing with the spoils of war. Among the most immediate problems were Pequot lands and, perhaps more important, Pequot survivors, including the few who had not been killed at Mystic and others who were captured in the months that followed. The Narragansetts had expected to receive hunting privileges in Pequot territory, along with some Pequot captives, as rights owed to them for having agreed to aid the English. Their expectations were met instead by conflicting claims about how Pequot lands should be used and who should use them. As late as a year after the attack, the disposition of Pequot war refugees remained unresolved. Those who were not sold into slavery were to be divided among the English and their Native allies, but there were accusations that the Narragansetts had sheltered Pequots without the consent of Massachusetts officials, along with counterclaims that earlier pledges had not been met.

In September 1638, Miantonomi was summoned by Connecticut authorities to appear at Hartford to negotiate a treaty that would formally end the hostilities caused by the Pequot War. He arrived in the company of Roger Williams and an escort of more than a hundred Narragansetts, including other sachems and his wife and children. Miantonomi and Uncas, the Mohegan sachem, entered into an agreement with the English. Any promises made to the Narragansetts before the Pequot War were superseded by the provisions of the new treaty. They lost all rights to the use of former Pequot lands. They were obliged to make an annual tribute payment in wampum for each Pequot they received. And in what was an unambiguous move by the colonists to establish control over Native affairs, the Narragansetts (and the Mohegans) were required have all intertribal conflicts resolved by the English.

After the Hartford treaty, there were reports of runaway Pequot captives and difficulties in meeting scheduled tribute payments in wampum. Colonial encroachment on Native homelands continued unabated. Dissatisfied with the conditions of the treaty and disgruntled over Connecticut's appropriation of Indian affairs in southern New England, the Narragansetts appealed to Massachusetts Bay. The colonists' sentiments toward the Narragansetts were no less hostile. They would, however, come to employ different tactics in attempting to control the Narragansetts. Preferring to err on the side of caution, they opted for a subject status for their former ally, whereas Connecticut urged nothing less than complete extermination. Suspicions that the Narragansetts were a threat to the security of the English colonies and that they were plotting a regionwide anti-English conspiracy grew deeper, but unlike earlier allegations, these seemed to be based more on probability than on innuendo.[30]

Although Narragansett country remained primarily "Indian territory," the English colonists continued to acquire additional tracts of land. Between the late 1630s and early 1640s, they obtained Pawtuxet lands lying to the south of Providence, along with several islands in Narragansett Bay, including Prudence and Aquidneck. Their presence was strengthened by the founding of new settlements at Portsmouth and Newport in 1638 and 1639 and at Warwick in 1642. The expanding colonial domain posed ever-tightening restrictions on the Narragansetts' way of life and raised an awareness of the potential for their extinction at the hands of the English.

No one was more aware of this than their sachem, Miantonomi, who one year before *A Key*'s publication had delivered a compelling and poignant speech to the Montauks. He had called upon them as brethren and friends to rekindle the enduring ties that linked them with other Native peoples in a wider regional Indian community, in order to confront the dangers posed by English colonial encroachments:

> For So are we all Indeans as y[e] English are, and Say broth[r] to one anoth[r]; So must we be one as they are, oth[r]wise we shall be all gone shortly, for you know our fathers had plentie of deare & Skins, our plaines weare full of dear, as also our woods, and of Turkeies, and our Coves full of fish and foule. But thes English having gotten our land, they with Sithes cut downe y[e] grass, and with axes fell the trees; their Cowes and horses eat y[e] grass, and th[r] hogs spoyl our Clambanks, and we Shall all be starved: therefore it is best for you to doe as wee, for wee are all the Sachems from East to West, both Mouquakues and Mowhauks Joyning with us, and we are all resolved to fall upon them all, at one apoynted day.[31]

Miantonomi realized that Native survival depended not only on mounting a counteroffensive but also on making short-term adjustments, which would require pragmatic departures from their accustomed ways. He urged them to "kill men, women, & children, but no Cowes, for they will serve to eate till our dear be Increased again."[32]

His eloquent plea for Indian unity and armed resistance is reminiscent of the translations of prophetic speeches given in later centuries by other Native American leaders who envisioned the restoration of their homelands and the revitalization of their culture.[33] Although his words may have been misunderstood, the voice that resonates in this speech seems all too familiar. It speaks of insults and cries for dignity, as much as it protests the loss of land and way of life brought about by English incursions. Miantonomi's call for a military offensive against the colonists, perhaps amplified and sensationalized, was rejected, at least temporarily, but it sealed his fate at the hands of the English, who arranged for his assassination by Uncas for his alleged plot.

For the rest of the Narragansetts and other Native peoples throughout southern New England, there would be no dramatic confrontation, nor would there be total resignation. Instead they continued to live their lives, in diverse and seemingly contradictory ways, within the conditions imposed by English colonialism.[34] They exchanged their corn, fish, venison, furs, and wampum for knives, hatchets, and brass kettles, often tailoring the English goods to their own liking. They inspected the quality of English cloth with a discriminating eye, some preferring English clothing to their own skins and furs.[35] They inquired about English muskets and came to possess them as payments for favors or through illegal trafficking, despite the colonists' repeated efforts to prevent their sale following the Pequot War.[36] They cared little for English livestock, especially pigs, but came to view them as an alternative to the dwindling supply of indigenous wildlife. Some developed creative alliances with the intruders, but most showed little, if any, interest in worshiping the Christian god.

So when Roger Williams appeared among the Narragansetts, they felt no sudden shock of confrontation with an alien visitor. Trade had brought about unanticipated exchanges of pathogens and alcohol, and colonization had raised opposing claims by those who vied for possession and those who challenged such boldness. The Narragansetts had come to know the English, at least provisionally, and had already entered into what would be a long-term strategy for survival, punctuated with resistance, defeat, political negotiation, cultural innovation, and renewal.[37] This was neither a pristine encounter nor a mythical moment. The Narragansetts were not untouched, but neither were they completely under the yoke of colonial domination when Williams came to live among them.

As an exile from his own community, Williams needed his hosts' cooperation to establish a new home and to carry on a reasonable trade to support his family. He needed them to guide him through the wilderness that lay beyond the gentle hills and marshland of the peninsula where he and his followers would settle. His survival depended on diplomacy, tact, and goodwill, but, perhaps even more important from a pragmatic standpoint, on observing them and learning their ways.[38] Prohibited from reentering Massachusetts, he found himself in a precarious position between those who had banished him and those on whom he depended for survival. For history writers who later championed Williams and dramatized his plight, he occupied a niche between two distinct worlds—savagery and civilization. At first homeless and at least partially estranged from his own kind, Williams satisfied the minimum prerequisites that characterized the lives of early ethnologists and other intermediary figures posed on the fictional and actual frontiers of American history.[39]

Figure 18. *Roger Williams Sheltered by the Narragansetts* (n.d.). Unlike other images of Williams's arrival at Narragansett Bay, this engraving portrays Williams as a weary and vulnerable figure receiving instructions from Narragansetts. Their posture dominates the composition, lending an impression of towering authority. (Courtesy of the Rhode Island Historical Society)

Described as someone who "might have been a hermit, a celibate, a solitary monk," he was, in fact, none of these.[40] Educated, intellectual, and driven by absolute principle, Williams felt increasingly solitary after his efforts at Puritan reform in Massachusetts had failed. By some accounts, he seemed to savor his roles as a dissident and outcast, which he "carried forever with him like a soldier's wound."[41] The conditions of his exile initially deprived him of many comforts enjoyed by his fellow colonists, but he soon made a reasonable, if not prosperous, living as a trader. Although ostensibly cut off from the social network of Puritan New England, he maintained personal and professional relationships with individuals from Massachusetts Bay, often providing them with information on Indian affairs as he had before the Pequot War. He bore the mantle of public life in Providence somewhat reluctantly and periodically retreated to Cocumscussoc. These periods of self-imposed isolation may have reinforced his singularity, but they also drew him closer to the Narragansetts.[42]

Although he began to observe the Narragansetts soon after his arrival in New England, his more sustained interactions with them, and with other Native peoples, began when he settled at Narragansett Bay. Between 1636 and 1643, not only Narragansetts, but also Pequots, Massachusetts, and others whose communities are not identified, visited Williams's home in Providence, carrying messages or goods. He received them and sometimes offered them lodging, but not without seizing the opportunity to converse with them. Occasionally he ventured to Native settlements. The letters that he wrote in the years immediately following his arrival in Providence indicate that he traveled (overland and by water) to Narragansett, Pequot, Mohegan, and Niantic homelands. By the time he had established his trading post at Cocumscussoc in the late 1630s, he had been a frequent visitor to Narigansett (Narragansett). Despite the haze of uncertainty surrounding his day-to-day activities and movements between Providence and his trading post at Cocumscussoc before *A Key*'s publication, Williams, in contrast to other early observers of Native life, was more than a temporary sojourner, whose brief and passing encounters became ethnographic facts.

Yet like others who wrote about Native cultures before the emergence of anthropology as a formal discipline, Williams had no special training that qualified him to tell the story of the Narragansetts. As a young boy, Williams could not have missed the triumphant returns of Capt. John Smith to his home parish in London or the arrival of Pocahontas and her retinue. It is unlikely that he would have been immune to the romantic extravagance surrounding popular tales of encounters with America's Native peoples. But neither "flesh and blood" displays of Native Americans nor the excitement generated by the talk of colonization, even by its most ardent proselytizers, would have provided sufficient encouragement to justify or to assist him in his undertaking.[43]

Williams, like other literate colonists, probably read the promotional literature about America before his migration. Works such as those of the younger Richard Hakluyt and Capt. John Smith had become standard references that shaped English colonists' expectations about America and its Native peoples.[44] Before his departure, he would have heard news about Massachusetts Bay Company's first plantation at Naumkeag (later named Salem) from Francis Higginson and perhaps even had the chance to read his immensely popular pamphlet *New-Englands Plantation*, published in 1630.[45]

None of these reports furnished him with a suitable prototype on which to model his account of Narragansett lives. Hakluyt had collected materials written by others and compiled them into an anthology that dazzled readers with a diversity of New World discoveries. Smith had traveled to Virginia and New England; Higginson had lived in Massachusetts. Having been there "on the ground," they could claim the authority of eyewitnesses. These assertions aside, this genre of reporting was full of colorful prose, rich in hyperbole and predictions about the potential of colonization. In general, these treatments of Native peoples projected characteristics based on the absence of familiar traits, rather than on knowledge gained by careful attention to detail.

Smith functioned as an ethnographer as well as a chronicler. In the former capacity, he provided important descriptive material about the Native peoples of Virginia, but less on those of New England. His interest in Native culture was motivated by the belief that this knowledge held the key to English colonial domination. He described their interaction with the environment at length, devoting much discussion to subsistence practices because he believed that the English could benefit from understanding Native peoples' survival techniques. He acknowledged the importance of acquiring Native language, but only to gain enough proficiency to conduct trade and diplomacy. Rather than commit himself to mastering the Algonkian dialects, his methods involved the practice of leaving English boys, sent to Virginia as indentured servants, in Native communities where they could learn language and customs and then be retrieved at some convenient time.[46] His *Generall Historie* includes words and phrases presumably acquired in this manner. Compared with his discussion of Native Virginia, Smith's ethnographic survey of New England offered little more than a partial inventory of groups and territories and accounts of several unfortunate incidents.

As the probability of active investment in New England colonization became a reality, perceptions of the region's Native peoples were altered. The "noble savages" admired in the pages of Hakluyt's volumes, but described by Smith as "pagans" exhibiting the vices Christianity condemned, were gradually transformed into targets of "civility" and anticipated conversion. Turgid descriptions meant to excite the curiosity of English readers became increasingly tempered by claims to literal certainty based on firsthand experience. Francis Higginson, whose writings had a powerful effect on recruitment for the Massachusetts Bay Company, professed to report the truth because he was not merely an idle traveler but an eyewitness, and moreover a minister, who made inquiries only of honest and religious persons to supplement his own observations. In spite of his claims of reliability, much of what he reported seemed to corroborate his inflated expectations about New England, rather than the testimony of his own limited experiences.[47]

As a "Preacher of Truth," Higginson offered an inaccurate account not only of the land but also of its people. In his brief description of New England Native Americans, he alluded to the effects of an earlier plague that left "very few to inhabit the Countrey." Unable to use more than a fraction of the land, these survivors "neither have any settled places, as Townes to dwell in, nor any ground as they challenge for their own possession, but change their habitation from place to place."[48] He implied that they "doe generally professe to like of our coming and planting here; partly because there is abundance of ground that they cannot possess nor make use of, and partly because our being here will be a meanes both of reliefe to them when they want, and also a defence from their Enemies." He urged those who were planning to colonize "to learne their Language" as soon as possible as "a meanes to do them good."[49] In his view, a knowledge of Native language was essential for conversion, not just for trade and diplomacy. Few heeded Higginson's advice, perhaps because they shared his view that the Natives of Massachusetts, though hardly posing a menace to the English, were not to be trusted. Roger Williams was an exception. Although he opposed Higginson's thesis about vacant lands, he agreed with his position on language acquisition and took the first serious step in remedying English ignorance of the Natives' language by writing *A Key Into the Language of America*.

It is unknown if Williams read, or had access to, descriptions of New England's Native peoples published after he migrated.[50] Although these were written largely for a middle-class, English audience and rarely made their way back across the Atlantic, his casual reference in *A Key*'s introduction to works written by fellow Englishmen who "have often, and excellently, and lately written of the Countrey" suggests that he was at least aware of the recent literature on New England. That he distinguished *A Key* from other works, which in his opinion had not described the place beyond "the goodnesse and worth of it," and thus had not dealt specifically with Native language and culture, raises the question of whether Williams read, or perhaps was inspired by, William Wood's *New England's Prospect* or Thomas Morton's *New English Canaan*, both written just a few years earlier.[51]

Wood's book, published in 1634, contained a description of the region's natural history and its Native peoples, plus a five-page vocabulary of their words and phrases. Written to dispel all misconceptions about the place because the author had lived there for four years (and hoped to return), *New England's Prospect* was typical reading for prospective immigrants. Wood offered not only a comprehensive inventory of available local plant and animal resources, but also a more balanced opinion of New England's promise compared with Hakluyt's and Smith's. His treatment of Native peoples, in the second part of the book, was comparative to the extent that he delineated the characteristics and territories of the Mohawks, Tarrantines (or Eastern Abenaki), Pequots, Narragansetts, and those he called the "Aberginians," his closest neighbors living in northern Massachusetts and southern New Hampshire. The comparative ethnology was based largely on information collected from other colonists, whose experiences and dispositions compensated for his limited personal contacts with the Native groups he wrote about.[52] Like other writers, he described their physical appearance, their institutions, such as government, religion, and warfare, and their daily life. His attention to mundane aspects of existence—how they swam, hunted, fished, and dressed hides, and especially, how women carried out everyday tasks—provided a different kind of accounting of Native New England compared with anything written previously.

Although it is tempting to speculate that Williams was fascinated by Wood's stories of Native life, he also may have been aware of the limitations of Wood's knowledge and preferred to produce an account based more on firsthand observations than hearsay, and one that would include a much more extensive vocabulary of Native terms than that appended to *New England's Prospect*—which some suspect that Williams helped compile.[53]

If Wood's *New England's Prospect* did not provide Williams with a model, then did Morton's lively *New English Canaan*? Morton's book, written before 1635 and printed in Amsterdam in 1637, was a combination of promotional literature, adventure tale, and anti-Puritan tract. It contained three books: "The Origins of the Natives; their Manners and Customs"; "A Description of the Beauty of the Country"; and "A Description of the People." Unlike Wood, his contemporary and literary arch rival, Morton began with a discussion of New England's Native peoples rather than its natural history. Instead of marginalizing Native peoples through erasure (e.g., Higginson) or disconnecting them from the land (e.g., Wood), he acknowledged their presence. He recognized their humanity but also accepted them as partners in trade, often preferring the companionship of these strangers to that of the English colonists. Compared with Wood, he conveyed a knowledge of Native life based on personal familiarity rather than on secondhand information. Although he described their houses, religion, apparel, trade, funerals, and many other elements of everyday life that figured into early accounts of Native cultures, his exposition provided intimate glimpses into aspects of their lives neglected and perhaps unseen by other English authors in the seventeenth century. His comments on their physical appearance, manner of dress, and experiences (e.g., puberty, childbirth) are more detailed and keenly sensual, revealing a more personal knowledge of New England Native peoples than that of other English writers.

Morton acquired this knowledge by living among Native people. Arriving in New England in 1625, he settled near Plymouth as part of a private colonizing venture known as Mount Wollaston. When the leader of the colony relocated to Virginia with the company's indentured servants, Morton stayed, taking over the plantation and its fur trade. In pursuit of trade, he learned the language and customs of Native people but also ate, sang, drank, and slept with them. In the colony, renamed Ma-re-mount, "mountain by the sea" (or Merry Mount, as it has been called since at least the nineteenth century), Native men and women interacted with Englishmen in a manner considered scandalous by the Pilgrims and, later, the Puritans. Such openly licentious behavior posed a threat to civil order and English culture, as did Morton's revelry around a maypole and his lucrative fur trade. The authorities of Plymouth Colony accused him of selling guns and in 1628 arrested him and deported him to England. He returned a little more than a year later, only to be arrested again by the newly founded colony of Massachusetts Bay and again banished to England. He remained there for ten years before coming back to New England for the last time.

Morton's *New English Canaan* was critical of those who had banished him. They in turn viewed the "infamouse and scurrilous booke" as seditious, because of its counterfactual interpretations of events in the early years of settlement, including incidents involving the Plymouth colonists' dealings with Native peoples. But *New English Canaan* was more than a diatribe written by a dissident. It offered a different kind of portrayal of Native peoples—one written from the vantage point of someone who did not maintain the social and spatial distance expected of an Englishman vis-à-vis Native Americans. Morton did not claim to be merely an eyewitness like other English authors. He was also a participant who had abandoned notions of propriety governing interactions between English colonists and Native Americans. With an eye on cultivating trade, he had committed the error of getting too close and risked becoming one of them. At the very least, his social vision had become blurred, causing him to make tentative and perhaps expedient gestures toward cultural amalgamation, or what might be called a "middle ground."[54]

Morton's knowledge of the Native peoples living at Passonagessit, the Massachusett name for the territory where Merry Mount was situated, would have appealed to Williams's intellectual curiosity. However, the matter of whether *New English Canaan* served as a prototype for *A Key* is much less certain. In many ways, the experiences of both men in seventeenth-century New England were remarkably similar. Both were considered opponents of the Puritan order and were ousted as a result. Both wrote books after their banishment from the English colonies. Morton, who supported the established Church of England, criticized the Puritans in *New English Canaan*, but for reasons that had less to do with differences in religious principles than with contesting Plymouth's and the Massachusetts Bay Colony's claims for complete domination over New England. Morton refused to subscribe to their sovereignty in a land so vast that there was room enough for many colonial enterprises and disparate Native communities. The charges he made against colonial authorities, narrated in the third book of *New English Canaan*, were laced with biting parody and sexual references, which he used as weapons in his assault on the colonists' hypocrisy in lieu of the guns he had sold to Natives. Williams, also an outspoken critic of Puritan New England, expressed opinions about Native peoples at odds with those of most colonists but would have been scandalized by Morton's innuendoes. He was appalled by the idea of "nativization," whether in everyday life or in the context of trade where, as Morton indicated, carousing sometimes became a prelude to business. In spite of the similarities between the two men—their expulsion from New England, their criticism of the Puritans, their roles as traders, and their living more closely with Native peoples than any of their counterparts—there were also significant differences. Morton could hardly be considered Williams's mentor, just as Williams could not be mistaken for him in appearance or manners. In *New English Canaan*, Morton described New England as beautiful and inviting, where he imagined the creation of a new place, neither wholly English nor Native American, but shaped by mutual interests rather than the dictates of colony building. Williams did not share that vision; his was a loftier, more idealistic view. *A Key* was intended not only as a means to help navigate New England's existing social and cultural landscapes, but also as a tool to facilitate the conversion of its Native peoples.[55]

Although *A Key* derived from the same general historical and cultural contexts as Wood's and Morton's accounts, these common threads fail to explain Williams's representation of the Narragansetts. Like others who wrote (and still write) about other cultures, his description of the Narragansetts was derived from and filtered through his experiences among them. Whether or not his immersion into Narragansett society approximated the experience that was later considered requisite for professional anthropologists—either in terms of duration or in the intensity of direct observation—Williams came to possess linguistic competence and a familiarity with local knowledge.

As a trader, preacher, and sometime translator and negotiator, he interacted with and came to rely upon a restricted group of individuals who acted as his informants. Some he traded with or employed as carriers; others served as messengers or guides or sought his skills in translation. Some of those mentioned in letters written in the years before *A Key* were indentured in English households— including his own servant, a Pequot boy he called Will, and Winthrop's servant Reprieve, so aptly named in terms of the Puritan mission—and had become accustomed to "civility," if only tentatively. In addition to these informants were the sachems with whom Williams negotiated and for whom he sometimes interceded in the context of seventeenth-century colonial politics. Among them were those of noted prominence, such as Canonicus and especially Miantonomi, whom he considered a friend, perhaps overstating the bounds of their relationship.[56] If these informants shared a common characteristic, it was that they were exclusively male. Although Williams might have had occasion to interact with Native women on a one-to-one basis, these were rare and isolated events.[57] In assessing *A Key Into the Language of America*, the effects of these interactions on Williams's representation of Narragansett culture and history, and especially the lives and experiences of women, need to be considered.

As with many other pre-anthropological interpreters of Native cultures, Williams's observations of the Narragansetts were tied initially to his study of local dialects. While residing at Plymouth and Salem, he began the arduous task of acquiring the rudiments of the Algonkian language spoken by southern New England Indians. Cast in the role of an eager student, he spent much time learning the names for common things and the phrases of familiar speech used in everyday interactions, repeating difficult words, stammering with pronunciation, and feeling otherwise helpless in an alien culture. Years after writing *A Key* he would state:

> How hard it is for any man to attaine a little proprietie of their Language in common things (so as to escape *Derision* amongst them) in many yeares, without abundance of *conversing* with them, in *Eating, travelling* and lodging with them. . . . I see not how without cons[t]ant *use* or a *Miracle,* any man is able to attaine to any *proprietie* of *Speech* amongst them, even in common things.[58]

By 1643 he had "so much converse with these Natives" that he decided to " write some little of them."

Although the degree of Williams's language proficiency is unknown, he was able to discern variations in regional dialects and was aware of the complexities of Native vocabulary.[59] In the directions he provided for the use of the vocabulary contained in *A Key,* he indicated that "sometimes there are two words for the same thing (for their language is exceedingly copious, and they have five or six words sometimes for one thing)." In committing his knowledge of what was a spoken language to print, Williams was, in the opinion of some experts, a less-than-accurate recorder, who had not mastered the anomalies of Native grammar.[60] Although he expressed a preference for learning languages through conversation rather than through the tedious study of grammatical rules, it is difficult to determine the extent to which problems in his transcription of the Narragansett dialect may have been linked to an inability to detect grammatical or semantic ambiguities in conversation.[61]

At times Williams's statements exude a tremendous sense of self-confidence in his ability to speak and to be understood by Native people. In a statement made to an assembly of commissioners in the late 1670s, he remarked that his ability to converse with Native people in their own language not only contributed to his acceptance but also afforded him considerable prestige within their communities.[62] In fact, Williams was the translator of choice for the sachems of the Narragansetts, who claimed that he did not distort the meaning of their words.[63] Unlike other interpreters, bilingual Indians or Europeans who sometimes acted as cultural mediators, Williams seems to have not only respected the Narragansetts' words but also captured their mode of expression.[64] Despite his claims of linguistic competence, however, he sometimes admitted to the limits of his comprehension and thus of his ability to understand completely what was being communicated in dialogues with Native people. His awareness of the potential problems of both receiving and giving misinformation is corroborated by examples in his letters, in which he tested the veracity of his informants by probing their statements to detect "any deceit or falsehood."[65] As he imputed in *A Key*, language imposed limitations that frequently caused communication involving an exchange of ideas and cultural knowledge to break down into one-sided harangues.[66]

Although mutual intelligibility was an ongoing concern, Williams's knowledge of local dialects may have allowed him to communicate with Native people in their own language with a proficiency that surpassed a rudimentary language of signs and pidgin speech. He would have had little need to engage in the stilted, sometimes ribald "trade language" often used in commercial, and presumably other, interactions between Natives and Europeans; he would have been able to conduct business through an exchange of questions and short answers.

Following the protocol of the trade, Narragansetts who wished to do business with him would have come to his post at Cocumscussoc. From what can be inferred from Williams's own statements, those who wished to trade came freely and frequently, sometimes in groups of ten or twenty persons, to exchange furs, corn, venison, fish, other provisions, and wampum for the manufactured commodities that he had to offer in return. Trade was not the primary pretext on which Williams ventured to nearby Narragansett settlements, but he may have made excursions to these places and others in order to maintain and broaden his business ties.

Anaqushénto.	*Let us trade.*
Cúttasha?	*Have you this or that?*
Cowachaúnum?	
Nítasha.	*I have.*
Nowachaūnum.	
Nquénowhick.	*I want this, etc.*
. . . .	
Cuttattaúamish.	*I will buy this of you.*
Nummouanaquish.	*I come to buy.*[67]

Although Williams left no business ledgers from which to estimate the volume of trade or annual fluctuations in the quantity of goods exchanged, he managed to earn a decent living from his trading activities, with an annual income eventually exceeding the amount a Puritan minister would have earned in England. As willing as any of his contemporaries to make his trading venture a going concern, his business—by his own appraisal—was not as prosperous as it might have been, because he had refused to engage in the lucrative trade in guns and liquor from which many had reaped a sizable profit, and he was willing to provide merchandise free of charge to friends and allies.[68] For Williams, trade was his livelihood, and most certainly it secured his survival in the years of exile from Massachusetts.

Besides giving Williams the means to survive in Narragansett country, trade also served as an important context for communicating with Native people.[69] In these verbal exchanges, Williams, the trader, would have been patient, wise, and unwavering in promising quality merchandise and value to make a profit and, like any able business owner, would have pursued his debtors to collect what was owed him—but perhaps with the added expectation of accruing new experiences and "some gaine of Language" for his efforts.[70] For their part, those with whom he traded would have questioned, hesitated, and even cajoled to get what they perceived as the best deal, fully realizing that trade did not make them equal partners. In the course of driving hard bargains, Native traders would have learned about market practices involving credit and price fluctuations, but not without much consternation. Mutually discouraged by misunderstandings, Williams and his customers might have lapsed into communicating in the clipped utterances of trade pidgin. As defenses were raised and accusations hurled, trade became not a neutral process but a prelude to the appropriation of land in exchange for nothing at all. Thus trade became a context in which much more was communicated than mere information about goods and exchange values. For Williams and the Narragansetts, trade confirmed the frustrations and struggles that were part of colonial life and the ethnographic experience.

Comaunekunnúo?	*Have you any Cloth?*
Koppócki.	*Thick cloth.*
Wassáppi.	*Thin.*
. . . .	
Etouwawâyi.	*Wollie on both sides.*
Muckŭcki	*Bare without Wool.*
Chechéke maútsha.	*Long-lasting.*
. . . .	
Mat Weshegganúnno	*There is no Wool on it.*
Tanógganish.	*Shake it.*
. . . .	
Tahenaúatu?	*What price?*
Tummòck cumméinsh.	*I will pay you Beaver.*
Teaúguock Cumméinsh.	*I will give you Money.*
Wauwunnégachick	*Very good.*
. . . .	
Cosaúmawem	*You aske too much.*
Kuttíackqussaûwaw	*You are very hard.*
Aquie iackqussaume.	*Be not so hard.*
Aquie Wussaúmowash.	*Doe not aske so much.*
Tashin Commêsim?	*How much shall I give you?*

Kutteaûg Comméinsh.	*I will give you your Money.*
Nkèke Comméinsh.	*I will give you an Otter.*
Coanombúqusse.	*You have deceived me.*
Kuttassokakómme.	

. . . .

Misquésu Kunúkkeke	*Your Otter is reddish.*
Yò aúwusse Wunnêgin	*This is better.*
Yo chippaúatu.	*This is of another price.*
Augausaúatu.	*It is Cheap.*
Múchickaúatu.	*It is deare.*
Wuttunnaúatu.	*It is worth it.*
Wunishaũnto.	*Let us agree.*
Aquie neesquttónck	*Doe not make adoe.*
qussish	

. . . .

Akêtash-tamòke.	*Tell my money.*
Now ánnakese.	*I have mis-told.*
Cosáumakese.	*You have told too much.*
Cunnoónakese.	*You have told too little.*
Shoo kekíneass.	*Looke here.*
Wunêtu nitteaûg.	*My money is very good.*
Mamattissuôg kut-	*Your Beads are naught.*
teaùquock.	

. . . .

Cuminanohamógunna.	*They will buy it of you.*
Cuppittakúnnemous	*Take your cloth againe.*
Cuppittakunnamì.	*Will you serve me so?*
Cosaumpeekúnnemun.	*You have tore me off too little cloth.*
Cummachetannakún	*I have torn it off for you.*
namous.	
Tawhìtch cuppítta-	*Why doe you turne it*
kunamiêan?	*upon my hand?*
Kutchichêginash,	*Your Hatchets will be*
kaukinne pokéshaas.	*soone broken.*
Teâno wáskishaas.	*Soone gapt.*
Natouashóckquittea.	*A Smith.*
Kuttattaúamish aũke.	*I would buy land of you.*
Tou núckquaque?	*How much?*
Wuchè wuttotânick	*For a Towne, or, Plantation.*
Nissékineam.	*I have no minde to seeke.*

Indiansuck sekineám- wock.	*The Indians are not willing.*
Noonapûock naûgum.	*They want roome themselves.*
Cowetompátimmin.	*We are friends.*
Cummaugakéamish.	*I will give you land.*
Aquìe chenawaûsish.	*Be not churlish.*[71]

As a preacher in Narragansett Bay, Williams had neither a formal church appointment nor an official congregation. Although he preached to any Native person who would listen—and apparently seized every opportunity to do so, whether in the aftermath of trade, when he traveled with them, or when he visited their homes—his role as a missionary is ambiguous and poorly understood. He learned the Native language because it was his "Soules desire to doe the Natives good," which in his view was to teach them Christianity. He indicated to John Winthrop in the late 1630s that he planned to send in short time "good newes of great hopes the lord hath sprung up in mine Eye of many a poore Indian soule enquiring after God."[72] Yet in his tract *Christenings Make Not Christians* (1645), believed to have been written around the same time as *A Key*, he stated that he could have "brought many thousands of these Natives, yea the whole country," to Christianity but failed to do so because of the apparent folly of converting Natives to a less-than-pure Christian church and also because of his developing ideas about the superficiality of overt ritual acts, such as mass conversions.

Despite his ambivalence as a missionary, Williams was less negligent about the welfare of Native souls than were other Puritans in the 1630s and early 1640s. Between 1636 and 1643—the period during which Williams observed the Narragansetts firsthand—he was content to hold the idea of religious conversion at bay, rather than to promulgate false worship. He directed his mission at facilitating future conversions, continually refining his knowledge of Native language so that he could discuss religious matters with Native people. Religion was a difficult topic of conversation, compared with verbal exchanges on mundane affairs, because it required conveying in an alien language a message that was, in itself, alien to the culture of the listener.[73] Nonetheless, it was a task that Williams seems to have relished despite his results, which seem lackluster if gauged solely on the basis of the number of Native converts.

In discussing religious matters, Williams, the tentative and hesitant missionary, assumed the confidence of an initiate making specific inquiries into their culture and beliefs. On such occasions, he was not a mere passive recipient of cultural knowledge, but an interrogator. His mode of ethnographic inquiry seems to have taken the form of an interview in which he elicited specific responses from his Native informants by asking questions that were preset, rather than ad hoc and curious. These "solemn discourses" were reminiscent of catechism lessons, in which Williams labored persistently in the hopes of evoking the Narragansetts' acknowledgment of the existence of the Christian god and, perhaps eventually, some confirmation of their piety.

Awaunkeesitteoúwin-cohòck:	*Who made you?*
Tunna-awwa com-mítchichunck-kitonckquèan?	*Whether goes your soule when you die?*
An. Sowánakit-aúwaw.	*It goes to the South-West.*
. . . .	
Nétop Kunnatótemous.	*Friend, I will aske you a Question.*
Natótema:	*Speake on.*
Tocketunnântum?	*What thinke you?*
Awaun Keesiteoû-win Keésuck?	*Who made the Heavens?*
Aûke Wechêkom?	*The Earth, the Sea?*
Míttauke.	*The World.*
. . . .	
Tà suóg Maníttowock.	*How many Gods bee there?*
Maunaũog Mishaúnawock.	*Many, great many.*
Nétop machàge.	*Friend, not so.*
Paũsuck naũnt manìt.	*There is onely one God.*
Cuppíssittone.	*You are mistaken.*
Cowauwaúnemun.	*You are out of the way.*[74]

How Williams's Native informants responded to the "varieties of *Intercourses*" on religion that he posed to them "Day and Night, Summer and Winter, by Land and Sea" can only be guessed. Initially, the limitations of language must have made his questions seem awkward. He may have had occasional breakthroughs when he learned something new from his informants.[75] But what they may have excused at first on the basis of his rudimentary language skills, they must soon have perceived as an intrusive, perhaps even confrontational, barrage of questioning about things they preferred not to reveal, and to which they responded with omissions, denials, evasions, and silences that even he could not penetrate.

Williams was not merely an observer of Narragansett life; he came to the Narragansetts as a trader and missionary. He frequently acted as a translator and mediator in their negotiations with colonial authorities and also furnished the latter with intelligence on Native affairs by serving as their eyes and ears on Narragansett

Bay.[76] In these different roles, he mingled behaviors that might have seemed inconsistent to the Narragansetts, who may have perceived conflicting aims between his attempts by day to make a profit by them and his efforts by night in exhorting them to give up their beliefs and embrace Christianity.[77] At times, even Williams's fellow colonists questioned his motives and objectivity, accusing him, at least indirectly, of complicity with the Narragansetts. On these occasions, he staunchly defended himself by assuring his critics that he had "not yet turned Indian, to believe all barbarians tell me."[78] Even long after A Key's publication, he continued to fend off rumors and innuendos about his relationship with the Narragansetts by asserting that his dealings with them were business arrangements, in which he sometimes placed himself in great danger.[79] Near the end of his life, when he was no longer constrained to defend his position, he depicted himself as neither an impartial observer of the Narragansetts nor an advocate for their cause, but as their victim.[80] He had lent them his boats and servant; given them lodging, goods, and gifts; and satisfied a dying Canonicus's request to be buried in cloth from his trading house. In sum, he claimed to have never denied them anything they desired. Perhaps his recollections were tarnished by disappointments and personal defeat, including assaults on his character in the contest over lands in Providence, his fading reputation as a persuasive figure among Narragansett sachems, and his losses in King Philip's War. But Williams's self-pity was tinged also with a bitter acknowledgment that he had not been as masterful in his dealings with the Narragansetts as he had sometimes portrayed by inflating the extent of his knowledge and influence. He had not dictated to them but instead had needed them for his very survival in Narragansett country, which was, in fact, an Indian place.

Williams did not willingly walk away from colonial society or choose to live his life as a Narragansett. Among the English colonists, "No civilized person in possession of his faculties or free from undue restraint would choose to become an Indian."[81] Although in his exile he was dependent on the Narragansetts and drawn to them for pragmatic reasons, his experience shared little in common with other colonists who took to Native life reluctantly or adopted it without any compulsion. From what little is known about Williams's personal life, nothing suggests that he adopted any aspects Native culture, except for acquiring their language. It is hard to imagine that Williams gave up his Puritan coat and breeches for a deerskin mantle and a breechcloth or that he cohabited with a Narragansett woman. In several letters written between the fall of 1637 and the spring of 1638, he adamantly registered his disapproval of William Baker, an English renegade who was accused of "uncleanenes with an Indian Squaw," and who, "after many whoredomes," had "turned Indian in nakednes and cutting of haire" and by marrying a Native woman.[82] Such behavior was perceived as a threat to the social order that the Puritans were attempting to create in New England, a risk of cultural and racial contamination that they, as well as Williams, feared. Given existing allegations about his fanaticism, he would have had many good reasons to avoid making it easy for his fellow colonists to spread rumors about his being a renegade or a "white Indian."

Williams evokes neither the image of someone who would have engaged in these sorts of behavioral improprieties nor the picture of an ethnographer-gone-native who would presume to tell the story of Native lives based on empathetic experiences. He was, as some have surmised, perhaps guilty of letting "the Narragansetts go to his head," because he had the audacity to propose that the English were not morally superior to Native peoples, and that Native peoples possessed some beliefs sympathetic to his own, especially concerning religious tolerance.[83] For some white Indians, the final and most difficult step in their enculturation was to acquire the ability to think like Native people and to share unconsciously their values, beliefs, and standards.[84] Williams did not make this transition, though at times his words came close to implying that he had. Roger Williams did not think as "Natives" thought (or think), nor should he have been expected to do so. He was as sympathetic to the Narragansetts as he was judgmental of them. At times, he seemed to express admiration for them, even awe. But as an ethnographer, his portrayal of them in *A Key* did not require him to see the world through their eyes, only to appreciate that they might have perceived things differently. Perhaps more important, he needed to capture the essence of why this was so, based on what he heard, as well as observed, in his interactions with the Narragansetts.

His record of words, phrases, and asides heard in conversations and of things he had seen in Narragansett country and the rest of New England became *A Key*.[85] He drew them together "in a rude lump at Sea" to aid in his recollection of the knowledge that he "so *dearely bought* in some few yeares of hardship, and charges among the Barbarians." Not the first European to have encountered the Narragansetts or to have written something about them, Williams played a crucial part in representing them to a white audience by deciding to cast what they said to him, and what he observed, into *A Key*. Although the degree to which Williams remedied memories flawed by distance and intervening experiences cannot be determined, it is possible, by examining *A Key*, to assess how much he was able to penetrate existing preconceptions about New England's Native peoples and to recount the lives and histories of Narragansett people.

5.

UNLOCKING *A KEY*'S SILENCES

A little *Key* may open a *Box*,
where lies a *bunch* of *Keyes*.[1]

This statement, taken from the preface of *A Key,* implies that Williams envisioned his book on Native America as an instrument of discovery. His words were clever metaphors that challenged readers to think about what might be learned by using *A Key*. As a dictionary or phrase book, *A Key* provided basic tools for communicating with Native peoples, to help other colonists avoid "what grosse mis-takes" Williams and others had made in attempting to navigate New England's social landscapes. As a textbook on evangelization, it offered ways of inquiring about beliefs and, perhaps more important, a means of discovering what constituted those beliefs.[2] As a manual of ethnological information, it contained a descriptive account of the "manners and customs" of Narragansett Indians. In the opinion of many later scholars, Williams did not simply offer an exposition of cultural institutions and attributes in *A Key;* he approximated the "nearest approach to an objective anthropological study that anyone was to achieve for a century or more."[3]

One could read *A Key* and conclude that it was a thorough and insightful account of Narragansett culture. Such a conclusion would not be unreasonable, given the breadth of topics covered in its thirty-two chapters and the great lengths that Williams went to in establishing his credentials as a commentator. He claimed a privileged understanding because his information about the Narragansetts was based on actual observations, instead of "armchair speculation" or hearsay. Throughout *A Key,* he bolstered his claims of originality by using a variety of stylistic conventions, including the first-person voice, anecdotes drawn from firsthand experience, and "implicite dialogues" that created the impression of conversations between Williams and "real" Native people.[4]

But neither the range of cultural institutions described nor the authenticity of the people and incidents portrayed could guarantee that *A Key* would penetrate preexisting expectations about New England's Native peoples. *A Key*'s strengths cannot obscure the fact that major portions of the world Williams attempted to portray remained silent (and invisible) to him. The purpose of this chapter is not to jettison *A Key* but to use it as it was intended—as an instrument of discovery— to identify aspects of Narragansett culture and history that Roger Williams did not discuss and perhaps simply missed.

The task is not easy. Unlike some others who observed and wrote about other cultures, Williams left no personal diaries filled with intimate revelations about his encounters with the Narragansetts. None of Williams's original fieldnotes have been located, so the contents of these records cannot be compared with what he wrote about in *A Key*.[5] A gap in his letters in the years immediately before and after *A Key*'s publication shrouds surrounding events with uncertainties. His surviving correspondence, if read straightforwardly, offers only a few backward glances into his frustrations with the complexities of the colonial encounter and, thus, limited insights into *A Key*.[6] But even if more resources were at hand, discovering *A Key*'s omissions and, more specifically, the meanings left hidden by its partialities, would not be assured.

In the absence of readily available answers and simple formulas, how is it possible to judge what Williams did not see or what he might not have recognized as important to those whose lives he attempted to represent? By reading *A Key* closely, one can hear the voices of the Narragansett people. No amount of overwriting or imposed meanings based on existing preconceptions has obliterated them completely. Whether pushed to the sidelines or reduced to faint murmurs, these voices, even in their silences, can be heard and used as differently positioned starting points in interpreting the archaeological record and exploring alternative histories of the Narragansett people.

In Williams's opinion, the Narragansetts were the people of America, or at least of that part of the continent familiar to him, a zone of English settlement that extended for about 200 miles (300 kilometers) "betweene the *French* and *Dutch* Plantations" (between New France to the north and New Amsterdam to the south).[7] As the people of America, they had, as Williams noted, been given many different English names: "*Natives, Salvages* [Savages], *Indians, Wild-men* (so the *Dutch* call them *Wilden*), *Abergeny men, Pagans, Barbarians, Heathen*."[8] All acknowledged their humanity but were misnomers that derived from attempts to incorporate them into an existing lexicon in ways that would make them intelligible to European readers. As savages and wild men, they were unruly and uncultured. As barbarians,

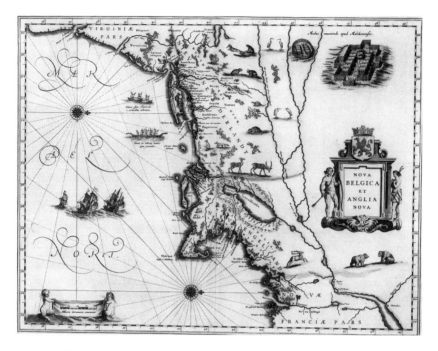

Figure 19. *Nova Belgica et Anglia Nova* (1635). This early-seventeenth-century map shows New England in relation to New Netherlands and New France, though with a somewhat inaccurate picture of the geography. (John Carter Brown Library at Brown University)

they were the inversion of civility because they did not conform to European social norms. As pagans and heathens, they were un-Christian, living in a depraved natural state under the devil's spell.[9] For New England Puritans in the seventeenth century, including Williams at the time he wrote *A Key*, these terms coexisted and were practically interchangeable in their usage, because the criteria on which they were based were inextricably associated.[10]

These English terms of reference confounded the Narragansetts. Williams admitted that they often asked him "why wee [the English] call them *Indians Natives*, &c.," when they did not have names to differentiate themselves from strangers. They had their own names instead, such as a general term that referred to all Native peoples (*Nínnuock, Ninnimissinûwock, Eniskeetompauwog*), which Williams translated as *"Men, Folke, or People."*[11] In addition to the term connoting shared identities across the region, they had specific names for peoples living at particular places (*Nanhigganeuck, Massachusêuck, Cawasumsêuck, Cowwêseuck, Quintikóock, Quinnipiĕck, Pequttóog*).[12] These dimensions of Native identity, as revealed by common terms of belonging for all people and distinctive ones tied to place, indicate the existence of a much wider and more diverse social and cultural scene than Williams portrayed in *A Key* and which he seems to have comprehended only minimally. Although he had known people whom he identified as Massachusett, Pequot, Nipmuck, and Niantic, his Native America—the one represented in *A Key*— was Narragansett.

The question of Native origins was far more puzzling and troublesome than the matter of what to call New England's Native peoples. Considered to be a subject of purely academic concern before the first English plantations were established, Native origins acquired additional significance as the colonial enclaves became more firmly embedded in New England soil. The question was important enough for Williams to include it as one of four main topics addressed in his opening preface to *A Key*. His opinions reflected the Christian belief that Native people were descended from Adam and Noah and, like all of humankind, were the product of a single creation. Although he stated this unequivocally, it was the problem of "their later Descent, and whence they came into those pars" that he found difficult to solve.[13] Imagined as a complicated series of deviations and transmissions from the Garden of Eden, and certainly from the postdiluvian travels of Noah's sons, their origins were as hard to define "as to finde the *wellhead* of some fresh *Streame*, which running many miles out of the *Countrey* to the salt *Ocean*, hath met with many mixing *Streames* by the way."[14]

The difficulty posed by this question was related at least partly to geography. The American continent was not contiguous to Europe or Asia, so any theory that did not disregard indigenous origins entirely had to account for how Native people arrived here. In the absence of clues from ancient texts, those who attempted to account for Native origins entered into long and complicated debates that lasted well into the nineteenth century. During the course of these arguments, a multitude of ancestors were identified in attempts to fit the Native Americans into a world created full and delimited in known space and time. Williams had heard different opinions on the subject from many he considered *"Wise* and *Judicious* men."* Some maintained that Native people descended out of the north from Tartaria.[15] While at New Amsterdam awaiting his departure for London in the spring of 1643, he learned "it pleased the *Dutch* Governour, (in some discourse with mee about the *Natives*), to draw their *Line* from *Iceland*, because the name *Sackmakan* (the name for an *Indian* Prince, about the *Dutch*) is the name for a *Prince* in *Iceland*."[16] Although somewhat circumspect in voicing his own view about Native origins, Williams seemed to favor theories that tied their lineage to the Jews or possibly the Greeks.

The idea that Native American origins could be traced to the Jews had gained popularity around the time of *A Key*'s publication.[17] For English Protestants keen on converting Jews, the conversion of those sharing Semitic heritage in America offered an opportunity to fulfill an essential stage in the millennial timetable: that of gathering the degenerate into the Christian flock. Like other English writers on both sides of the Atlantic, Williams seized on any hint of a resemblance between Native American and Jewish customs to infer a genealogical relationship. He itemized these points of similarity in *A Key,* noting that some Narragansett words were similar to Hebrew and that Native peoples "constantly *annoint* their *heads* as the *Jewes* did," give "*Dowries* for their wives, as the *Jewes* did," and "constantly separate their Women (during the time of their monthly sicknesse) in a little house alone by themselves for foure or five dayes, and hold it an *Irreligious thing* for either *Father* or *Husband* or any *Male* to come neere them," a practice he had not "observed amongst other *Nations* as amongst the *Jewes,* and *these.*"[18]

Although he found reason to suspect (and perhaps advocate) Jewish origins, Williams also identified evidence to suggest that Native Americans might have been descended from the Greeks. He stated in *A Key* that he found greater affinity between the Narragansett language and the Greek tongue than Hebrew. An additional corroboration was deduced from the similarity of the Native and classical names for the northern constellation Ursa Major, or "Great Bear." Williams considered it profoundly significant that the Narragansetts, like all mariners since the time of Ulysses, called these northern stars "the bear" (*Mosk* or *Paukunnnawaw* in Narragansett). He believed that this resemblance implied the existence of a set of symbols and myths shared with the Greeks and other peoples of the Northern Hemisphere.[19] Similarly, Native allusions to a mythical figure, "one *Wétucks,* a man that wrought great *Miracles* amongst them, and walking upon the waters,, &c." bore, in Williams's opinion, "some kind of broken Resemblance to the *Sonne* of God."[20]

His proposals about a Jewish or Greek pedigree were not prompted by any interest in accounting for Narragansett history in its own terms. These alleged ancestors were unknown to the Narragansetts; besides, they knew nothing about the biblical story of Creation until Williams told them about it:

Kukkakótemous, wâ- chit-quáshouwe.	*I will tell you,* *presently.*
Kuttaunchemókous.	*I will tell you newes.*
Paûsuck naûnt manít kéesittin keesuck, &c.	*One onely God made* *the Heavens, &c*
Napannetashèmittan naugecautúmmo- nab nshque.	*Five thousand yeers* *agoe and upwards.*
Naûgom naûnt wuk- kesittínnes wâme taêgun.	*He alone made* *allthings*
Wuche mateâg.	*Out of nothing.*

Quttatashuchuckqún-
  nacaus-keesitínnes wâme.
Nquittaqúnne.
Wuckéesitin wequâi.
Néesqunne.
Wuckéesitin Keésuck.
Shúckqunne wuckée-
  sitin Aūke kà
  wechêkom.
Yóqunne wuckkéesi-
  tin Nippaūus kà
  Nanepaūshat.
Neenash-mamockíu-
  wash wêquanantígansh.
Kà wáme anócksuck.
Napannetashúck-
  qunne Wuckéesittin
  pussuckseésuck wâme.
Keesuckquíuke.
Ka wáme namaūsuck.
  Wechekommíuke.
Qutttatashúkqunne
  wuckkeéssittin pena-
  shímwock wamè.
Wuttàke wuchè
  wuckeesittin pau-
  suck Enìn, *or,* Enes-
  kéetomp.
Wuche mishquòck.
Ka wesuonckgonna-
  kaûnes Adam, túp-
  pautea mishquòck.
Wuttàke wuchè,
Câwit míshquock.
Wuckaudnúmmenes
  manìt peetaūgon
  wuche Adam.
Kà wuchè peteaúgon.
Wukkeesitínnes pau-
  suck squàw.

In six dayes he made
  all things.
The first day Hee
  made the Light.
The second day Hee
  made the Firmameut.
The third day hee made
  the Earth and the Sea.

The fourth day he
  made the Sun and
  the Moon.
Two great Lights.

And all the Starres.
The fifth day hee made
  all the Fowle.

In the Ayre, or Heavens.
And all the Fish in the
  Sea.
The sixth day hee made
  all the Beasts of the
  Field.
Last of all he made one
  Man

Of red Earth,
And call'd him Adam,
  or red Earth,

Then afteward, while
  Adam, or red Earth slept.
God tooke a rib from
  Adam, or red Earth.

And of that rib he made
  One woman,

Kà pawtouwúnnes	*And brought her to*
Adâmuck.	*Adam.*
Nawônt Adam wut-	*When Adam saw her,*
túnnawaun nuppe-	*he said, This is my*
teâgon ewò.	*bone.*
Enadatashúckqunne,	*The seventh day hee*
aquêi.	*rested.*[21]

They told Williams that they had never heard any of this before and offered him a different explanation of their origins: "And then [they related] how they have it from their Fathers, that *Kautántowwit* made one man and woman of a stone, which disliking, he broke them in pieces, and made another man and woman of a Tree, which were the Fountaines of all mankind."[22]

From these beginnings, Williams reported that "they say themselves, that they have *sprung* and *growne* up in that very place, like the very *trees* of the *wildernesse*."[23] Like nature's plantings, they believed that they were firmly rooted in Narragansett country.

Williams, like other English colonists, disregarded the Narragansetts' beliefs about their origins in lieu of arguments that situated the Native past within the framework of Western European history. The assimilation of their history countered the claims of their knowledge and disallowed the possibility that their history might extend beyond the temporal limits of a European past as it was conceptualized in the seventeenth century. If Native people had simply grown up "like the very *trees* of the *wildernesse*," as they claimed, then they could not be "unregenerates" who had migrated to North America as a result of a number of historical accidents. If this indeed were true, the logic of the Puritan mission in New England would be undermined. Without the specter of cultural degeneration, Native conversion would become a more perplexing problem. Any acknowledgment that Native people had a separate history would create more than an intellectual crisis: it would pose a serious threat to English colonization. Williams was reticent on this point and, in all probability, simply could not fathom its implications.

The particulars of Native American origins notwithstanding, Williams was resigned to the opinion that Native peoples were spiritually lost but that their salvation was a possibility. He did not extend the same guarded optimism to his ability to comprehend the social, cultural, and sacred landscapes of Native New England, however. In *A Key*, he characterized all the territory beyond the enclaves of English colonial settlement, including the lands of Narragansett Bay, as a "wilderness." In describing this wilderness, Williams offered a less comprehensive and less calculated view of the natural landscape than other seventeenth-century authors, but a view that also misrepresented it.

From a simply practical standpoint, Williams was dependent on Native people in making his way through this wilderness. He acknowledged the Narragansetts' intimate familiarity with the physical landscape of southern New England and admired "what paths their naked hardned feet have made in the wildernesse in most stony and rockie places."[24] He commented on, and seemed impressed by, their precise knowledge of territories. "The *Natives*," he said, "are very exact and punctuall in the bounds of their Lands, belonging to this or that Prince or People, (even to a River, Brooke) &c."[25] He noted their terms for "house" (*wetu*) and "at home" (*wetuómuck*) and stated that the phrase "I am going home" (*Nickquénum*) was "a solemne word amongst them; and no man wil offer any hinderance to him, who after some absence is going to visit his Family, and useth this word *Nicquénum* (confessing the sweetnesse even of these short temporall homes)."[26]

He was baffled by their practice of moving from the houses "where they winter" toward the "fields where they plant Corne" as the weather gradually warmed, and again moving "to a hunting house in the end of the yeere," if not before, because of an infestation of fleas, a fallowing schedule, a death, or an approaching enemy.[27] In his opinion, they were so quick to move from one place to another that "in halfe a day, yea, sometimes at few houres warning to be gone and the house up elsewhere."[28] Although some of their moves from place to place appeared to be regular and cyclical, others seemed sudden and unpredictable, leading Williams to remark that he once "in travell lodged at a house, at which in my returne I hoped to have lodged againe there the next night, but the house was gone in that interim."[29]

To depict Narragansett country as a remote wilderness filled with ponds, hills, rivers, woods and trails, and discrete houses and towns, and what seemed to be a constant ebb and flow of people, would be only a partial picture, obscuring what were more complicated connections between people and the land. Within this wilderness was a composite of stable and permanent cultural landscapes that can be defined as Native homelands. These homelands were not neatly circumscribed "tribal" territories. Similar to what others have called "locales" or "lived spaces," homelands encompassed "seasonal, interactive, and cosmological dimensions," but also much more.[30]

A typical homeland would have contained one or two important settlements and meeting spots, planting fields, sacred sites such as communal cemeteries, and locations for fishing, collecting shellfish, and gathering food and other resources. Dispersed throughout the homeland area would have been "dozens of wigwams, alone, in pairs, or clustered in small hamlets."[31] These homelands were not just territories that Narragansett people traveled through, settled on, and subsisted from; they were places steeped in long-term histories, enduring social relations, and sacred traditions. They were landscapes shaped by geography, history, beliefs, experience, and spirituality. As active and animated spaces, rather than simply static

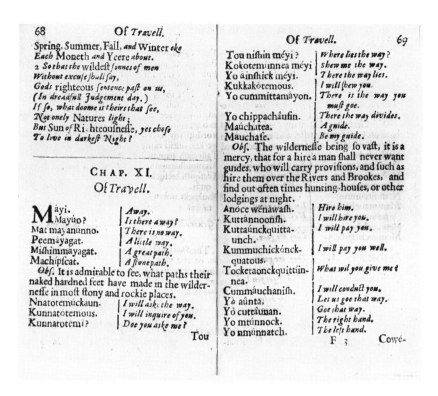

Figure 20. Pages 68 and 69, *A Key Into the Language of America* (London, 1643). Using words rather than graphic images, the dialogue indicates Williams's dependence on the Narragansetts' knowledge of the land in navigating his way through Narragansett country. (John Carter Brown Library at Brown University)

backdrops, homelands were important not only in sustaining the Narragansetts' daily lives but also in maintaining their social and historical identity as a people.

More was involved in the Narragansetts' use of and attachment to the land than Williams portrayed in *A Key*. Although he observed that "the sociablenesse of the nature of man appears in the wildest of them, who love societie; Families, co-habitation, and consocation of houses and townes together," he did not comprehend the basic principles that underscored these connections.[32] The "sociablenesse" to which he alluded was neither derived from, nor manifested in, the nuclear family or domestic residence. Rather, it was rooted in bonds of kinship that linked people of a homeland together and to kin living in other homelands across southern New England. Although *A Key* contains no specific references to kin groups besides "families," Williams's comments about obligations among family members imply the existence of a different kind of social connectedness.

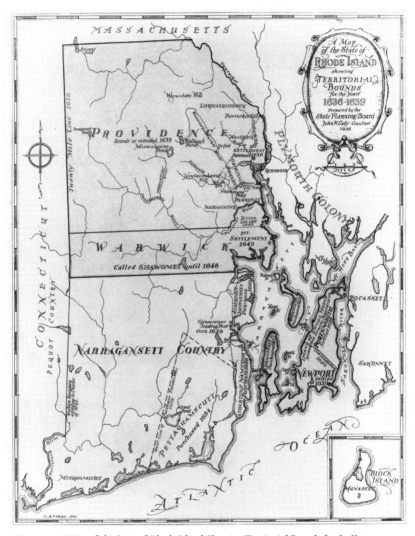

Figure 21. *A Map of the State of Rhode Island Showing Territorial Bounds for the Years 1636–1659,* by John Hutchins Cady (1936), traces English settlement history around Narragansett Bay. (Courtesy of the Rhode Island Historical Society)

He indicated that they "hold the band of brother-hood so deare, that when one had committed a murther and fled, they executed his brother; and 'tis common for a brother to pay the debt of a brother deceased."[33] Such mutual responsibility in avenging wrongs, paying debts, and "if a man be poore," contributing toward brideprice (what Williams interpreted as "contributing Money toward the Dowrie") is generally a feature of lineage or clan organization.[34]

Figure 22. John White's *Drawing of the Indian Village of Secoton* (1585) (63915PD) provides a model of settlement places and planting fields within Narragansett homelands. (Copyright The British Museum)

The nature of these lineal descent groups—that is, whether they were patrilineal or matrilineal—was not addressed in *A Key*. One could suppose this was because Williams had little interest in whom Narragansetts married. Or perhaps the difficulty of conceptualizing Native kinship terms, apart from seemingly analogous categories within the English nuclear family, precluded inquiries about the intricacies of descent.[35] Implicit in *A Key*'s silences on this matter is the assumption that Narragansett society was patrilineal. Although patrilineality and matrilineality do not necessarily equate with male-dominated and female-dominated societies, *A Key* impresses on the reader the opinion that the Narragansetts embraced a "patrilineal" ideology. It is possible that some of Williams's male informants might have chosen not to tell him the importance of matrilineal kin simply because they were not asked. Like most other seventeenth-century Englishmen, Williams's patriarchal background would have precluded any serious inquiries about women's role in formal kin relations and their influence (and authority) in politics and consensus building in their communities.[36] Also, aside from Williams's own cultural bias, some of his male informants might have had a vested interest in advancing their own prominence and, indirectly, the idea of patrilineal descent and patriarchy. To those who wished to appear as absolute monarchs—and, especially, to those predisposed to portraying them as such—uterine ties mattered less in the construction and maintenance of status and authority.[37]

In conveying the idea of male dominance (and patrilineality), Williams muted the voices of Narragansett women and deprived their actions of the energy and significance attributed to those of men. Although women's opinions were rarely sought, evidence in *A Key* suggests the possibility of alternative understandings about their roles in Narragansett society and their importance in reckoning lineal descent. In several parts of the text, Williams commented about Narragansett women's strong connections to the land, through their involvement in all facets of agricultural production—planting seeds, nurturing immature crops, and gathering and storing the harvest. In contrast, men's participation in cultivating food plants generally was limited to breaking up the earth before planting. Only in rare instances would "the man himself, (either out of love to his Wife, or care for his Children, or being an old man) help the Woman which (by the custome of the Countrey) they are not bound to."[38] Women's labor brought "in all the increase of the Field &c." and supplied the people of a homeland with a major source of food, especially corn, their principal source of nourishment. Williams estimated that, per woman, yields of dried corn amounted to "two or three heaps of twelve, fifteene, or twentie bushells a heape."[39] This was more than enough to allow some portion of the surplus to be exchanged with other Native groups and the colonists in the local subsistence trade.

The importance of horticulture in daily life—buttressed by the observation that women were entrusted with the care of gardens and communal planting fields, where they cultivated the gifts of corn and beans bestowed on Narragansett homelands from the Great Spirit, Cautantowwit—is compatible with matrilineality.[40] At the very least, Narragansett women's role in horticultural production would have reinforced what might be termed a matrilineal "ideology" that emphasized commonality, collective relationships, and lineage or clan affiliation.[41] These relationships may have permeated Native homelands before the advent of horticulture (around a thousand years ago) and continued into the later historic period, but they may also have afforded women in the seventeenth century greater independence and power than they had enjoyed previously. Narragansett women's horticultural connections to the land and their roles in biological reproduction and socialization made them a visible and profound presence in their homelands, thus tempering insinuations and claims about male dominance.

Regardless of the question of how descent was reckoned, these lineal kin groupings were organized into clans based on claims of descent from a common ancestor. Within every Narragansett homeland, a particular clan was represented by localized segments. Longer houses having two to three fires (*Nées quttow* or *Shwishcuttow*) probably were occupied by clan leaders of the dominant lineages and their close kin and located at important settlement places.[42] Small round houses (*puttcukakâunese* or "a little round house"), occurring alone or in groups, were occupied primarily by members of one clan, but as men and women did not marry within their own clan, others also would be represented.[43] Because individual clans were not specifically territorial—that is, members of the same clan might be found living in different homelands within "Narragansett country" as well as in other homelands throughout southern New England—clanship was the basis of many social and economic connections that linked people across space and through time. Accordingly, a clan member could expect to find hospitality among fellow clan members in distant homelands. If separated from an ancestral homeland of near kin, because of economic necessity (or "tribal" dispossession), a clan member could (and would) return for varying lengths of time in order to enjoy familiar company, visit ancestral and other sacred places, and participate in ceremonies.[44]

If the English concept of "wilderness" failed to capture the complexities of Narragansett homelands, the same was true for the ability of the term "ceremony" to express the richness and meaning of their ritual traditions. In *A Key*, the "ceremonial" consisted of what Williams referred to as religious devotions and "publique *Games*." His descriptions of these rites derived largely from secondhand information provided by informants, for he confessed that "after once being in their Houses and beholding what their Worship was" that he "durst never bee an eye witnesse, Spectatour, or looker on, least I should have been partaker of Sathans Inventions and Worships."[45] He echoed similar sentiments after having once seen what he referred to as the folly and evil of their "publique *Games*."[46] Although Williams surmised that the Narragansetts' religious devotions and public games were forms of devil worship, there was perhaps more to his disdain of Narragansett rituals than his perception that these acts were inspired by Satan.

Like other Puritans, he had repudiated the extravagant rituals and visual symbolism associated with Anglican Christianity as corrupt and superstitious and had hoped that the Puritan church in New England would be devoid of any vestiges of such idolatry. Believing that Puritan ritual reforms did not go far enough, Williams became embroiled in conflict with the magistrates of Massachusetts Bay on issues concerning mandatory oaths, public prayer, and worship services when he was living at Salem. Although one could argue that Williams was targeting issues of conscience and the relationship between church and state, and not ritual per se, his disfavor of idolatry and false worship made him wary of all spectacle and ceremonial pageantry.[47] These sentiments may have contributed to the paucity of detailed information in *A Key* on Narragansett sacred rituals.

Williams characterized the Narragansetts' principal religious devotion (*nickòmmo*) as a feast or dance. Although his accounts of these rituals are sketchy, *nickòmmo*s seem to have involved a basic set of rites, spanning a variety of performative genres, which can be traced in outline. Each *nickòmmo* began with an invocation led by a *powwaw* (or shaman) whom Williams identified as a priest and chief religious practitioner. Others in attendance, numbering fewer than fifty to maybe a hundred, and at other times nearly a thousand, "follow, and joyne interchangeably in a laborious bodily service, unto sweatings, especially of the Priest, who spends himselfe in strange Antick Gestures, and Actions even unto fainting."[48] Although Williams did not describe the sequence of events following the invocation, an essential part of a *nickòmmo*—regardless of its scale—was the exchange of material things through feasting, gifting, and ritual destruction. The participants gave away large amounts of money—white and black shell beads, which Williams identified as their currency—and various goods "according to and sometimes beyond their Estate" in several parcels valued at "eighteen pence, two Shillings, or thereabouts to one person."[49] Using the monetary values Williams provided in *A Key*, the amount of beads given away by those hosting a *nickòmmo* would have been in the hundreds or even thousands. He observed that the "person that receives this Gift, upon the receiving of it goes out, and hollowes thrice for the health and prosperity of the Party that gave it, the Mr. or Mistris of the Feast."[50]

According to Williams, *nickòmmo*s were of two sorts: "publike" events hosted by shamans or privately sponsored rites. Among the former were calendrical rituals performed to mark different seasons of the year. Although *A Key*'s information concerning the scheduling of these rituals is vague, the Narragansetts apparently conducted these ceremonies in the late spring at planting time, in the summer before the harvest, at the harvest, and in the winter. He commented on games and devotions coinciding with the planting period, which could have been any time between May and June, depending on weather conditions. *Keesaqúnnamun*, an event described as a "kinde of solemne publike meeting, wherein they lie under the trees, in a kinde of Religious observation, and have a mixture of Devotions and sports," may be the "solemne meeting for play" that he mentioned in a letter written to John Winthrop dated circa early June 1638.[51]

Toward harvest time, the Narragansetts conducted what Williams said was "their chiefest Idoll of all for sport and game." They prepared for this occasion by setting up a *Qunnèkamuck*, a longhouse 100–200 feet (30–60 meters) long, "upon a plaine neer the Court (which they call *Kittcickaúick*) where many thousands, men and women meet, where he goes in danceth in the sight of all the rest; and is prepared with money, coats, small breeches, knifes, or what hee is able to reach to, and gives these things away to the poore, who yet must particularly beg and say, *Cowequetúmmous*, that is, *I beseech you*."[52]

Based on Williams's comments about when these rites were scheduled (i.e., toward harvest time) and the amount of preparation involved, this probably was a "green corn" ceremony, celebrated in August when the first corn ripened. This is corroborated by information furnished in two of Williams's letters dated to about August 12, 1637, and August 20, 1637, in which he reported having been told that the Narragansetts were busy for about two weeks keeping "a kind of Christmas," in which they "were in a strange solemnity when the sachems eat nothing but at night, and the Natives round the country were feasted."[53]

Williams provided little detailed information on the harvest ritual itself, but like the ceremonies that accompanied the ripening of the new corn, this was an occasion for thanksgiving. In the winter, when they still enjoyed "a caulme of Peace, Health, Plenty, Prosperity," they held a *nickómmo* in which "(as the Turke faith of the Christian, rather the Antichristian,) they run mad once a yeare) in their kind of Christmas feasting."[54]

In addition to these calendrical rites, Williams referred to other *nickòmmos* that were conducted on a private or ad hoc basis for any variety of reasons, such as curing an illness, bringing relief from drought or famine, ensuring success in war, or celebrating a successful hunt or good fortune. The limited information provided in *A Key* suggests that the different rites may have been varied; certain repertoires were perhaps more appropriate in some situations than others, or some degree of improvisation occurred in the performance of a basic set of rites. Shamanistic rituals conducted in times of drought, for example, were "great and solemne meetings from all parts at one high place, to supplicate their gods; and beg raine" that would continue for "ten days, a fortnight; yea, three weekes, untill raine come."[55] In curing ceremonies, Williams recalled that "the Priest comes close to the sick person, and performes many strange Actions about him, [and] threaten[s] and conjures out the sicknesse" because "they conceive that there are many Gods or divine Powers within the body of a man: In his pulse, his heart, his Lungs, &c."[56]

In commenting on these rituals, Williams questioned the effectiveness of the *powwaws'* curing techniques, registering his harshest criticism against what he perceived as their vulgar materialism rather than their unconventional methods:

> These Priests and Conjurers (like *Simon Magus*) doe bewitch the people, and not onely take their Money, but doe most certainly (by the help of the Divell) worke great Cures though most certaine it is that the greatest part of their Priests doe meerely abuse them and get their Money, in the times of their sicknesse, and to my knowledge, long for sick times: and to that end the poore people store up Money, and spend both Money and goods on the *Powwâws*, or Priests in these times, the poore people commonly dye under their hands, for alas, they administer nothing but howle and roare, and hollow over them, and begin the song to the rest of the People about them, who all joyne (like a Quire) in Prayer to their Gods for them.[57]

In voicing his disapproval of the large expenditures of money (wampum) spent on the services of the *powwaws* in the hope of a cure, Williams neglected to see a connection between the exchange of material things in curing rites and other *nickòmmos*. In these ritual contexts, actions in which wampum (but also other material goods) were given away, consumed, or destroyed were not simply forms of payment, which could be refunded if the anticipated outcome was not achieved, or usury, as Williams insinuated about the *powwaws'* curing rituals. Wampum in particular was not just "money" or, for that matter, a commodity to be bartered in the fur trade or paid as fines, but an object that had more profound social value. Material acts involving wampum and other items reiterated the importance of generosity and exchange among the Narragansetts. Like other Northeastern Native peoples, they associated generosity with health, general well-being, and peace and believed that gift giving was essential to "satisfy the hidden desires of peoples' souls and cure them of illness."[58] Therefore, exchanges of material goods would have been an essential part of individual and collective curing rituals and other sacred activities through which the Narragansetts cultivated and maintained relations within their communities, with other groups, and with generations of ancestors instead of a crass ploy for material gain.

A Key contains virtually no information on life-cycle rituals, except for a discussion of rites associated with death. The absence of evidence is puzzling. Although one could reasonably surmise that the Narragansetts did not conduct rituals to mark critical transitions in a person's life, this seems improbable. It is more likely that the lack of evidence can be explained by the experiential basis of Williams's inquiries into Narragansett culture. From what can be reconstructed, it seems that he might have had only limited opportunities to observe these rites. Living at some distance from Narragansett settlements, he would not have seen many of the ordinary events and struggles of their everyday lives, such as birth, puberty, or marriage, or the cultural logic they applied to them. Admittedly, some rites of passage, such as initiation (or puberty) rites and perhaps birth, might have remained hidden because of cultural taboos surrounding them or because the Narragansetts wanted to shield these private rites from Williams's gaze.[59]

Although one might have the impression from A Key that birth was a biological event, puberty a nonevent, and marriage a contractual event (involving the payment of brideprice to the woman's family and the "consent of Parents and publique approbation"), death was portrayed as an event of critical cultural importance.[60] Neither Williams nor the Narragansetts he described in A Key viewed death as an end. Instead, they perceived it as a transition. For Williams and other Puritans, it meant the acceptance of an everlasting fate that had been predetermined at birth; hence, death was an occasion marked by resignation and the absence of ceremony. For the Narragansetts, death was considered a transition between states of being and between two worlds: that of the living and that of the dead. At death, a person's soul left the body and went to join the souls of close kin and friends in the world of the dead, located in the southwest where the god Cautantowwit and the spirits of the ancestors dwelled.[61] For the Narragansetts, death was not a mere biological act; it was a profoundly social event.

Information in A Key suggests that Narragansett death rites focused on the corpse, the mourners, and the society as a whole. Although the length of time that elapsed between death and burial is unknown, it probably did not exceed more than a few days. Clan members and kin would gather for prayer and mourning when a person was gravely ill and death seemed imminent.[62] Female members of a household, including both "Women and Maides," blackened their faces with soot and other substances. When death came, "the father, or husband, and his neighbours, the Men also (as the English weare blacke mourning clothes) weare blacke Faces" and joined in the mourning.[63] A person of chief esteeme, typically "some wise, grave and well descended man (a Mockuttásuit)," prepared the corpse for burial by wrapping it "in winding mats or coats."[64]

When the corpse was brought to the grave, those in attendance would "sit downe and lament" the deceased, lament again after the corpse was laid in the grave, and "sometimes (in some parts) some goods cast in with them." "Upon the grave," they placed "the Mat that the party died on, the Dish he eat in; and sometimes a faire Coat of skin hung upon the next tree to the Grave, which none will touch, but suffer it there to rot with the dead."[65] After burying his son, the sachem Canonicus "burn'd his owne Palace, and all his goods in it, (amongst them to a great value) in a sollemne remembrance of his sonne, and in a kind of humble Expiation to the Gods, who (as they believe) had taken his sonne from him."[66] Their grieving over the death of a child was so great, Williams reported, "that I have knowne a *Father* take so grievously the losse of his *childe*, that hee hath cut and stobd himselfe with *griefe* and *rage*."[67]

The mourners continued to blacken their faces and lament the dead for "divers weekes and moneths; yea, a yeere, if the person be great and publike."[68] According to Williams, these lamentations were "very solemne amongst them morning and evening and sometimes in the night" when they cried out for "their lost husbands, wives, children, brethren or sisters &c."[69] He reported hearing "a poore Indian lamenting the losse of a child at break of day, call up his Wife and children, and all about him to Lamentation, and with abundance of teares cry out! O God thou hast taken away my child! thou art angry with me: O turne thine anger from me, and spare the rest of my children."[70] During the mourning period, they considered it inappropriate "to play (as they much use to doe) or to paint themselves, for beauty, but for mourning; or to be angry, and fall out with any, &c." unless a special dispensation was given.[71]

Along with the ritual wailing and behavioral expressions of grief, Williams recorded that the Narragansetts engaged in acts of condolence directed toward the living. Family members and neighbors visited the bereaved frequently and consoled them with the words "*Kutchimmoke, Kutchimmoke*, Be of good cheere" as they stroked their cheeks and heads.[72] They used these expressions of sorrow because they "abhorred" mentioning the deceased by name. The apparent unwillingness to invoke the names of the dead was reinforced by strong sanctions. According to Williams, "if any man beare the name of the dead he changeth his name; and if any stranger accidentally name him, he is checkt, and if any wilfully name him he is fined; and amongst States, the naming of their dead *Sachims*, is one ground of their warres; so terrible is the King of Terrors, Death, to all naturall men."[73]

Statements in *A Key* suggest that Williams may have attended Narragansett funerals, but his description of these rites is meager. He provided more information about mourning practices than about burial rituals. Although the lack of detailed description can be attributed to Williams's disapproval of ritual displays, and particularly to the belief that burial rites were beneficial to neither the dead nor the living, another factor might account for the fragmentary reporting. Imagine for a moment what the scene must have been like. A corpse is carried out of a mourning house to a cemetery and placed at the "Grave's mouth," where a crowd of Narragansett men, women, and "little children in abundance" have assembled. With their faces blackened and tears pouring down even "the cheekes of stoutest Captaines," the mourners sit around the grave and engage in ritual laments, making woeful sounds and chanting.[74] After the corpse is lowered into the grave, some of the deceased's personal possessions and gifts from grieving relatives and friends might be added to it. As the grave is filled, the wailing and crying reach a climax.

The *Mockuttásuit* and perhaps others overseeing the ceremonies mark the grave in a gesture whose meaning can only be guessed. Soon after, the mourners depart, followed by the rest of those in attendance. It was a ritual of overwhelming proportions, full of sounds and actions that perhaps were too much for an accidental witness to take in, especially an outsider like Williams.

In all probability, there is much that Williams did not see at Narragansett funerals. He was not trained in the methods of modern fieldwork, in which visual observation ideally corroborates information derived from discursive events, and certainly he observed these rites only on a few occasions. Given the spectacle of funeral ceremonies, he would have needed to collect evidence from repeated performances, occurring over the course of time, to appreciate let alone fully describe these rituals. Without cumulative information, Williams's account of Narragansett funerals would be based on arbitrary impressions and insecure evidence.[75] Seeing only what may have appeared to him as a series of disconnected images, he did not mention, for example, that graves were part of communal cemeteries, nor did he report that these places were used and visited by successive generations of Narragansett people. Thus *A Key* presents an "observed moment" masked as a "generalized possibility," in which much is left unsaid about funerals, and about the importance of burial places in Narragansett homelands and the sacred traditions associated with them.

A Key is only a partial account of Narragansett culture and history. It simplifies the complexities of the Narragansetts' lives and those of the Native communities that shared their social environment. It portrays their experiences in the seventeenth century as unrelated to antecedent events and processes, whereas they were the products of long-standing traditions as well as contemporary developments and would continue to be so beyond the colonial period. It merely hints at the social nexus that intertwined individuals, families, and groups across regions and generations. Moreover, what Williams described as ritual behavior was only part of a much richer repertoire of sacred activities performed by Narragansett people. In addition to the more obvious omissions (e.g., life-cycle ceremonies), other rituals were conducted outside the "spectacle" of public/calendrical and private/ shamanistic ceremonies mentioned in *A Key*. These sacred customs and traditions were conducted at various localities within Narragansett homelands, including cornfields, sweat lodges, cemeteries, and other sites where people had strong and enduring attachments. At these sacred places, sometimes located beyond the venues of the ceremonies discussed in *A Key*, Narragansetts fulfilled their ritual obligations, rekindled their ancestral memories, and nurtured their cultural identities, often in inconspicuous acts unnoticed by non-Indian observers like Williams.

PART THREE

Beyond *A Key*

6.

UNDERTAKING
NARRAGANSETT GRAVES

The junction of Routes 4 and 102 in North Kingstown, Rhode Island, is just a few miles from Roger Williams's trading post at Cocumscussoc. In 1982 the area southwest of the intersection opened onto a large meadow that had been recently scoured by a bulldozer. All that appeared to be left was a barren, sandy field and a large pile of backdirt. The scene was all too familiar. Land formerly farmed—with a few small and large trees in the distance, a fieldstone wall, outbuildings, and a silo—was under development for modern construction. Except here, pieces of human bone, shell and glass beads, and a tarnished spoon, apparently of some age, littered the newly exposed surface and revealed vital information about the now-invisible history of this place.

The sequence of events that followed the bulldozing is difficult to reconstruct. Someone walking through the field to retrieve spent cartridges collected the bone and the artifacts and delivered them to the Rhode Island Historical Preservation Commission.[1] Although neither the informant nor the archaeologists at the commission knew exactly what had been found or its full import, they surmised that the "discovery" was significant. What then transpired was in many ways at odds with the usual procedure in such situations. As a matter of course, the commission notified the landowner that an archaeological site of some potential importance had been located on the property. In this case, however, the state archaeologist also contacted the Narragansett Tribal Council on the presumption that the Narragansetts would be interested in the "discovery."

The first matter was to figure out exactly what had been discovered. The general opinion was that a Narragansett grave or graves had been unearthed, or possibly a Narragansett "village" dating to the contact or colonial period. But official files showed no record of a cemetery, and the Narragansetts were said to be unaware of one at this location.[2] Glenn LaFantasie and Paul Campbell, historians at the Rhode Island Historical Society, indicated in conversations that a "village" ruled by a Narragansett "squaw sachem" named Matantuck was burned somewhere nearby in 1675.[3] A preliminary inspection of the bulldozed property indicated that further investigation could produce evidence that might help to determine whether a Narragansett cemetery or "village" had been discovered and also to answer questions raised by those who, for different reasons, wanted some concrete answers.[4]

The initial field investigations quickly dismissed the possibility that preparations for the planned construction had disturbed a Narragansett "village." Signs of Native settlement were few and did not meet expectations of what a burned village might yield. The only visible evidence of the site's former history was a few scattered quartz and argillite flakes and traces of subsurface pits. Some of the features appeared to be graves. This possibility was confirmed as the disturbed area was cleared of loose soil. All that remained of some graves were shallow depressions, whose contents had been scraped up by the bulldozer. The outline of one grave shaft appeared to be intact. Fragments of a broken skull with a double string of brass beads, pieces of wood, and iron nails were visible. The individual's identity and cause of death were unknown. It was an ambiguous death, plagued by even more uncertainties as those involved in the field investigations debated what should be done about it. Crushed by the weight of the bulldozer that had passed back and forth over it, and afforded only minimal protection by a covering of plastic and dirt placed there by the archaeologists, the burial could not be restored, nor could the indignities be erased. Ella Wilcox Sekatau, at that time the Narragansett tribal coordinator, advised removing the remains with the expectation that at some time and place they would be given a decent reburial.

The size and robustness of the bones suggested that the remains were those of an adult, possibly male. The wood and iron nails raised the question of whether the fabric- and bark-shrouded corpse had been buried in a coffin. The multiple rows of brass beads encircling the mutilated skull hinted at a headdress conveying a distinct cultural code. A signet ring with an anchor-and-heart motif and another with a stone setting presumably had been worn on fingers whose delicate bones had long ago decayed. A European latten spoon, an English kaolin pipe, and a brass buckle, possibly from a sword belt, were the only other traces of offerings in the grave. The evidence suggested that the individual had been buried in the latter half of the seventeenth century, perhaps even in the last quarter, in what seemed to be a communal burial ground. Despite what seemed knowable, if not fairly certain, many questions were still unanswered.

If this one grave was relatively intact, were there others? How much of the cemetery had been disturbed? Were there other clues that could be collected about those whose remains had been disinterred so unceremoniously? Exploratory coring identified soil profiles suggestive of grave fill beyond the bulldozed area. Based on this evidence, the burial ground was estimated to cover an area of less than one-half acre (approximately 2,000 square meters) and included as many as thirty to sixty graves.[5] The mound of backdirt created by the bulldozing, thought to contain the contents of maybe a half-dozen graves, yielded a large quantity of human bones and a variety of artifacts. The number of skeletal parts recovered indicated that the contents of nine individual graves had been completely or almost completely removed.[6] The diversity of the artifacts connoted that a rich assortment of European commodities and Native-crafted items had been incorporated into the graves of the deceased, presumably as offerings made during funeral rites.

This was the beginning of the story of a seventeenth-century Narragansett cemetery that came to be known as RI-1000. The "proof of its discovery"—the pieces of human bone, the shell and glass beads, and the tarnished spoon from graves accidentally unearthed by the bulldozer— and the evidence gathered during preliminary field investigations lead to the conclusion that this was a communal burial ground associated with the history of Narragansett Indians. Based on these initial findings, the Narragansett Tribal Council, the Rhode Island Historical Preservation Commission, and the owner of the property agreed that the burial ground should be left alone.

However, there were no legal restrictions to prevent the planned construction. With the necessary notifications having been issued, the landowner had satisfied existing Rhode Island state law concerning the accidental disturbance of unmarked cemeteries on private land and could have gone ahead with construction.[7] Because the design plans called for construction directly over the cemetery, a seemingly reasonable way to ensure the burial ground's preservation would have been to cover the area with a large quantity of dirt. For a variety of reasons, this proposal for protecting the site was unsatisfactory to all interested parties. The developer questioned the feasibility of filling, given the existing topography and the design plans for the construction. The Rhode Island Historical Preservation Commission expressed concern about how altered drainage patterns might adversely affect the in situ preservation of human bones and artifacts, especially highly perishable items such as textiles. And the Narragansetts voiced serious doubts about whether any amount of dirt could provide sufficient deterrence to thieves intent on robbing the graves of their ancestors.[8] Because no preservation plan seemed satisfactory, all agreed, even if somewhat reluctantly, to have the cemetery excavated.

The decision signaled the beginning of another chapter in the story of the RI-1000 burial ground. The timing of this decision came within months of the federal government's formal acknowledgment of the Narragansetts as an Indian tribe (and within just a few years of the one-hundredth anniversary of the state of Rhode Island's official proclamation of their extinction).[9] The timely juxtaposition of these events seemed almost beyond mere coincidence, even to the most jaded outsider. In agreeing to have the RI-1000 burial ground excavated, the Narragansetts seized an opportunity to reverse the consequences of their loss of communal land and sovereignty a century ago. It was a chance to tell an alternative version of their history and help extinguish, perhaps once and for all, myths about their disappearance and their cultural amnesia concerning tribal traditions that had lingered as rumors since the end of King Philip's War and were accepted as facts by the nineteenth century.

The Narragansetts' ties to North Kingstown and, more specifically, to the ancestral homeland centered around Wickford Harbor and extending north and west of modern Wickford Village, were complicated to say the least. European Americans had begun to claim places within this homeland as gifts or purchases well before the end of the seventeenth century. Sales of "vacant" lands west of Wickford, which Ninigret II had agreed to quitclaim to the colony of Rhode Island in 1709 in return for a legal guarantee of protection for a 64-square-mile (166-square-hectare) tract in Charlestown, gestured even further toward the Narragansetts' erasure from North Kingstown.[10] In the process of seizure and settlement, they were steadily divided from the land in acts that foreclosed their ancestral title to this homeland region and, ostensibly, sacred sites located within it. Given this history of dispossession, any outright assertions that their connections to this homeland were uninterrupted or that their cultural knowledge was intact, recalling the most intricate details about sacred traditions and the lives of those buried at RI-1000, would have evoked criticism and disbelief from most European Americans. Taking a more conservative position—favoring historicity and the possibility that cultural memory may not survive unscathed under conditions of colonial displacement—had its risks, however. Silences might be interpreted as ignorance and pauses as uncertainties, whereas they might originate in a wide range of experiences. Even a wait-and-see attitude could be construed as the Narragansetts' expecting revelations rather than anticipating confirmation. But the potential gains of a cautionary stance outweighed its risks, because much remained to be reclaimed about their past. Coupled with federal acknowledgment of their "Indianness," the excavation and study of the RI-1000 burial ground became part of the process of revealing concealed stories about Narragansett struggle and survival.

These stories offer a counterpoint to histories condoned by *A Key*. In framing and informing interpretations of the Narragansetts, *A Key* has led scholars to ask

Figure 23. *Portrait of Ninigret II, Son of Ninigret I, Sachem of the Eastern Niantics* (ca. 1681). The Niantics, allies of and identified with the Narragansetts, lived along the coast of Rhode Island and Connecticut to the west of Narragansett country. (Museum of Art, Rhode Island School of Design, gift of Mr. Robert Winthrop)

certain kinds of questions and to generate certain sorts of answers. Its uncritical acceptance has caused many to trivialize what can be learned beyond it and thus to deny the possibility of writing alternative narrations that strive to grasp the historical realities of Narragansett people and their struggles to survive. These stories are not easily tracked, especially if they are fettered by an unwavering preoccupation with *A Key* as a source of evidence on Narragansett culture and history. The challenge posed by the excavation and study of RI-1000 was to confront *A Key*'s

silences and the misrepresentations reinforced by it, rather than simply to under-
write them. To have attempted anything less than recovering the lives of those
interred in this burial ground, from a documented past that neglected them and
rendered their struggles inconsequential, would have made this undertaking utterly regrettable. Taking these fragmentary remains and "restoring" them to life
were necessary steps in telling this other story.

This counterstory began decades, maybe even centuries, earlier, although exactly when is a matter of conjecture. Perhaps it began as early as 1524, at the sheltered harbor that Verrazzano called his Refuge; or on the peninsula now known
as Providence, where Roger Williams and his small band of followers set foot in
1636; or maybe on the shore of eastern Long Island in the summer of 1642, when
Miantonomi delivered his impassioned speech to the Montauks. Other beginnings
are possible, and all certainly contributed to this other story in one way or another.
Some have not been entered into recorded history, but they are at least as important to the construction of this alternative narrative. Imagining what the setting
of RI-1000 must have been like in the 1600s illuminates other possible beginnings
to this story.

It would be a mistake to envision this burial ground as an isolated cemetery, separated from the places where Narragansett people lived. Matantuck's "village," believed to have been located in the vicinity of RI-1000, was part of a large ancestral
homeland that extended from a stone fortification known as Queen's Fort, situated
4 miles (6 kilometers) west of Cocumscussoc, to a distance of about 15 miles (24
kilometers) to the south.[11] Within a 5-mile (8-kilometer) radius of this "fort,"
named for its historical association with Matantuck, whom the seventeenth-century English sometimes called the "Old Queen," were the dwelling places of other
Narragansett sachems related to her through blood or marriage, such as her husband, Mixanno, who was the son of Canonicus.[12] To the northeast was Sawqoque,
"the home of Canonchet," where Canonicus had once resided, along with
Miantonomi (Canonchet's father). East of the "fort," in the neighboring portion
of present-day Exeter, was Bassokutoquage, inherited by her son Scuttop at the
time of Mixanno's death in 1658. Pessicus, Canonicus's nephew and Miantonomi's
successor, who for a time ruled in tandem with Mixanno over this homeland, may
have lived in a settlement located farther to the southeast on the Shewatuck
River.[13] Dozens of wigwams belonging to other kin were situated near these core
settlements and the surrounding spaces of this homeland. When war with the
English broke out in Narragansett country in December 1675, many of these wigwams were overrun and burned. Among the 150 wigwams said to have been destroyed in the attack were those in Matantuck's own "village" near Queen's Fort,
which had earned a reputation as a formidable pocket of resistance to colonial ad-

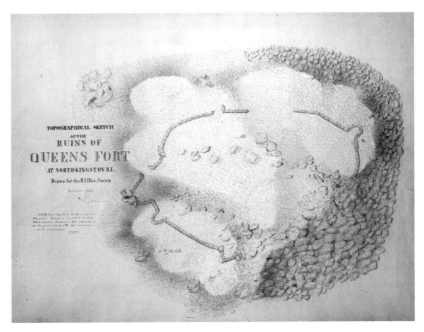

Figure 24. *Topographical Sketch of the Ruins of Queens Fort, North Kingstown, Rhode Island* (1865). The fort was built and occupied by Narragansetts as a place of refuge. (Courtesy of the Rhode Island Historical Society)

vancement because of the sachem's steadfast refusal to sell land to English entrepreneurs and settlers.

Based on archaeological evidence, this homeland area has a record of use by Native people going back at least eight thousand years. By five thousand years ago, they began to settle into some locations more permanently. Small freshwater streams, which earlier had been used only intermittently, became the sites of permanent fishing stations. Other localities offering a rich diversity of natural resources, which they visited perhaps on a seasonal basis at first, to gather plants and to hunt, were eventually frequented for longer durations. Near the core area of this homeland, they would have found a mixed-oak upland forest, offering an abundance of hickory nuts and acorns and game such as white-tailed deer and wild turkey, and low-lying wooded swamplands extending as far as Narragansett Bay, presenting a variety of shrubs, herbaceous plants, sedges and rushes, and small mammals, including muskrats, otters, and beavers.[14]

The archaeological record points to increasing residential stability around two thousand years ago. With sea levels stabilized, coves and estuaries also became

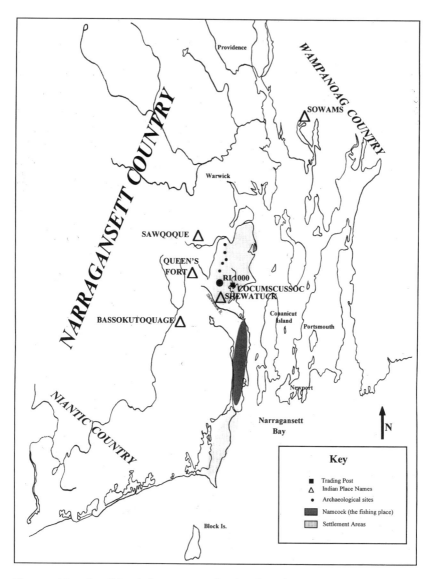

Figure 25. Map of traditional place-names and archaeological sites in Narragansett country. (Drawn by Desiree D. Zymroz)

attractive residential locations. Some areas along the coast became places of permanent, year-round settlement. Throughout the homeland are archaeological signs, including hearths, storage facilities, and ceremonial structures, which suggest that ties to the land were becoming more enduring than casual. The presence of a large storage facility containing eight deep pits filled with the charred remains of hickory nuts indicates that surpluses of this labor-intensive and seasonally abundant resource were being processed and stored in great quantities. Hickory trees, located in the upland forests, were managed prudently to cull their nutritious fruits. Studies of charred wood samples from archaeological features suggest that hickory had only limited use for construction and none at all as firewood, even though it exhibited properties that made it suitable for these purposes.[15]

Projectile points and chipped bifaces made from a variety of lithic raw materials and conforming to different manufacturing traditions found at some site locations imply activity diversification and time depth. But this diversity also may be viewed as evidence of regional procurement and exchange networks for maintaining social and political alliances with peoples living in other homelands, in what could be interpreted as an emerging clan system that formally linked local groups over a wide area.[16] The majority of lithic raw materials at sites within this homeland area and a nearby one centered around Greenwich Bay were available locally, however, suggesting that regional exchange complemented increased sedentism within more fixed, stable territories.[17]

A communal cemetery located on Conanicut Island and dating from about 3,200 years ago lends additional, if not compelling, support to the interpretation that the social geography was becoming formalized. The stone blades and projectile points, ground-stone axes and gorgets, steatite bowls, graphite pebbles, red ochre, incised amulets and shells, and charcoal found in these graves hint at the elaborate mortuary ceremonialism that accompanied cremation burial and, on one occasion, possibly a secondary burial rite, in which an individual's remains were exhumed, cremated, and then reinterred.[18] The material evidence associated with this ceremonial site shows affinities with other early cremation burials in southeastern Massachusetts and Long Island, providing one more expression of regional consciousness among increasingly localized communities in southern New England at least three thousand years ago.[19]

The long-term archaeological evidence provides undeniable testimony of a history that predates the arrival of Roger Williams and that has little, if anything, in common with the tales that he and other Europeans told about postdiluvian migrations of lost tribes, Greek odysseys, and other transoceanic journeys. As Williams's Narragansett informants explained to him, they knew from their elders that they had *"sprung* and *growne* up in that very place, like the very *trees* of the *wildernesse."*[20] A tree was their fountainhead; it was from a tree that Cautantowwit, the Creator, had made them. Without a doubt, they knew their family tree, the oak (*Paugautemisk*), which Narragansett oral history identifies as the seed of their inception.[21] Like the oaks of the southern New England forest—the majestic whites, the tawny reds, the gnarled blacks—their roots ran deep. They had been firmly rooted in place for at least three or four thousand years, or as long as anyone could remember.

Within this homeland, some locations were used repeatedly over long periods of time. Others appear to have been lived in almost continuously for successive millennia, based on the spatial and temporal patterning of archaeological features. One such site is located just a short distance northwest of the RI-1000 burial ground. Its long-term pattern of use, dating from around 2,500 years ago, is represented by a diversity of overlapping features, including trash pits, postmolds, hearths, and a sweat lodge.[22]

Based on carbon-14 dates, the sweatlodge was used over a five-hundred-year period that preceded the arrival of Roger Williams by more than a millennium.[23] The roughly circular feature contained fire-reddened and fire-cracked stones suggestive of having once been heated. When splashed with water, the heated stones would release steam conducive to sweating, which was an integral component of personal hygiene and curing rites among Native peoples in later centuries.[24] Williams wrote that "ten, twelve, twenty more or lesse, enter at once starke naked, leaving their coats, small breeches (or aprons) at the doore, with one to keepe all: here doe they sit round these hot stones an houre or more, taking *Tobacco*, discoursing, and sweating together" in order to purge their bodies of whatever ills afflicted them.[25] Sweat lodges were used for more than cleansing and therapeutic purposes, however. They were places of spiritual and social transformation, where those gathered, perhaps including clan leaders and *powwaw*s, would have communicated with the spirit world through steam emanating from the stones and perhaps through other acts of ritual exchange.[26] The presence of this sweat lodge in the archaeological record provides persuasive evidence that the immediate environs of the RI-1000 burial ground may have had a long history of sacredness to Native people.

The postmolds, hearths, and trash pits (containing a mixture of Native and European artifacts) associated with the sweat lodge suggest that by the seventeenth century, if not earlier, this locale may have become the residence of an important clan leader. The density of postmolds implies the presence of perhaps not more than a pair of dwellings at this location. Although archaeological evidence reveals little about the size, shape, and other formal characteristics of these dwellings, nothing suggests that this was a palisaded village or that these structures even remotely approximated the scale of an Iroquoian longhouse.[27] Instead, this was a small settlement, or perhaps a hamlet, inhabited primarily by members of a single clan.

Narragansett men and women would have carried out many of their mundane activities in these dwellings. Here they would have ground hickory nuts and acorns as they had for more than a thousand years; dried, mashed, and brewed wild plants, like the cherry, parsley, sumac, mustard, and mint recovered in small quantities from archaeological contexts, for use as seasonings and medicines; and prepared meals mixing beans, presumably with corn and squash, in Native-made ceramic pots or European brass kettles. At these living spaces they would have repaired worn kettles, perhaps refashioning some into ornaments, as is suggested by the presence of small fragments of brass in the trash pits; sharpened and chiseled the edges of stone and iron tools, judging from the small lithic flakes and the minute bits of iron found; and tanned and sewed hides into items of clothing, perhaps even embroidering some with glass beads, as might be supposed from a single glass bead recovered from the archaeological excavations. Here they would have conducted their everyday lives, in much the same manner as did their mothers and fathers and the generations who had preceded them, despite the incorporation of foreign commodities and the acquisition of new technological skills.

Critical pieces of physical evidence are missing from the archaeological record of this settlement place, because of agricultural plowing and the removal of the tilled soil (known as the "plowzone") in the initial stages of field investigations.[28] There are no floors or traces of partitions to shed light on the organization of work, task specialization, or other patterns and relations that might be inferred from archaeology. Although scant, the surviving remains of these dwellings suppose the sort of evidence that could provide additional details about the unwritten past of the Narragansett people. But it is unrealistic to think that years, even decades, of plowing could be undone, or to wish that the plowzone had been retained so that it could be combed for more clues about the lives of those who resided at this settlement. Although it is impossible to cross the thresholds of these wigwams to examine what Roger Williams might or might not have seen or heard, the graves of Narragansett men, women, and children located about 600 feet (183 meters) to the southeast provide a unique opportunity to gain more than a passing glimpse into their lives and sacred traditions.[29]

Geographically, this burial ground was not remote from the world of the living but was integrated with other places within this ancestral homeland. The dead shared the cultural landscape with the living, for whom this sacred space served as a constant and visible reminder of communal ties that linked generations and connected people to their ancestral homelands. Although archaeological evidence suggests that dwelling places and burial grounds were interwoven into the spatial fabric of the homeland, *A Key* provides few specific clues about the location of cemeteries and their siting. With the surface of the burial ground and much of its immediate surroundings altered by subsequent land use, including the removal sometime before 1982 of topsoil and sand in preparation for the proposed construction, it was difficult to imagine how this sacred space might have appeared from the vista of these dwellings or what it might have looked like to those who walked between and around the graves when gathered there for a funeral. With so much of the original detail in the vicinity of the burial ground erased by European Americans, its environmental setting and historical context offered the only clues for understanding how this sacred site might have appeared in the seventeenth century.

From the living area, the view of the burial ground would not have been obstructed by any prominent feature of the natural landscape. The moderate slope of the land surface on which the wigwams were situated rose to the west and north, where it formed a distinctive topographic boundary; to the east and south, in the direction of the burial ground, it gave way to a relatively featureless plain. This flat terrain was marked by woody marshes and freshwater streams that meandered toward the coast to dilute the salt water flowing into Narragansett Bay from the open sea. No well-worn footpath can be traced from the wigwams to the burial place on the basis of surviving archaeological evidence, so it is impossible to gain a sense of the visual experiences of Narragansett people as they approached the graves. In the short distance between the wigwams and the burial ground were found only occasional postholes, a few broad hearths containing charcoal and some lithic artifacts, and a possible burial pit devoid of human remains.[30] The spatial proximity and the relative contemporaneity of the hearths, the possible burial pit, and RI-1000 suggest an association, and one in all likelihood directly related to funeral rites.

Located within an ecotone (an edge zone between two distinctive natural communities), the burial ground was posed between an upland, mixed hickory and oak forest and a coastal plain of lowland plant communities, where the Narragansetts fished, hunted, collected wild resources, and planted corn, beans, and squash. The burial ground's geographical setting suggested another kind of transition zone, blanketed with additional layers of meaning. Posed between the clearing surrounding the wigwams and a watery edge defined by the Shewatuck River just 576 feet (175 meters) away, the burial ground was aligned symbolically to a metaphorical threshold between this world and the other in terms of Northeastern Woodland Indian cosmology.[31] Viewed in this manner, its location underscored the belief that human beings along with plants and animals do not simply occupy "a *natural* world comprised of inorganic astronomical, meteorological, and geological phenomena." Instead, they "inhabit and maintain through ritual a *social* world, comprised of grandmothers, grandfathers, aunts and uncles, and sisters and brothers of other-than-human kinds of man beings" dwelling at the points farthest from their settlement places.[32] At such places, they could cross from this world into the other through rituals of physical, spiritual, or social transformation in order to encounter these other-than-human beings, especially the more powerful *manitos*.[33] Within this conceptual framework, even the Shewatuck River, flowing to the south and west of the RI-1000 burial ground, is a spatial analog representing the body of water that the soul was required to cross in its long and arduous journey to the afterworld.[34]

What the RI-1000 burial ground looked like close-up is a matter of conjecture. Williams is as silent about what burial places looked like through a narrowly focused lens as he is about how they might have appeared from a distance. His only reference to Narragansett graves is his comment that at the conclusion of the burial rites "the Mat that the party died on, the Dish he eat in" were placed upon the grave, "and sometimes a faire Coat of skin" hung upon on a nearby tree.[35] Instead, answers to questions about how the RI-1000 cemetery might have appeared to an eyewitness—whether its boundaries were defined by a palisade; or whether individual graves were marked by woven mats, wooden boards, piles of raw earth, or the hollows of partially filled grave-pits; or whether its surface was littered with the unburied corpses and weathered bones of individuals ravaged by catastrophic illnesses—must come from archaeological evidence.[36]

During the first two weeks of the 1983 excavations, archaeologists identified the outlines of forty-eight graves.[37] The process of discovery involved the exhausting and monotonous task of shovel-scraping the modified surface of burial field to the depth of sterile soil in order to reveal the discolored stains of grave fill. Each grave was recognizable as a distinctive patch of yellow-brown soil, mottled with grey silts and dark-brown organic materials, occasional large cobbles, and flecks of charcoal that stood in stark contrast to the homogenous palette of the surrounding soil matrix.

The arrangement of graves was orderly. With only two exceptions, all were oriented southwest–northeast along their long axis. Most were arranged one near the other; only one grave was superimposed on another. The spacing between the graves was visibly even, with just a few burials occupying outlying areas. The majority appeared to be organized in parallel rows, as if each grave had been dug in an ordered sequence according to some rule of cultural logic. Presumably, those who visited this burial ground could discern an order, perhaps based on kinship, or on knowing the names, characters, and even idiosyncrasies of the dead, that was not apparent to the outside observer.

Most of the graves were rectangular with rounded or angled corners; only one grave was oval, and another nearly so. Most were of uniform size, but several exhibited measurements at the high end of the range for both dimensions, and one was noticeably smaller than the others.[38] Although the significance of grave shape is unknown, it has been suggested that rectangular and more oval shapes resulted from the use of different digging tools.[39] Rectangular graves, presumably dug with "square European shovels" instead of wooden digging stakes, have been interpreted as a conscious attempt to emulate the European grave shape, rather than merely the consequence of using a new kind of tool.[40]

Regardless of what tools they might have used, the Narragansetts dug these graves to depths that did not reach more than about 3 feet (1 meter) into the subsoil from the cleared surface of the burial ground.[41] Even at this depth, the bottoms of some graves extended into a substratum of glacial cobbles. Some graves seemed to have been deeper than others, but the altered topography made it impossible to determine absolute depths with any precision, let alone assess the reasons that might have factored into these decisions, including the desire to protect the corpse (and grave goods) from intrusions by burrowing animals, or marauding vandals. Yet sometimes even the grave diggers' attempts to conform to what seemed to be an average grave depth (as gauged from archaeological evidence) apparently were thwarted. For example, the bottom of one grave was abruptly defined by the presence of a large granite boulder. Rather than terminate the excavation, those digging the grave excavated around the contours of the rock, incorporating it as part of the burial facility.[42]

The graves were simple earthen shafts, devoid of constructional enhancements. There were no traces of evidence to suggest that they had been lined with stones or logs. Only in a single instance were the sides of a grave shored with wooden planks to form what seemed to be a makeshift coffin for the deceased. A dark, stratigraphic layer exposed in most of the graves, initially described in the field-notes as "possibly burned or reduced earth" or "a greasy, black stain," was actually decayed organic matter that came to be recognized as an archaeological signature of the excavators' proximity to buried ancestral remains. Although the composition of the layer appeared to be indecipherable, preservation was sometimes good enough to reveal the structure and nature of the contributing materials: Native textiles made from the fibers and stems of grasses, sedges, rushes, cattails, "Indian hemp," cornhusks, and the inner bark of basswood and possibly cedar.[43] Most had been sewn or twined. Many seemed to have been constructed using more than one technique and more than one type of material.

Archaeological evidence suggests that these Native-made textiles were used to cover the bottom of the grave, the deceased, and the grave goods. They do not appear to have been used as winding-sheets in preparing the corpse for burial, except perhaps for more finely woven mats, which may have been wrapped around the body before burial. Some graves contained only a single layer of matting either above or below the interment; in others, mats were used as both grave linings and covers. The matting sometimes appeared thicker near the edges of the burial shaft because the textile had been carefully folded over. In a few instances, the excess length or width of a mat was used instead to line the sides of a grave.

Although the grave was not the ultimate destination in the Narragansetts' life journey, it provided what they envisioned as a final and secure resting place for their physical remains, deep in the fertile, well-drained, silty loams of their homeland. Although digging these graves in arable ground, rather than on marginal land, might simply have been a matter of convenience, Narragansett traditions suggest an alternative interpretation. According to their beliefs, the corn and beans were gifts from Cautantowwit. By burying the bodies of the dead in fertile soils where corn and beans grew, the Narragansetts may have given physical or spatial expression to the idea that the relationship between life and death was a cycle of continuous renewal between the community of the living and that of the ancestors dwelling at Cautantowwit's house in the southwest.[44]

Archaeological evidence from southeastern New England suggests that this relationship may have been reinforced through time, because pockets of arable soil became places of communal burial, rather than the location of single, isolated graves or small clusters of a few burials, only in the contact period.[45] In the case of RI-1000, the existence of a formal, bounded, communal cemetery on arable soil does not appear to predate the middle of the seventeenth century. The appearance of this communal burial ground in the archaeological record of this ancestral homeland at this time tends to support the interpretation that this sacred place may have been used primarily by a localized segment of a particular descent group or clan claiming exclusive access to land, corn, and other resources of increasing social and cultural significance in the seventeenth century.

In fact, the RI-1000 burial ground may have been one of several burial clusters in the core area of this homeland. One of these other burial areas is suggested by at least two or three mid-seventeenth-century graves salvaged from a nearby gravel pit in the 1950s.[46] Another is implied by numerous features northeast of RI-1000, which in outline mirror the shapes of graves.[47] The presence of separate burial areas close to each other reveals a kind of sacredness and sociability that Williams poorly understood and paints a picture different from that which might be conjured from the pages of *A Key* or, for that matter, imagined if the RI-1000 burial ground were viewed as detached from the context and history of this ancestral homeland.

7.

RETELLING NARRAGANSETT LIVES

The silhouettes that emerged from the RI-1000 graves were those of Narragansett men, women, and children. Their names are unknown or, at least, were not entered into any records of vital statistics kept by English colonists. Some were probably born when Roger Williams was compiling lists of words and phrases and observing behaviors that he subsequently entered into *A Key*. However, even this effort offered little assurance that the stories of these Narragansetts would be made known to later European Americans. Except for the information that he furnished to colonial officials about the identities and actions of prominent men in Native New England, Williams provided few details about the lives of other Narragansetts. For him, biography was neither a comfortable mode of expression nor a literary genre that suited his purposes in writing *A Key*. This reticence, if not reluctance, to tell about Narragansett lives is mirrored in the works of later historians who chose to lavish attention on a few named persons of "royal" or "noble" stature but cast the majority anonymously and impersonally.[1]

For those interred in this burial ground, these graves offer a poignant counterpoint. They contain the neglected stories of the Narragansetts' struggles to survive in the second half of the seventeenth century. Set against the pages of *A Key*, these graves give meaning to much of what has been obscured, marginalized, and silenced about how they conducted their lives within the tangled web of colonialism. To assume that the material inscriptions in these graves merely confirm and extend Williams's ethnography minimizes their importance, but that assumption also makes these deaths and, more important, the lives which preceded them, unremarkable.[2] The archaeological evidence, though ambiguous and at times halting and mute, provides a subtle, even provocative, picture of the lives of these people. This chapter will use the evidence contained in these graves to tell about the complexities and contradictions of Narragansett lives in late-seventeenth-century New England.

The forty-seven graves contained ancestral remains.[3] Each was a single interment, with no evidence to suggest double or multiple burials.[4] Each body was laid out on its right side, facing east, with the legs bent at the knees in a flexed posture, suggesting that the body had been prepared for burial (including being bound and possibly anointed with red ochre) before being transported to the grave. The arms were crossed with the hands cupped and positioned near the face, usually at the mouth or chin. The dead, like the earthen graves that held them, were aligned to the southwest. Exceptions to these observed patterns were few: Two graves contained individuals placed on their left sides facing west, and a third held a corpse oriented on a north–south axis that conformed to the anomalous alignment of the grave itself.[5]

Although Roger Williams did not comment specifically on the relationship between the Narragansetts' burial practices and aspects of their cosmology in *A Key*, recent scholars have explored these connections. William Simmons was the first to detect a meaningful link between attributes of the corpse and Narragansett cosmology. He reasoned that the alignment of the buried corpse, with the skull pointed toward the southwest, corresponded to the direction that the soul exited when it left the body to travel to the land of Cautantowwit and Narragansett ancestors. He also proposed that the arrangement of the body in a flexed (or fetal) position signified a symbolic connection between death and birth, much in the same way that burying the dead in fertile soil reiterated this relationship.[6] By arranging the corpse in a posture like that of a fetus in a mother's womb, the Narragansetts reenacted birth in death and denied the finality of mortal endings by giving symbolic expression to a belief in the process of continuous renewal between the communities of the living and those of the ancestors residing in the afterworld in the southwest.

Similarly, George Hamell linked the corporeal aspect of sidedness to ideas about social and spiritual well-being among Northeastern Algonkian peoples.[7] According to these beliefs, the placement of the corpse on the right side facing east—both life-associated, social directions—would have affirmed Narragansett well-being. Paul Robinson has extended these ideas by arguing that the increased rigor exercised in positioning the corpse to the right and east in late-seventeenth-century burials served as a symbolic declaration of the Narragansetts' political unanimity and dominance over other Native peoples in southern New England.[8] Yet regardless of the scholarly interpretation imposed, the careful and consistent treatment of the corpse as revealed in these graves suggests ordered ceremonies, presumably carried out under the guidance of clan elders versed in sacred traditions. In a time of so many uncertainties, these ceremonies not only expressed the community's respect for the dead but also offered reassurances about shared interests in generations of ancestors. Even allowing for improvisations, these traditions were meaningful and comforting to grieving Narragansett survivors.

Like the bodies of the dead, material items were placed in the graves in an orderly manner. Except for body ornaments, grave goods were situated to the east of the corpse and concentrated near the upper half of the body, implying that the well-being inferred from the corporeal aspect of sidedness might have been extended to grave goods. Only rarely were objects positioned opposite the side that the corpse faced. However, the placement of objects in the graves may also have had other meaningful associations, such as expressing symbolic links between objects and particular parts of the human body. Pipes, for example, were typically placed near the mouth of the deceased. Other items seem to have been placed in or between the hands so that they appeared to be held. Spoons were often positioned this way, with the bright and reflective bowl section pointing toward the individual's face or chest, the anatomical site of the soul thought to sustain a person's vital energy.[9]

Similar things were sometimes tied together with cordage or nested one on top of another. In some cases, dissimilar things appear to have been bundled together before being placed in the grave. Some objects found close together may have been placed in animal-hide pouches or bags, along with other perishable substances that had long since disintegrated. Others were wrapped in fabric, judging from the fibers and swatches adhering to them or the skeumorphs (impressions) of weaving preserved in the surrounding soil. Bottles, perhaps originally sealed, had held unidentified liquids. Kettles frequently were buried upside down and sometimes over other grave goods.[10] In one instance, an inverted kettle held soil described as having a "dry sawdust-like consistency," perhaps suggesting offerings of food, which had later become infested with earthworms. Thus the placement of objects within the graves, like that of the corpse itself, was not casual or random but was, at least in certain instances, imbued with more elaborate connotations.

The objects that had been placed in these graves with such orderliness, presumably with the intention of sacralizing them, included Native-made and European-manufactured artifacts.[11] Most were foreign items, typically found in seventeenth-century ships' cargoes as "trade goods." These included such things as cloth; iron hoes, awls, and knives; brass kettles and bells; and looking glasses and glass beads mentioned in *A Key*, all goods that the Narragansetts could have procured from Roger Williams during his short-lived fur trade but also from others into the later decades of the seventeenth century.[12] No account books document other stock that Williams or his successors at Cocumscussoc, Richard Smith and his son, might have sold to Narragansetts who came to there to trade, but artifacts recently excavated in the vicinity of the trading post and the blockhouse (later known as Smith's Castle) are representative of many of the things found in the RI-1000 graves.[13] In fact, the site's trash-filled deposits speak volumes to contact and trade.[14]

Some items found at the site include columella bead blanks, beaver teeth, a brass tinkling cone, a lead casting sprue shaped rather like a turtle, stone tools, and an occasional sherd from a shell-tempered clay pot, unattributable to any particular time. They offer a furtive glance at Native people who once came here to bargain or perhaps even settle a score, and who, when they departed this world, probably were buried at RI-1000. The European artifacts yield a crude and partial inventory of what Williams and the Smiths might have traded for the Narragansetts' goods and, beginning in the decade or so before King Philip's War, paid for their labor. Half of a lead bale seal tells of the bolts of coarse, thick woolens (or "trucking cloth") and fine worsteds whose quality and price were haggled over, and whose surviving fragments appear in some of the RI-1000 graves.[15] A clear blue, medium-sized seed bead and a sugary-textured, gilded oval one hint of the hanks of beads that the traders dangled before the eyes of their discriminating customers and that eventually came to be threaded by Narragansett weavers onto strands of sinew and cordage. The broken stems of latten spoons matched some that were presented whole and unused; weathered earthenware sherds, with traces of white tin glaze, resemble cups and jars that complemented Native pottery, wooden dishes, and gourds; and numerous fragments of kaolin pipestems alluded to the ready supply of mass-produced pipes that were traded as alternatives to those carved from local stone by Native craftspeople.[16] The shattered green glass from thick, "globe-and-shaft" wine bottles and square-bodied case types, made iridescent by time, speaks of an illicit trade in spirits conducted in spite of restrictions by colonial authorities, though allegedly never by Williams, who denied having any role in selling liquor to the Narragansetts (except in small amounts for medicinal purposes).[17]

The Narragansetts incorporated these and other items into their everyday lives and sacred traditions. They adapted them to suit their purposes, in ways unimagined or considered unattainable to them by Williams and other Europeans, and infused them with meanings that frequently were all their own. As early as 1642, Miantonomi spoke to clan leaders about the dangers of colonialism and urged war against the English, advising them to kill "no Cowes, for they will Serve to eate till our dear be Increased again."[18] At the time, they dismissed his proposal for war, but some must have thought well of his other recommendation, enough to per-

Figure 26. Items of trade from archaeological excavations at Cocumscussoc. Top row: lead bale seal, blue glass bead, latten spoon (bowl and stem). Bottom row: kaolin pipe bowls, glass bottle rim. (Photo: Copyright 2000, Cathy Carver, N.Y.)

suade their people of the wisdom of compromise and the need to make certain trade-offs, especially if these adjustments might help them avoid starvation and give them a chance at a Narragansett future. Toward this end, they continued to live and work in the manner of their ancestors and to follow their sacred traditions, although with some differences.

They acquired brass kettles, repaired damaged ones with sheet-brass patches and rivets that they made themselves, and even replicated these seemingly unreproducible objects using scraps of sheet brass. With other broken pieces of brass, possibly from kettles that were beyond repair, they made rings, combs, beads, bracelets, and spoons. They formed these in a Native style by cold hammering, bending (or folding), cutting, annealing, and brazing.[19] In some instances, they combined cold and hot metalworking techniques to produce objects that provide undeniable testimony of their skill and ingenuity. One such item is a spoon—a hy-

Figure 27. Metal objects from archaeological excavations at Cocumscussoc. Top row: cast lead cylinders, lead shot, lead sprue resembling a turtle. Bottom row: cut brass arrowhead, brass tinkling cone (sometimes made from kettle pieces), iron nail with flattened rosehead, iron horseshoe. (Photo: Copyright 2000, Cathy Carver, N.Y.)

brid in form, material, and manufacturing techniques—that they created by fusing a Native-made handle, cast in the form of an elongated, open keystone, to a European spoon bowl.[20]

Native craftspeople decorated the lustrous surfaces of their brass combs, bracelets, and spoons with the familiar geometric, zoomorphic, and other stylized motifs that they used on clay pots, baskets, and mats. They incised trails of zigzag designs on a small brass bracelet and hammered the same into a raised-relief pattern on the stem of a spoon. They stamped (or engraved) circles or dots resembling a bull's-eye pattern onto the handle or extension of an elaborate comb and punched out others on small side projections so that they could be used to hold thin strands of hair or decorative feathers. They cut the projecting ends of delicate combs and the tip of at least one spoon into identical flaring bifurcated (whale-tail) finials and impressed a small, domed piece of sheet brass, perhaps a decorative tack (or maybe a button) used on clothing, with an intricate, raised medallion-like motif. The design incorporated a central dot surrounded by V-shaped fields defined by arrowheads and a dotted border that resembles the painted designs appearing on woodsplint baskets made by Native peoples in southern New England during the nineteenth century.[21]

They cast lead stock into ammunition for the muskets they used in hunting fowl, turkeys, and deer—and maybe occasionally pigs and cows kept by the English—and in fighting their enemies. They poured molten lead, and perhaps pewter or brass, into molds to make buttons and other decorative ornaments, some in shapes derived from their totemic clan symbols. They put iron tools to good use, sometimes employing them in a multitude of tasks, including those intended by their original manufacturers as well as quite different ones. They deliberately modified some iron implements, tailoring them to their own needs and tastes, and converted broken tools into usable ones. They did this in a variety of ways (dismantling, reducing, hammering, and forging) that demonstrated their ingenuity and technical skills. In sum, their metalwork was anything but crude.

They used the glass trade beads for ornamentation. Glass beads, the "blue crystals" mentioned by Verrazzano in 1524, were the items that caught the Narragansetts' eyes in early colonial encounters and continued to hold their interest as consumers even in later decades.[22] They strung and wove glass beads on tightly twisted two-ply cordage and strands of sinew to make bracelets, necklaces, headbands, and other personal ornaments. They sewed glass beads onto deerskin clothing, sometimes using brass hoops to frame their designs, and wrapped strings of beads around other objects as decoration. Using beads of different sizes, shapes, and colors—mostly dark blue, yellow, white, green, and black, but very little red—Narragansett women created designs unseen in the imaginations of bead makers toiling in the factories of Amsterdam or merchants trading them by weight on this side of the Atlantic.[23]

The patterns of the ornamental beadwork display the skill and creativity of Narragansett women in using glass to supplement existing decorative traditions based on shell, quills, seeds, and brass. They used glass beads mostly to make neck and wrist ornaments. The pattern was always one of contrasts, dark and bright. They often interspersed glass beads with shell and occasionally brass. In one exquisite show of artistry, they laced small, cylindrical black glass beads on thin strips of sinew as a background for white wampum beads arranged in an open diamond pattern to form a tiny bracelet, crafted whole or from a segment of a longer woven belt. Although they had small, colorful seed beads, they never incorporated them into the designs for their necklaces. Their artistic creations were not whimsical; instead, they imply the existence of decorative traditions.

The patterns Narragansett women embroidered—on clothing and small leather accessories, such as pipe and tobacco bags, quivers, and awl and knife cases—have almost all been lost, except on one item; probably a leather pouch, it is completely covered with identical small, spherical beads. Their hide and textile canvases have disintegrated, leaving the beads of their once-intricate designs randomly scattered. However, the unstrung seed beads of various colors found in some graves, often in association with other kinds of beads, hint at the beauty of their patterns. One example is a skin shirt, decorated with brass spirals, mica ovals, seed and shell beads, and glass tubes forming an epaulet on one of the garment's shoulders. The mica ovals were backed with paper printed with an engraved picture of "Ecce Homo," an image of Jesus Christ, quite possibly cut from a larger engraving in an illustrated Bible.[24] Thinly veiled in mica, the icon was appropriated as a canvas for beadwork.[25] The women took glass beads, drawn and wound by European craftspeople and traded to them by colonial merchants, and made them their own. Attached to the hides they had worked, the pieces of sinew they had removed from an animal's flesh, and the cordage they had twisted from plant fibers, the beads became inseparable elements of the women's own creations.

The European trade goods uncovered in the RI-1000 graves were much more than an index of how accustomed those buried in this cemetery had become to new forms of technology and material culture, or of how they unwittingly acquiesced to more profound changes in their lives and surroundings. These items suppose a much more complicated scenario than one that can be captured in a "continuous narrative" with an inevitable outcome of emerging Anglicization and disappearing "Indianness."[26] The Narragansetts buried at RI-1000 had embraced new things, even more so than Williams had observed at the time of *A Key*. Even by that time, they had altered their way of life to incorporate elements of English material culture and practices. Some had modified their wigwams, substituting doorframes they made from *"English* boards and *nailes"* or *"Burch* or *Chestnut* barke" for a "hanging *Mat,"* or had furnished them with *"English* Chests."[27] Others wore English clothes, hunted with guns, and rode horses. They came to rely on many of these things for their survival, but they also imposed their imprints on them. As part of their everyday lives and sacred traditions, they became the tools of their resistance.

Scrutinizing the contents of the graves in the RI-1000 burial ground affords insight into how some Narragansett Indians lived their lives and responded to English colonialism in the generation after *A Key*. Although the stories inscribed in these graves have passed through filters of time and discovery, these factors do not present insurmountable obstacles in trying to learn about the lived experiences of the Narragansetts buried here. Beyond documenting the extent of foreign acquisitions, the artifacts in the RI-1000 graves provide evidence of how the Narragansetts incorporated these goods into their sacred traditions and used them with more traditional objects to identify connections to kin and community, as they struggled with the perplexities of living their lives as Indians in late seventeenth-century New England.

The Narragansetts buried in the RI-1000 graves ranged from about two and a half or three years to more than fifty years old.[28] Of those whose sex could be determined from their skeletons, females outnumbered males by almost two to one.[29] The population imbalance raises questions about marriage practices, especially polygynous arrangements, and about the effects of disease and war. But it also seems to prefigure the demographic composition of small communities of Native Americans that persisted throughout southern New England, and elsewhere along the eastern seaboard, in the later colonial period. The populations of these later communities were disproportionately female, largely because many of the men had died fighting in colonial wars (ironically often on the side of the colonists), and others had left for periods of time to work in seafaring occupations or as laborers on others' farms to help support their families.[30] Although the Narragansetts buried at RI-1000 had not yet been stripped of their ancestral lands or suffered the full brunt of cruelties that befell Indian survivors of King Philip's War, the demographic profile of the cemetery suggests a community under stress.[31]

Of the forty-seven individuals whose remains were recovered within graves, nine were children aged from about three to four years, whose immature skeletons revealed nothing about their sex. The absence of fetuses, newborns, and infants in the burial ground suggests that these individuals were not buried with other Narragansetts. Exactly where and how their remains were disposed of is unknown, but babies who had reached their third year were afforded the same death rites as other members of the community, suggesting that they had passed a cultural or social watershed in their young lives. The significance of this turning point is illuminated by Narragansett oral history, which tells of babies being nursed for three winters "after which time they began to learn all the ways of their adult counterparts."[32]

For all these children, death had come much too soon, but perhaps not altogether unexpectedly. Although there are no figures available on infant mortality rates, the deaths of very young children would not have been uncommon in New England's Native communities. At RI-1000, the mortality level for those between birth and the age of three may have been as high as 40 percent, so for infants and toddlers the chances of survival were inordinately low.[33] Although the causes of their mortality cannot be determined with certainty from their skeletal remains, the primary pathogens were probably gastroenteric and infectious diseases, including tuberculosis, which may be fatal to young children.[34] Only in one case could the probable cause of death be attributed to a congenital disease.

As with other misfortunes, the Narragansetts must have perceived the causes of early childhood mortality to be the consequence of Cautantowwit's anger or acts of sorcery. The behavior that triggered Cautantowwit's wrath often was unclear, but forgiveness, and perhaps the restoration of the child's health, could be achieved by ritual supplication, such as hosting a feast in which property was destroyed.[35] If sorcery was believed to be the source of a child's illness, then it is likely that a shaman was called upon to effect a cure. But when the shaman determined through divination that a child's condition was incurable, the prospects for survival must have seemed much less certain. How Narragansett women who had borne these babies and were responsible for nurturing them responded to such dire projections can only be guessed. They had taken their pregnancies and deliveries in stride. They had gone about their normal activities until the beginning of their labor, which, according to Williams in *A Key*, was a "more speedy and easie Travell, and delivery then the Women of *Europe*" and experienced with hardly a complaint, and for many, scarcely a groan. Within a few days after delivery, they resumed many of their activities and soon thereafter were back at work.[36] However, the mundaneness of childbirth, as it appeared to Williams, does not provide a gauge of maternal attachment nor does it help predict how a Narragansett woman would care for a child whose survival seemed unlikely.

Narragansett traditions tell about the abandonment of some newborn infants. According to a story described by Ezra Stiles in 1761, Narragansett mothers who gave birth to "illegitimate" children would do so in the woods, presumably in isolation, and then kill the infant near the rocks, "where they killed so many infants, & their Bones lay about so thick, that they go by the name of the Bastard Rocks."[37] Stiles learned of this practice from a Narragansett who claimed that infant abandonment under these circumstances dated to before the arrival of the English. More than two centuries later, another Narragansett, the Reverend Harold Mars, reported a similar story about a place where the cries of deformed and handicapped children, abandoned because they could not survive the hardships of Native life, could still be heard.

> Now one of the older Indian men who was a member of the family would tell of passing by these rocks late at night, and perhaps, if the wind happened to be in the right direction and he would hear what sounded like babies crying and we have heard that story all of our lives and that's how it got its name, the Crying Rocks. Now the story behind that is that, the legend is, that the Indian recognizing the fact that they were exposed to life in the raw so to speak, that when a child was born deformed or crippled in any manner, it was the plan and practice of the Indian people, with proper ceremony, to put that child to death because obviously the child would be handicapped. If he was a man child he would be handicapped as a boy and as a hunter or as a fighter, and so it is said for that reason why they would put a child to death, and this thing having gone on for many years, why there was a build up of little skeletons.[38]

Narragansett oral history offers yet another reason for infant abandonment. According to Ella Wilcox Sekatau, ethnohistorian and medicine woman for the tribe, some Narragansetts also considered infants fathered by non-Natives "imperfect." Rather than incorporating these children into Narragansett communities, where they might be perceived by Rhode Island officials as additional proof of the Narragansetts' loss of "Indianness," some women abandoned them at "Crying Rocks" with other "handicapped" infants or buried them in unmarked graves. Other Narragansett mothers left their "imperfect" babies of mixed heritage as foundlings on the doorsteps of European American houses, where they were adopted through indenture contracts that bound them until adulthood as a supply of household labor.[39]

One could easily read cruelty and indifference in the accounts of "Bastard Rocks" and "Crying Rocks." Imagining a woman abandoning or killing the baby she had carried within her for nine months seems shocking and horrifying, though not unfathomable, to non-Indian thinking. But could the same not be said for enabling a sickly or handicapped infant, surrounded by the premise of death, to survive for only a few months or maybe a year or more? Or allowing a baby who carried the stigma of mixed blood to grow up in a world where its life would be defined by worthlessness and degeneracy in the eyes of European Americans? Or permitting such a child to become the possible object of mounting frustration and uncontrolled rage among close relatives and members of their natal communities?[40] Infanticide, as intimated in these stories, was perhaps as much a necessary evil for some Narragansett women as it was for those of their gender in the communities of the English colonists.[41]

Aside from the circumstances described in these stories, Narragansett babies were accepted and nurtured.[42] According to Williams, no children were fatherless, none for whom the community did not provide.[43] His observations on the subject of *"Relations* of Consanguinity, &c."* suggest that the Narragansetts loved their children dearly. A child's death could evoke inconsolable grief and profuse emotional despair that no self-inflicted wounds could relieve. Not even mournful wailing at dawn and dusk, or during the night, could erase the reminders of the lost child. Although emotion and sentiment are considered to be unanswerable from archaeological evidence, the evidence preserved in the RI-1000 graves provides telling glimpses of how some Narragansett children were cared for during their brief lives and, most especially, in death in late-seventeenth-century New England.[44] Evidence shows children who had been recognized as provisional members of the community but who, as unfortunate as it might seem, came to represent an unfulfilled hope for a future generation of Narragansetts.

The younger children—those between three and four years of age—formed a cohort. They had survived infancy, but not early childhood. They had been weaned and, presumably, named. The act of naming would have marked a change in the child's personal status, one of many he or she would undergo in the course of an uninterrupted life.[45] With each new stage in life, a new name would be adopted and an old one left behind.[46] Naming conferred new status, but it also bestowed identity by distinguishing the child from generic, unnamed infants.[47] Although the humanity of any Narragansett child was never questioned, naming expressed unequivocally that the child was now a person with unique characteristics.

Naming was not the only means of distinguishing members of this cohort. The material culture in their graves served as another way of marking these individuals. Of the nine three-to-four-year-olds, the graves of eight contained material goods and one did not. The material items in the marked graves appeared to be deliberate inclusions, rather than the result of random events or sheer coincidence.[48] As purposeful and, therefore, meaningful objects, these were of two sorts: objects placed on the person as body ornamentation and those put in the grave presumably as ritual offerings or as personal possessions.

The remains of six young children were ornamented or clothed. Their small wrists were adorned with bracelets, their throats with necklaces; sometimes a child's head was encircled with a headband or an ear embellished with ornaments. Their decorated corpses come as a surprise when one recalls Roger Williams's remarks about the bodily "nakednesse" of children. "Their male children goe starke naked," he said, "and have no Apron untill they come to ten or twelve yeeres of age; their Female they, in a modest blush cover with a little Apron of a hand breadth from their very birth."[49] Whether their little bodies came to be covered with the clothing in the years following *A Key*'s publication is unanswerable; but in death, their "nakednesse" was not to be seen.

Among Native Americans, the surfaces of the human body singled out for cultural, and specifically decorative, elaboration may provide insights into a variety of concerns about social identity.[50] Bracelets or wristlets, for example, are believed to bind a person to the earth. The wrists of newborn babies among the Algonkian-speaking Delaware were tied with strings of deerskin or cornhusks so that their spirits could not travel far.[51] Bracelets effectively, and metaphorically, connected the individual to the world, much in the same way as do the human body's extremities.[52] Bracelets, as symbols of community and socialization, presumably would have been given to a child at a naming ceremony, so that bracelets given in rituals distinguished the child just as much as a name. Necklaces may be analogous to bracelets; functionally, the neck serves a purpose comparable to that of the wrist to the hands, in that it connects the trunk to the head. Necklaces then may be to the neck as bracelets are to the wrist.[53] Similarly, earrings also may have been linked with imbuing social capability and, more specifically, with activating a child's capacity to receive social information. Thus ornaments, as artifacts that impose a social form on the individual, are important signatures of the cultural process of socialization.

The ornaments that adorned the three- and four-year-old children were beaded with shell and wampum, either alone or woven with glass and brass. On the left wrist of one child (Burial 10) was a multistrand bracelet made of alternating rows of white and purple wampum. The child's head bore a headband also made of wampum, but instead of alternating bands of white and purple, it had four rows of purple beads to one of white. The headband appeared to have an extension (possibly part of a fastener) at the back made of colored (yellow, turquoise, and clear dark blue) glass seed beads combined with dark (blue and black) tubular ones.

The bracelet that apparently had been placed around the wrists of another child (Burial 11) is suggested from a thread of sinew found in association with mainly brass and glass beads plus one cylindrical shell bead. Some of the brass beads were wedge shaped or triangular and Native cast; others were small and barrel shaped. The glass beads included seed beads in an array of colors and tubular beads in black and white. The remnants of a purple and white wampum headband, perhaps of no more than one or two strands, extended across the cranium of a child buried in another grave (Burial 36), and a bracelet of the same had been placed at the wrists. Ten buttons (five glass and five metal) were clustered nearby. Although the buttons were found in association with a fragment of coarse woolen fabric, it is unclear whether the buttons were sewn onto clothing or were part of an ornament (or even a child's rattle). The head of another child (Burial 21) was wrapped three times around with a band of double rows of small, tubular brass beads. Brass hoops, suitable for attaching beadwork and found in association with wampum-like shell beads in purple and white, suggest that the child was buried in an embroidered shirt. Small shell beads formed part of a poorly preserved earring that had been placed over the left ear of the child in Burial 34.

The most elaborately ornamented child (Burial 37) had wrists tied with several bracelets. Two were made of small, cylindrical black glass beads woven with white wampum onto sinew in a design that resembles those appearing on wampum belts exchanged on ritual occasions. Strands of small brass beads (both barrel shaped and tubular) had been wrapped several times around one of the child's wrists. Another bracelet, of sheet brass, rounded and finished at one end but broken at the other, was etched with a zigzag design centered between borders of deeply incised lines. Three strands of long, tubular black glass beads and white shell beads in different varieties (wampum, long cylindrical, and hourglass) encircled the child's neck, and a delicate spiral of tiny shell beads (none of which survived excavation) appeared to have been worn as an earring. A belt of tubular, dark blue glass beads girdled the child's waist and extended between the legs to form a small apron. Both forearms were enveloped in a deerskin garment richly embellished with seed beads, brass spirals, mica ovals, and tubes of dark blue glass beads. A pouch made of identical glass beads of white with bright blue and red stripes strung on twine was placed at the back of the individual's head. A cluster of small brass bells (described as "hawk's bells" because their size was similar to those traditionally used by falconers) was attached with Native cordage and found near the hands, forming what may have been another bracelet or perhaps a rattle.

All but two of the ornamented three- and four-year-olds were buried with grave goods. A spoon of European latten metal had been placed in each of their graves, but one child had been given three, plus a small brass spoon (almost teaspoon size) of Native design. Other items found in their graves included bells, hoes, a cup or apothecary jar of white tin-glazed enamel, a tiny, castellated Native-made clay pot with a single corn effigy, a very small glass bottle, a pair of scissors, a metal container or two, and a swivel. Bells, found with two of the three- and four-year-old children, may have been ornamental. Bells were not found in the graves of adults; however, the other items were found with individuals of other ages and genders. Some, like the Native pot and glass bottle, appeared to be scaled-down or miniature versions of the objects found in other graves, but the other items hardly seem like children's things. The hoes, for example, had short, rounded bits that were extremely worn and may well have been reused after part of the original blade had broken. Although these might represent artifacts of socialization, they also may be read as especially poignant offerings, gifts left by a mother or some other close female relative, whose identity was tied to this seemingly mundane object.

Measured in terms of body ornamentation or the number of items per graves, three- and four-year-old children's graves were among the most lavish in the cemetery. Even within this group, five had more things in their graves than the rest.[54] Although such disparities might be taken as evidence of a social inequalities, and even material signatures of inherited ranking (because these children had little opportunity to attain things in their own right), other explanations seem entirely plausible, especially when these graves are compared with those of other young children, whose bodies were unadorned and whose graves were virtually devoid of offerings. An alternative interpretation considers the role of maternal expectations concerning a child's survival. Although many factors might help to determine with reasonable certainty whether a child will remain with the living (e.g., birth spacing, multiple births, maternal health), the circumstances surrounding the child's death, as read from the biological and material evidence in the RI-1000 graves, sheds some light on how the Narragansetts might have attempted to reconcile themselves to the loss of a child in the climate of late-seventeenth-century New England.[55]

Included among the unadorned was a child with hydrocephaly (Burial 42), a congenital condition that manifests itself soon after birth and signals premature death.

It was an unusual burial, not only because of the absence of personal ornaments but also because the grave's shape and orientation were anomalous. This was the only oval grave and the only one oriented north–south. The single "offering," if it could be construed as such, was a sawblade placed behind the child's cranium, perhaps a tool abandoned at the site after preparing the grave or maybe the coffin, as suggested by the presence of a few iron nails. Here then was a sickly and visibly imperfect child, but one who was nurtured for three or four years, perhaps in the hope, however tentative, that death might not come so early. Perhaps not named because of all the uncertainties, the child was still enough a part of the community to be buried in the ancestral cemetery.

The remains of another very young child (Burial 13) without ornaments or grave goods of any kind bore spinal lesions signaling tuberculosis. A skeletal signature suggests that the child may not have died immediately after contracting this highly infectious disease. Instead, the pathogen settled in the child's lung, where it eroded the nearby spinal bones, a sure sign of what medical specialists call a "postprimary" case of tuberculosis. Spared a sudden death, the child lingered until the disease-causing pathogen became reactivated, no doubt because of reduced immunity.[56] For this child, who had withstood this illness and clung to life, even if on a thin thread, this bout of "delayed hypersensitivity" proved to be fatal. In all probability, the child's death did not occur unexpectedly.

In both instances, the deaths of these young children were neither sudden nor entirely unanticipated. The prospects for life at the time of birth were never assured, but if a child survived the first year or a second, then maybe there was hope for another or even more. Although these children were weak and vulnerable, they might have had a chance, however slim, of surviving into adulthood. Their short lives presumably had been lived in an environment of "watchful waiting" by their mothers and the Narragansett community.[57] When they died, they were not excluded from the ancestral burial ground.[58] The absence of bracelets and other body ornaments suggests that they were still nameless, but they were mourned nonetheless.

The causes of death for other three- and four-year-olds buried in RI-1000 are less certain. Without any visible manifestations of disease detectable on their fragile skeletons, one could suppose that their deaths were sudden. These were otherwise healthy babies who for some reason, perhaps not easily pinpointed, became fatally ill. Although the causes of their rapid deaths cannot be diagnosed today with any certainty, gastroenteritis and a host of other infectious diseases, such as influenza, measles, smallpox, and even tuberculosis, would not be unreasonable culprits. For a mother who had nursed a child for three winters, and who had every reason to believe that this one was a survivor, so much so that she asked the elders to name the child, death must have evoked disbelief and inconsolable sorrow. The uncertainty about why Cautantowwit had taken the child, the one with a name, must have been haunting. This was not the kind of pain that was eased by going through the motions. Following the traditions gave reassurances, but in cases like these more medicine was needed: perhaps the shiny, mirrorlike English spoons and, certainly, the beads. The glass ones, many as bright as the daytime sky and as deep as nightfall; the brass, glistening and lustrous; and especially, the shell, white and purple in equal proportions, placed on the body to restore the harmony and balance that had been upset.

The burial ground held remains of other children, whose ages ranged from about six or seven to thirteen years. They had passed the first transitional stage of social life. Many of their graves were erased by the bulldozer; among those that remained intact, several were empty except for the remains of the children themselves. Although their lives had not been menaced by the hazards that posed risks to older members of the community, the conditions of life in late-seventeenth-century New England did not exclude them from susceptibility to chronic illnesses. Five had suffered (and probably died) from chronic tuberculosis, perhaps reactivated because their own poor, age-specific immunity had been compromised.

Although not immune from chronic illness, two younger children, whose ages were estimated at around six to seven or eight years, had exceptional graves. Both were buried with items of personal adornment, but little else. One of the children (Burial 24) was buried wearing a garment profusely embroidered with brightly colored seed beads and some tubular ones. Two small, brass hawk's bells may have been attached to the beaded garment to create a jingling sound as its wearer walked on home ground and, at death, traveled the long and arduous path to the afterworld. The child also wore a delicate bracelet made of translucent yellow glass beads, resembling grains of corn, arranged with white wampum in an alternating pattern. The other child (Burial 41) was buried with a cluster of lead or pewter buttons, which may have been cast by a Native craftsman. The thirteen buttons were placed close to where the child's hands had been positioned, suggesting that they may have been part of a bracelet.

From the material evidence in these two graves, one can suppose that the emphasis at this stage of life was on individual, rather than a shared, identity. Children were permitted to express themselves freely and engage in mischief in ways considered inappropriate for most members of the community.[59] Little in these two graves would suggest that material things played an active role in a child's discipline and training in the late seventeenth century, except perhaps in a most subliminal way. Glass corn-beads threaded on a bracelet may have reminded the child of Cautantowwit's sacred gift. Sounds made by bells and jangling buttons protected the child and offered reassurances that their ancestors had traveled the same ground and made the same journey to the spirit world. Perhaps they were "sawcie, bold, and undutifull" as Williams had insinuated, but they certainly did not "want of *learning*."[60] They watched, imitated, and most of all listened to the stories told to them by the elders. They were works in progress. As provisional members of the community, they were unfinished and uncensored, but most of all they were deeply cherished and indulged, because they were the key to future generations. Unfortunately, the lives of these children were cut short before they had a chance of becoming full-fledged members of the community. Their early deaths must have cast an ominous shadow on the prospect of a Narragansett future.

Some Narragansett children at RI-1000 survived until adolescence. Those from roughly eleven to fifteen years old had begun to show signs of biological and sexual maturity. Measured with a biological yardstick, they were almost men and women. However, their maturity was not simply about chronological age and biology. In a social and cultural sense, it had more to do with character, responsibility, and knowledge. As culturally contingent and socially determined, their coming of age did not simply mean that they had reached puberty. Rather, it marked them as members of a group, having certain responsibilities in the community.

For many Northeastern Native American groups, puberty involved private rituals and public acknowledgment. The private component entailed the grown child's physical separation from the community. Girls were secluded in a small house reserved for the use of menstruating women, where they were cared for by an older woman.[61] Boys were expected "to go forth into the forests and hills," unaccompanied by their fathers or clansmen.[62] According to oral Narragansett traditions, it was during such seclusion that the girl or boy learned "the great mysteries of life" through some combination of fasting, instruction (for girls), prayer, and perhaps the gift of a vision from a *manitou*. These revelations came at the different ages for girls and boys. Even among them, different individuals would have demonstrated their readiness to their parents and the community at slightly different ages. At the end of the period of isolation, young adults were given a new name that was different from their childhood name. The elders chose these "new" names from the pool of available clan names. Thus, they really were not new names, but used and old ones that offered continuity and protection. These names would define the young adults in a kind of verbal shorthand fitted to their appearance and personality. They would bear these names throughout their lives, or at least until the names no longer suited them.

Besides gaining another name, the young adults were given other gifts in acknowledgment of their newly acquired maturity. According to Narragansett tradition, girls were given baskets woven by their mothers and filled with "many useful articles" contributed by the female members of her clan.[63] The gift-filled basket was the young woman's "hope chest," full of "all the useful dainty things . . . required of her society."[64] These articles became her very own, the badges of her readiness to assume new responsibilities in the society. The graves of females be-tween the ages of fourteen and twenty-six provide some indication of what these material signatures of this stage of maturity were in the late seventeenth century.

Nine of the ten "young women" were buried with body ornaments, such as necklaces and bracelets. Some had rings on their fingers; one young woman had both a headband and a comb. Necklaces were more common among young women than children, suggesting that these ornaments may have been part of the decorative code of their new status. Worn around the neck, necklaces represented the body part associated with communication, but also the head, the locus of un-derstanding. A headband and comb would have similar connotations. All three or-naments—necklace, headband, and comb—pointed to the acquisition of cultural knowledge about adult responsibilities. The rings found with adolescent women were not part of the decorative paraphernalia in children's graves. Rings were worn on the part of the body associated with dexterity. Worn on the hand of a young woman, they might signify that she had learned tasks of adult women and had cast off the things of childhood.

As with ornaments found in the graves of children, those of young women were made of glass, shell, and brass. The most elaborately adorned young female (Burial 22) wore a headband of multiple rows of small, barrel-shaped brass beads inter-spersed with some purple and white wampum. Her neck was adorned with two necklaces made of a variety of glass, shell, and brass beads. The glass beads in-cluded dark-colored cane beads, a few longer ones of the same hue, and some clear, resinous ones with impressed designs and gold overlay. The shell beads oc-curred in both purple and white, and in a variety of shapes, including wampum. The more complex shapes were rare in the RI-1000 graves. The few brass beads in the necklaces were similar to those found in the headband. The design of the neck-laces is unknown. A sheet-brass comb with eight short tines and a broad handle, with flared projections resembling the bifid motif found on other examples of Na-tive brasswork at RI-1000, was also part of the young woman's adornment.

Another (Burial 40) was placed in her grave with a necklace and two bracelets. The necklace was made of dark blue tubular beads mixed with purple and white wampum.[65] The bracelet on her right wrist was made of about four rows of pur-ple and white wampum. The left wrist was wrapped with a long strand made en-tirely of dark blue tubular beads (similar to the ones in the necklace) and green-ish-yellow seed beads, except for the inclusion of a single white, almost colorless, tubular bead. The tubular and seed beads were arranged in a ratio of one to seven.

The necklace encircling the throat of one young woman (Burial 29) was made of glass beads, dark and clear with overlaid brick red stripes, and cylindrical pur-ple and white shell beads slightly larger than wampum. The design also incorpo-rated a small, tubular black bead and a spherical white shell bead. According Ella

Wilcox Sekatau—who is, among other things, an artisan known for her weaving—the pattern was one glass bead to three shell. In another grave (Burial 48), a young woman wore a necklace made of tiny, barrellike brass beads, still strung together. A necklace composed of similar but slightly smaller beads, remarkably also still threaded on what appeared to be twine cordage, was placed on the individual in Burial 18. Eight brass rings, in a variety of "Jesuit" and signet styles, were also among her personal ornaments.[66] Similar rings were found in the grave of another young woman (Burial 19), along with a large assortment of glass beads in different sizes, shapes, and colors—solid and striped (black with white, black with brick red and white, brick red over clear with blue and white)—and even a corn-grain effigy. Fragments of two brass rings, one possibly in a signet style, were found in association with another adolescent (Burial 17) in addition to brass hoops, which may have been used to attach quillwork to clothing. Of the remaining decorated females, one (Burial 47) had a bracelet of white and dark medium-sized seed beads; the other (Burial 49) had a mass of purple and white wampum plus some shell beads in cylindrical and more complex forms.[67]

Some of their beads were similar to the children's, like the clear, deep blue tubes. Other colors and shapes also were found with young women and children, even corn-beads. Perhaps it was just a matter of supply—that is, what merchants had on hand to trade. But the beads of the young women also could have been acquired on some previous occasion. For girls on the brink of adulthood, these might be beads they had been given when they were first named as three- and four-year-olds. Some might have been lost, others could have been restrung. These beads were personal history, what could be called "life-to-date" beads. Other beads associated with young women were different. They were not incorporated into the glass-beaded ornaments adorning the bodies of children. Some were brick red with the dark centers or the brick red over clear cores with stripes. In fact, any tube bead with stripes in some combination of red, black, or blue with white belonged to their age group alone. Children's beads had stripes, but they were sky blue with brick red stripes, clear and light compared with the opaque and deeper-colored striped beads of young women. Beads seemed to deepen with the age of the wearer. They went from light (and sometimes bright) to darker, richer, even redder shades, as if to announce that the young woman's social responsibilities within the community, like the colors of her beads, had intensified.

Of the grave goods buried with individuals belonging to this category of womanhood, some were especially telling of their new responsibilities as clan members. The graves of two young women contained objects depicting clan emblems. One (Burial 17) held a brass spoon made by a Native artisan that in outline resembled a European latten spoon but was decorated with cutout forms of zoomorphic figures located on either side of the point where the bowl and handle were joined. The two facing figures appeared to represent bears. The bear was (and is) the totem animal of the bear clan, one of several descent groups connecting Narragansetts with other Native peoples across southern New England and the greater Northeast. The other clan emblem placed in the grave of young woman (Burial 22) was that of a turtle, carved into a piece of graphite. Like the bear, the turtle is associated with a clan that has enduring social and spiritual significance for the Narragansetts and other Algonkian peoples. These bear and turtle symbols, the only recognizable clan symbols in the RI-1000 burial ground, were badges that identified clan membership for these young women, much like the adult clan names they had been given to replace their childhood names. Clan organization, which may have begun several millennia earlier to facilitate exchange between peoples living in different homelands, designated appropriate marriage partners, defined their sacred duties, and, in general, created both a broad and profound network of kinship and community for them. That these clans' emblems were associated with adolescent women makes a compelling statement about the importance of women in Narragansett society and especially about their role in reckoning descent.

The objects encoded with clan totems along with the beads and other items would have been given to young women at the rituals marking their transition from children to adults. The bear-effigy spoon and the graphite turtle were sacred objects. The turtle effigy carved into graphite is especially evocative of more esoteric cultural meanings. Graphite is a substance used to paint or smudge on the face for ritual and perhaps other occasions. For example, Roger Williams noted in *A Key* that mourners blackened their faces to lament the dead. However, among other Algonkian peoples, the child at puberty wore a blackened face. Boys especially were said to wear a blackened face as sign that they were entering adolescence, but girls also were known to have been "smudged" in acknowledgment of their transition from childhood to womanhood. In design and substance, the turtle effigy placed in the young woman's grave conveys information about clan membership, personhood, and sacred traditions.

A diversity of other items also accompanied adolescent women in their graves. Spoons, in addition to the one with the clan emblem, were common, especially European latten varieties. Glass bottles appeared in the majority of graves within this group. The latten spoons and the glass bottles exhibited few signs of wear resulting from ordinary use, suggesting that they were special offerings for the deceased.[68] The other grave goods were single occurrences of a miscellaneous array of objects. Some, like white tin-glazed cups (or jars), also appeared in a child's grave, as did a pair of scissors.

The grave of one young woman (Burial 17) held an unusual assortment of objects. In addition to body ornaments, and the glass bottles and spoon diagnostic of her age group, her grave contained iron kettle hooks, an iron pot or kettle, brass clips, and a wooden mirror box. The hooks and kettle tell of the responsibilities of a mature woman, not one having recently acquired the knowledge to assume this place in Narragansett society. Here was someone who, judging from her grave lot, was both a young woman and a mature one. She was a person inscribed with two female identities, one superimposed on the other, much like the inverted iron kettle that covered the glass bottles in her grave. Double identity implied that she was in two social places at once: She was poised on the brink of womanhood but also had ventured beyond it. She had acquired the gifts typically given to young women at puberty, but her ornaments were few and seemingly worn. She wore only the fragments of two rings, but no beads. Her simplicity was perhaps more than a matter of personal style. Viewed in the context of the other elements of her grave's material assemblage, it conveyed something more. Although she was only recently versed in the responsibilities of her gender in Narragansett society, she had a scar on her pelvis, a mark of pregnancy and parturition. She was not the only young adult woman to have this chiseled groove etched onto her skeleton, but in her case the imprint confirmed what her ornaments and grave goods implied: She had a history in her own right, however brief.[69] Before her fertility and purpose were cut short, she had carried a pregnancy into its later stages and perhaps had even experienced childbirth, along with fulfilling other responsibilities to her clan and community.

The grave of one seventeen-to-eighteen year old female (Burial 26), whose chronological age was within the range of the category of "younger women," lacked ornaments or grave goods of any kind. However, her burial also was unusual in other respects. Her torso, though right sided, almost appeared to be in a prone position; her hands were crossed in front of her face, a position not seen in other individuals buried at RI-1000. The bones of her nasal area exhibited extensive destruction. The erosion is suggestive of a treponemal infection, probably in the form of venereal, rather than congenital, syphilis that was acquired sometime after she had reached puberty. These skeletal lesions, characteristic of the tertiary stage of the disease, could have developed as early as two years after an infective contact or maybe even sooner.[70] Whatever its timing, the infection wreaked havoc on her body. Skeletal stress markers such as traverse lines on the long bones (which in her case were significantly higher than the averages calculated for females within the RI-1000 burial population) and severe dental caries suggest that she may have been already weakened because of malnutrition before becoming infected and most certainly subject to further synergistic responses as a result of it.[71]

Clearly, her condition was far from asymptomatic. The severe erosion of her nasal bones suggests that neither sweating nor medicinal potions cured her of the disease she had acquired.[72] The infection had taken its toll by inflicting pain, depleting her energy, and leaving her defenseless to other diseases. Rather than looking forward to a future in the company of older women and to giving birth to children who would live to become the next generation in her lineage, she gazed at death.[73] She was deathly ill and must have known it, as did others who could not have failed to notice signs of disease. Yet despite the disfigurement to her face, she was buried with the care and respect given to all Narragansett ancestors. The beads and other gifts she had been given at puberty, when her prospects for this life seemed hopeful, did not accompany her to the grave, however. Perhaps they had been destroyed, shed along with her name and other aspects of her identity, in hopes of restoring her to health and keeping her in the community of the living.

By crude estimates, a young Narragansett woman in the late seventeenth-century could expect to live to the age of about thirty-five or forty. In fact, some women buried at RI-1000 lived much longer, a few even well into their fifties. Their bodies showed the wear that comes with age: Their pelvises were scarred by pregnancy; their joints exhibited degenerative arthritis, especially of the spine, elbow, and wrist. One woman's foot showed the consequences of stress imposed by habitual kneeling. A few had Colles' fractures, the technical term for a broken wrist, the kind that could result from attempting to break a fall with an outstretched hand. Several had evidence of osteoporosis, the loss of bone mass that frequently occurs in postmenopausal women. All had poor dental health. In general, they had more caries, abscessed teeth, and antemortem tooth loss than men of comparable age.[74] They had suffered bouts of malnutrition and perhaps had felt pangs of hunger. And like so many others in the community, they too bore the signs of tuberculosis.[75]

Their bodies had earned the insults that come with age. The women had lived through many things that come with longevity. They had grieved over the death of a parent, a spouse, or even a child and learned to deal with life's unfairness and uncertainties. The older ones had lived beyond their years of strength and fertility. Their losses were not only personal; they had seen much change during their lives. There were new tools for doing old things, clanspeople made homeless by disease and war, encroachments on their ancestral lands by the English, tensions caused by alcohol and greed, pressures to convert to the foreigners' religion, and the questioning of cultural traditions. Some probably even remembered Roger Williams.

Their maturity, unlike the acknowledgment of their coming of age, was not marked by ceremony. It did not require a change of name, but it enabled them to name others. Maturity was about assuming adult responsibilities and growing in wisdom. Marriage was part of the package, a requirement for full adulthood and a commitment to fulfill the obligation to reproduce. The marriage itself would have been formally recognized by the consent of the couple's parents and the en-

dorsement of the community. The groom would have presented gifts, which according to Williams were payments of wampum, as a "dowrie" to the woman's
family.[76] Whatever the material form, these gifts, perhaps more correctly thought
of as a brideprice, were offered in gestures of exchange intended to strengthen the
relationship between the two households and clans joined in the marriage.

As wives, Narragansett women were expected to be "loving," "proper," "sober
and chaste," and "fruitfull."[77] Although many couples were known to have stayed
together for most of their adult lives, some marriages, however well intended, undoubtedly failed.[78] The reasons were probably as simple and as complicated as in
any other time or place. Native oral history and colonial records indicate that
women sometimes left their husbands because of abandonment but also for political expediency.[79] In cases of adultery, the wronged party could separate from
(i.e., divorce) the offending spouse. According Williams in *A Key*, "if the Woman
be false," the husband was allowed to take revenge on "the offendor, before many
witnesses, by many blowes and wounds," even to the extent of murder.[80]

In the course of their reproductive careers, Narragansett women were said to
"abound with Children, and increase mightily," but even at the time of *A Key* epidemic and chronic disease had taken the lives of many and reduced the number
of births.[81] However, other factors also would have compromised their fecundity.
Lactation would have affected the time between pregnancies; its contraceptive effect was ensured by culturally prescribed sexual abstinence, which lasted until the
nursing child was weaned three years after birth. This long period of lactation
would have regulated birth spacing for any healthy woman to at least three years.
Demanding physical labor also could have restricted a woman's reproductive capacity by causing infrequent menstrual periods and by placing enormous burdens
on her ability to care for young children. Thus, although physical labor may have
contributed to "their extraordinary ease of childbirth," and children were thought
to increase agricultural yields, Narragansett women's role in production may have
had both unintended and intended consequences for their childbearing histories.[82]
In all likelihood, even fertile seventeenth-century Narragansett women were not
always pregnant.[83]

As important as children were to Narragansett life, so too was corn. Indeed,
much has been made of the ways in which activities of Narragansett (and other
Native American) women in southeastern New England intersected with corn.
They not only planted the seed but also weeded and hilled the immature plants;
gathered and dried the harvest; and ground stored kernels into flour, keeping some
as seed for the next year's planting. They were almost solely entrusted with the
care of the plant that was much more to them than an important food, considering the symbolism surrounding its place in their daily lives and sacred traditions.
In addition to tending the corn, women gathered wild food and plants, including

grasses, sedges, herbs, and dyes. They also collected shellfish, which provided an essential source of protein in their diets and the raw material for bead making. Like the mats woven from cornhusks, bulrushes, and cattails, beads made from shells served as a creative medium through which Narragansett women expressed their artistic skills and their knowledge of cultural traditions. Beadwork and weaving (though certainly not limited to shell or cornhusks and marsh reeds) were as much a part of a woman's burden as their work in the fields and gardens, mud-flats, and the other spaces of the homeland. They were all expressions of women's identities and their contributions to the reproduction of Narragansett society.

In death, as in life, older women were distinguished from younger women. Among the women buried at RI-1000, those whose ages ranged from twenty-nine to fifty-eight were undecorated. Unlike younger Narragansett women, they wore no beads. No necklaces or bracelets encircled their limbs; no rings adorned their fingers. Without exception, all eleven "older" women lacked any type of body ornamentation. They were marked, in a sense, by their decorative invisibility. The absence of personal ornaments in their graves suggests a silent discourse in which adult women, in contrast with younger ones and children, were not defined in relation to someone else, such as a parent. Instead, their social position within the community had become redefined in terms of their own life experiences and increasing sense of independence.

Seven of eleven adult women's burials contained some type of grave good.[84] In general, they were mundane objects used in everyday life: tools associated with horticulture, such as iron hoes and stone pestles; items linked with cooking, such as brass kettles and iron pothooks; and still others, like awls (or muxes) and a bone- (or antler-) handled knife, possibly used in beadwork or basketry or other tasks. The hoes showed damage from heavy use; they were not pristine objects obtained or curated for the specific purpose of placing them in the graves of the dead at the time of burial.[85] The brass kettles also exhibited signs of wear. They were battered, heavily charred, and in some cases patched. The stone pestles presumably had been used as well. On ground stone tools, it is often difficult to differentiate use-related wear from that resulting from the manufacture, but the surfaces of these items implied use in pounding and grinding. Two surfaces of one particular pestle exhibited wear. It was smooth and flat on one side of its shaft, and its handle end was worn and chipped, suggesting multipurpose use.

The distribution of these objects among the women's graves suggests that hoes and pestles were buried with women past the age of forty. Among the nine graves containing remains of women of this age, three held hoes, and two, pestles. Three of the graves did not contain any grave goods. The women buried with these objects included a woman aged between forty and forty-five years (Burial 51), whose exceptionally short-bladed hoe exhibited a lifetime of use. It was reused or reworked after the original blade had been broken. The grave of another woman, between fifty-six and sixty years old (Burial 32), contained a hoe with a broken haft. It retained part of its wooden haft and a wedge that once held it in place. The graves of both women also contained pestles. The other hoe was buried with a woman in her midfifties (Burial 31); it was similar in size and shape to the hoe found with Burial 32. Its longitudinal cracks, visible in X rays, revealed a history of heavy use.

The presence of such tools in the graves of these older women underscores the association between Narragansett women, the land, and cultivation. These items, all well worn from years, even lifetimes, of use, embodied women's activities in providing sustenance and in nurturing cultural traditions. In the time since Williams commented on Native women's preference for "their naturall Howes of shells and wood," they had adopted iron ones and put them to good use.[86] That such items were buried with older women suggests an intimate, if not inalienable, link, between these objects, the duties and knowledge they imply, and those who possessed them. Thus, these heavily used and highly curated hoes may have been much more than everyday tools. The same may also be true for pestles. Although effigy pestles found in contact period females' graves have been interpreted as symbols of Algonkian women's importance as food producers and spiritual leaders, because of their lack of wear and their zoomorphic and anthropomorphic representations, noneffigy pestles may have had similar connotations in the context of the RI-1000 burial ground.[87] By taking these undecorated and worn pestles out of circulation and appropriating them for use as grave objects, these ordinary objects became sacralized.

Of the two women buried with pestles at RI-1000, one (Burial 32) was the oldest woman in the burial ground. Between fifty-six and sixty years, her age would have made her old enough to be respected as an elder and imbued with the authority that comes with seniority and accumulated knowledge. Her grave goods—the pestle, hoe, and awl—were objects of her position as a woman in Narragansett society, but they are also simple yet eloquent reminders of her wisdom, confidence, and leadership in matters of social intelligence and cultural traditions.

In contrast, the other woman buried with a pestle (Burial 51) was not an elder. Her skeleton suggested an age between forty and forty years. She may have been old enough to have gained experience and esteem as a clan mother, but she was still what might be called a "young forty," even in that time when forty was not considered young. Besides a pestle and a hoe, her grave included objects not buried with women past forty, such as brass kettles and a bone-handled knife.

The brass kettles in her grave ranged from large to small. The medium-sized kettle exhibited evidence of multiple instances of repair. A sheet-metal patch fastened to its wall appeared to have three other patches riveted to it in subsequent attempts at repair.[88] The smallest kettle (or perhaps pan), like the others, was damaged from use and heavily charred on its exterior surfaces. All of the kettles had been placed in her grave upside down; the largest partially covered the hoe. The presence of two nearly complete iron bails suggests that the handles of the larger kettles had been deliberately removed before being placed in the burial, perhaps with the intention of depriving them of their utilitarian value and thus reinforcing their close identification with the deceased.[89] Sections of iron rods, which appeared to be parts of kettle-rim reinforcements, may have been associated with similar acts of ritual destruction. The only other brass kettle recovered in a woman's grave at RI-1000 was found with a twenty-seven-to-thirty-year-old (Burial 28) who, like other "mature" women at RI-1000, was not decorated with beads or other ornaments.[90] The bone-handled knife in Burial 51 was similar to that found in the grave of a preadolescent girl.

The array of objects in Burial 51 included womanly things, such as brass kettles, that connoted an adult woman's duties to her household and her responsibilities in childbearing and nurturing, but in addition items like the hoe and pestle marked increasing maturity and heralded her entry into the company of clan matrons. These objects were symbolic of the more profound power and understanding that often came with age. Here was a woman in transition, posed between fertility— and the duties attached to it—and the rewards of longevity. Like other mature women and the elders, she had persevered. She had been raised in the ways of her community and clan and had put these lessons to use during the course of her adult life. Along with others of her age, her life experiences gave her the license to share with the next generation of Narragansett women the survival skills so fiercely won in the brutal arena of seventeenth-century New England.

The material inscriptions in the graves of women buried at RI-1000 tell about more than women's roles in motherhood and cultivation. The graves of some older women indicate that they engaged in other activities equally important to the reproduction of the society. Two graves of women past the age of forty (Burials 9 and 32) contained slender iron rods that have been interpreted as drills or muxes used in perforating wampum, much like the ones Roger Williams said they used to bore "their shell money" decades earlier.[91] Although wampum production and trade in seventeenth-century New England were certainly important and widespread, these metal tools may possibly have been awls or needles, rather than drills. Using these needles, which like their hoes were made of European iron, Narragansett women strung, stitched, and wove beads manufactured from local shell or imported brass, and Dutch glass beads obtained from traders, into patterns that were neither casual nor idiosyncratic. Their beadwork—found in the graves of children and adolescent women and their male relatives—was the thread and sinew that joined the young to the community and connected the generations.

These women had passed from youth to maturity, survived childbirth, and become old and wise. Although their deaths may have come as no surprise, the causes are not readily diagnosed. No evidence of trauma suggests that they had met violent deaths. Some may have died from tuberculosis or other respiratory diseases, such as pneumonia or flu, common in late-seventeenth-century New England. Dysentery, smallpox, or any number of things could have killed them. Some may simply have died from what might be described as natural causes. Despite the spareness of facts surrounding how these women died, there can be no doubt that their deaths left a void in the lives of those who survived them.

Unlike the lives of these women, those of men buried at RI-1000, especially those in their twenties and thirties, should be familiar to European Americans. These were the members of Narragansett communities who typically interacted with the English colonists. These are the ones whom Roger Williams would have written about in *A Key* or mentioned in his letters. This is the cohort that furnished his travel guides, diplomatic contacts, trade partners, and those with whom he occasionally shared food and lodging. It was from these public, male characters that he learned about the Narragansetts and their way of life. Whether identified by their Algonkian (or English) names or left nameless, these are the people who came to represent Native culture in southeastern New England in the seventeenth century.

Despite the aura of familiarity, very little is known about the lives of these men or of younger ones and elders. Even a high-profile individual like Miantonomi, perhaps the best known of all prominent seventeenth-century Narragansetts, is chronicled for only an eleven-year period from 1632 to 1643, when he was between his midthirties and forties.[92] He emerges from the written documents as honorable, charismatic, tough minded, politically astute, vocal, and angry—and the victim of an assassination. Like that of other sachems, this profile derives from textual references that tie him largely to specific events and diplomatic negotiations. However, his life was not played out merely in the arena of intercultural politics.

Like other men in his community, Miantonomi was a son (of Mascus), a nephew (of Canonicus), a brother (of Yotash, Pessicus, Cojonoquant, and possibly others), a husband (of Wawaloam), a father of three sons (among them Canonchet and Moosup), and a close friend to others, perhaps some since adolescence.[93] In the context of these relationships, he was expected to emulate, to respect, to provide, to teach, to share, to travel, to fight, and sometimes to risk his life or die. Yet fulfilling these social obligations became increasingly difficult in seventeenth-century New England. The English had interfered with hunting privileges, limited access to fishing areas, and in general threatened to disrupt his and other Narragansetts' way of life. Surely survival was at stake, but also life as the Narragansetts knew it. There was a possibility that the balance of daily life, the complementarity of tasks, and the duties and obligations that were part of the pattern would all be upset. The aspects of Miantonomi's life that were overlooked by the English had little to do with intercultural politics, or, in some ways, perhaps everything. Over the next generation or two, these concerns would continue to be important to Narragansett men—including those whose remains were interred at RI-1000.

The men buried in these graves, eleven in all, ranged in age from their late teens to late forties. Most were in their late twenties and thirties. A few were older, and two were in their late teens or early twenties. Compared with women of about the same age, younger men were conspicuously underrepresented among the mortalities. The appalling imbalance is not easily explained. The recruitment of teenage boys as warriors or as farm laborers and servants in English households may have been a contributing factor. However, their removal from family and community for periods of time does not provide an entirely satisfactory explanation for their virtual exclusion from the ancestral burial ground. Their underrepresentation hints at the more complicated patterns of community commonly found in Native New England in the eighteenth and nineteenth centuries but rarely mentioned in written narrations about Narragansetts of the late seventeenth century.

The material inscriptions in the men's graves at RI-1000 suggest that their life histories were different from those of women. Life passages were not as clearly marked, which seems to imply that transitions in the life cycle were not as meaningful for them as they were for women. For example, unlike the women buried at RI-1000, younger men were not distinguished from older ones by the presence of decorative ornaments. Rather, some younger and older men were buried with body ornaments such as headdresses, rings, and a buckle. These personal ornaments suggest complicated individual histories instead of shared group identities forged at critical junctures in the life cycle.

That the heads of some men were singled out for decoration suggests a link between men and the part of the body associated with knowledge, understanding, and speech. Men were the talkers, the interlocutors, and often the spokespeople. They gave the speeches, told the jokes, and uttered the prophecies. Women may have done much of the same, but it was expected of the men regardless of whether anyone was listening (or would admit that they were). Their beaded head ornaments were made of shell and brass but, unlike those of young women and children, never glass beads. The headband of one adult male (Burial 2) was made of multiple strands of small, standard-sized beads cut from expertly prepared sheet-brass tubes. Others were made of wampum. One (Burial 38) was a modest, single strand of purple and white wampum beads. The most elaborate, constructed of many more purple and white wampum beads arranged in rows, was worn by a sixteen-year-old (Burial 3) along with a comb, as is suggested by two fragments of a bone comb found in his grave.

Rings were buried with two adult men in their late twenties to midthirties. The man in Burial 15 wore six engraved "Jesuit" rings, all on his right hand. Three exhibit identical "IHS I" motifs found in Jesuit symbolism. The others are embellished with variants of a generally similar "L-Heart" design. Rings exhibiting similar motifs also appeared in the graves of adolescent women (Burials 18 and 19). Although Jesuit rings are generally associated with French missionary activity, they hardly seem to be artifacts of a praying Indian, especially a Catholic one, in the context of this Narragansett grave. Here were objects of exchange, perhaps not with the French themselves, but more likely with their Native trading partners, the Mohawks, who had become strong allies of the Narragansetts in the second half of the seventeenth century. From exchange goods, the rings were transformed into personal ornaments that accompanied their new wearer to the grave and into the afterlife, where their earlier symbolism disappeared.

The rings buried with the other adult male (Burial 2) included a brass ring with a thin band and an ornate bezel designed to hold five small, round stones, the only one of its kind among the RI-1000 graves, and a heavy, European-style signet ring engraved with an anchor and heart. A European cast-brass double-style buckle suitable for use on a belt, possibly for a sword, completed his ornaments. Although signet rings were found in other graves at RI-1000, none bore the heart-and-anchor motif. The anchor has been an emblem of Rhode Island since 1647, and hearts appear in a variety of Rhode Island family seals dating from the second half of the seventeenth century.[94] One could suppose that this signet ring was used by a prominent colonist who affixed it to a document, perhaps even a deed, along with a signature.[95] Its presence in this grave alludes to a more complicated cultural history. Perhaps given to a Narragansett leader to seal a land transaction thought to involve the transfer or sale of property, rather than certain use rights, the ring was a symbol of misunderstandings. Recovered in the grave of the individual identified so unconventionally and so imperfectly as Burial 2, who wore the brass ring on one of his fingers, it was much more than simply a fashion statement. It was an expression of personal and tribal history, of autonomy and submission, and of appropriation and rejection; it was an artifact with complex and multiple meanings, here all equally valid.

The four decorated males were all buried with spoons. Most of them were Native made of brass and were either badly corroded or fragmentary. One was a miniature, scooplike spoon, 2 inches (5.3 centimeters) long, with a rolled handle unlike any other Native-made brass spoon found in the burial ground. In only a single instance (Burial 2) was a European latten spoon buried with one of the decorated males. One of the spoons had stains of red ochre and fine fur adhering to one end; others were associated with fragments of European woolen textiles, perhaps suggesting that these brass spoons, like their European counterparts, were ritual objects serving as special offerings for the deceased.[96]

The majority of adult men were buried with pipes; some had more than one. Pipes were found only with men. Most were typical of common English pipes shipped to New England in the second half of the seventeenth century, but some were similar to imported pipes that reached America from the late seventeenth into the eighteenth centuries. However, one with an outward flaring bowl, round heel spur, and flattened stem was presumably molded by a Native craftsman to resemble a European-style pipe. The decorative incisions on the bowl mimic the impressed rouletting which often appears on imported pipes.

All of the pipes showed evidence of use. Their bowls were charred, and their stems showed incisor marks. Some of the European pipes even appear to have been cut down and smoothed after their bowls and stems had been broken. The teeth of two men (Burials 25 and 38) had wear facets on their lateral incisors and canines, confirming what the pipes themselves implied about the association between adult men and tobacco. According to Roger Williams in *A Key*, they alone were responsible for cultivating tobacco.[97] Smoking was a male activity: it was something that men did when they gathered in formal councils, in sweat lodges, and in chance encounters in their travels.[98] It facilitated communication, allowing words and ideas to flow between them and to the spirit world. But other times they smoked tobacco as a tonic for their bodies, rather than for their senses. For example, they took tobacco to relieve the discomfort of toothaches, which Williams said caused even "their stout hearts to cry" in pain.[99] The condition of their teeth would not deny this.[100] With a few rare exceptions, "men throughout the Countrey" were said to have "a *Tobacco-bag*, with a *pipe* in it, hanging at their back."[101] Those buried at RI-1000 were accompanied by their pipes. In death, however, their pipes were always placed near their heads, sometimes close to their mouths, never at their backs.

With few exceptions, most of the other objects buried with men were tools. Among them were iron knives, adzes, and craft-related tools that reflected their activities as wampum makers, leadcasters, and metalworkers. These objects typically were buried with younger adult males, rather than older men, whose graves rarely contained any tools. The grave of an adolescent male (Burial 3), for example, contained wooden-handled iron knives, a trade ax, a stone mold, and wampum blanks that tell of his responsibilities and promise as a Narragansett man. These tools relate to skills he would have been taught since childhood (e.g., how to use a knife to skin a deer or an ax to fell a tree), but also to those he would have acquired since becoming an adult. The stone mold and wampum blanks comment on survival skills in a complex cultural universe, things he would have to do in this life and in the next so that his community could continue. Another young man, in his early twenties (Burial 16), might not have shown the same abilities as a hunter. Tall, yet with a gracile build, he was buried with only an iron container.[102]

The grave of an adult male in his late twenties (Burial 25) held ten iron awls sheathed in decayed wood. X rays disclosed two discrete clusters, each with large and small awls. The larger ones were longer than the awls found in women's graves, lending support to the interpretation that they may have had a different function, perhaps as drills or muxes used in manufacturing wampum. The sets of different-sized muxes were carefully maintained and securely held in a wooden case. These things were curated and even treasured, rather than casual and expendable things used once or twice and simply discarded. They were important enough to have been placed in the grave of this individual, who presumably had invested much time and energy in using them during his lifetime. In another grave of a Narragansett man in his late twenties (Burial 15) were cast-lead cylinders and a musket ball, all of the same diameter. The lead castings, which could have been used as ammunition, were made without a ball mold, perhaps by a Native craftsman (even the warrior himself). The other tools in his grave included an adze, a grooved abrader, and an iron hoe with a broken edge. The adze does not exhibit any real signs of use damage, and the broken hoe does not appear to have been reworked, unlike so many others found in the RI-1000 graves.

Burial 38 contained a remarkable assemblage of tools used in the repair and manufacture of iron implements and in other types of metalwork. The tool kit of this twenty-eight-year-old Narragansett man included a claw hammer, a horseshoe, a chisellike wedge, various reworked iron artifacts, assorted hardware (perhaps usable scrap iron), a stockpile of recyclable pieces of sheet brass, knives, a flint (or possibly a gunflint), and a whetstone. Among the reworked objects was a kettle-rim reinforcement straightened into a heavy rod; an iron spike tapered to a chiseled edge; and a strip of wrought iron bent into a shape that resembled a handle, possibly intended for use on a heavy wooden object or a tumbler for a very large stock-lock.[103] An iron wedge was recycled from a broken ax or adze. Another with a chisellike end was made from an iron bar that had been forged into a very low-carbon steel or wrought iron suitable for working wood.

The sophistication evident in reworking this object and some of the others in this grave suggest technical skills not very different from those of European smiths.[104] The individual in Burial 38 was a skilled craftsman.[105] His grave goods give evidence of traditional knowledge in working native copper, practical experience with imported brass, and adeptness in forging iron. He had both the equipment and the ability to repair and adapt brass and iron implements, including firearms, and thereby extend their use life. A clay pipestem (noticeably heavier than those of other European pipes) and a latten spoon—both objects of ritual significance—found with a pile of tools containing many materials and implements for blacksmithing, including a horseshoe, suggest that his powers of transformation may not have been confined solely to metal.[106] Instead of speaking to trade, acculturation, or possibly a youthful apprenticeship among the English, the items in Burial 38 tell a compelling story of Narragansett resourcefulness and resistance in late-seventeenth-century New England.

The men had been prepared for burial with many of the things they had used in this life and presumably could also use in the next. The hunters and warriors were equipped with knives and musket balls they could use for fish and game (and warfare), and axes and adzes for taking the forest and its many resources. They had the tools of their trades for fixing broken axes, patching kettles, repairing guns, and making shell beads. Warriors as well as those past that stage in their lives had their pipes positioned close to them, as if readied to smoke. The old men were buried with neither tools nor pipes, however. Instead of having these objects in their graves, they had the knowledge and memory of these things, and of course the stories to go with them. They could chronicle events, name the English they had guided, speak of long-running feuds, tell of exploits and deceptions, enumerate troubles, and catalog losses. These intangibles they took with them to their graves and to the community of the ancestors.

They were perhaps ready to die. Their aged bodies had become frail with arthritis and severe osteoporosis. In the end, one elderly man may have been unable to conquer the chronic tuberculosis that had plagued him on and off for so long. In spite of their elders' readiness to leave this world for the next, those who survived them still had many reasons to mourn. The elders had contributed so much, and so much would be gone with their passing. Younger men also would have been missed, but perhaps for other reasons. They had not racked up the years. To their way of thinking, they had not survived as many winters. Most were strong and able. Hardly a trace of arthritis was to be seen among them, though more than a few had spondylolysis, a defect in their spines resulting from strenuous activity or even an inherited predisposition, which could have caused chronic back pain or given them considerable discomfort.[107] Only two men seem to have died from tuberculosis.

Why had these men died so young, in the prime of their lives? They showed no blatant signs of trauma, such as fractures, amputations, multiple lesions, or musket balls imbedded in their bones. Some had evidence of periostitis, however, indicating the bone tissue's response to infection. In two cases the periostital infection was associated with traumatized ribs, but most often it had a nonspecific origin. The lesions on two men's tibias resembled syphilis, or they could have been part of the disease syndrome, but the diagnosis is ambiguous. So, in short, the causes of their deaths are a mystery. Cold, hunger, the indignities of the "bloody flux," spoiled meat, and hunting accidents are all possibilities, but so too is violence perpetrated by human agents. Such mortal wounds cannot always be ascertained in skeletal remains, let alone autopsies, but this does not eliminate them as possible, and in some cases probable, causes of death. Circumstantial evidence would suggest that such violence was as endemic in late-seventeenth-century New England as tuberculosis, dysentery, and other chronic illnesses that plagued the region's Native peoples long after the first waves of viral epidemics had subsided. The lying-in-wait for ambushes and raids, the preparations for and talk of war, and indeed the bloody skirmishes, surprise attacks, and torture made them weary before their time and sometimes surely killed them.

Even before the fatal blows were struck, some might have begun to think of themselves, and perhaps even of the society, as tired, worn-out, and old. Maybe some doubted the continuation of their way of life. Their sachems had wrestled against incursions on their cultural, political, and economic autonomy; some had entered into treaties intended to gain protection for them from the colonists, including an act of voluntary submission to the king of England. This kind of fighting had gone on for decades, even back to when Roger Williams was in Narragansett country. At times, it must have seemed like a losing battle. They still had their land, at least some or most of it, depending on who was keeping track. They could use it to negotiate with the English by giving use rights, maybe even selling some parcels, in order to gain promises. They knew the dangers of famine, but also the threats posed by disorder and chaos. They had struggled against both in very different ways and yet for the very same reason: to preserve their "Indianness." They had taken jobs among the English; some had left their children in their care temporarily; but most, if not all, had clung tenaciously to their Native traditions. The sacred rituals offered reassurances, the comfort of the familiar, the hope that the pattern set in motion long ago would continue to repeat itself. But even when the vision of the horizon looming before them was clouded, the bonds of kinship and the sense of community were still strong enough to overcome the dissension that might have occasionally surfaced among different factions and individuals.

In summary, the evidence in the RI-1000 graves reveals stories about Narragansetts in the late seventeenth century that have not been told in historical narratives. These are stories about their struggles to survive, make sense of the transformations taking place around them, and maintain kinship connections and community. They bring to light the lives of women, children, young men and women, and elders who were at the margins of Roger Williams's field of vision in the 1630s and 1640s and would barely be noticed by most later scholars. They also reveal people in different dimensions than simply those of politics and entrepreneurship. They tell as much about historical consciousness, and a continuing sense of identity as a people, as they do about material acquisitions and new technological skills. The RI-1000 graves do not confirm predictions about the disappearance of the Narragansetts' "Indianness" which come from A Key. Instead, they do much to challenge these notions.

8.

REMEMBERING THE DEAD

Buried according to the sacred traditions, the dead would depart this world for the other. After a long and difficult journey, they would arrive at Cautantowwit's house in the southwest, where they would be welcomed by ancestors—the ancient ones, the dear ones, and, like them, the recently arrived. Passing through the gates under the watchful eyes of a ferocious guard dog whose job was to ward off unworthy intruders, they would find companionship and solace. Here was a paradise overflowing with nature's bounty, where they could wander through lush green meadows, bask in productive cornfields, drink from cool streams, and find shelter in houses free of smoke, drafts, and fleas. Here they would be unencumbered by worry or pain. They would never feel hungry, because the storehouses were filled with an abundance of corn, beans, and squash; strawberries were always in season; and the clams were more succulent than any they had ever tasted.[1]

Although the southwest was envisioned as an everlasting abode, the spirits of the dead could pass through its gates time and again to return to earth. Unlike the unworthy, who were sentenced to wander restlessly abroad, these souls could appear at will at their gravesites and presumably anywhere else they chose in what was their former and still present homeland.[2] The oral narratives of southern New England Native peoples dating from the late seventeenth century are rich in folklore that illustrate beliefs in this phenomenon. These stories, legends, and myths suggest that the reasons why the ghosts and spirits moved between their new home and their earthly one was to convey messages, especially warnings and

reminders about who people were and how they should behave. They had the uncanny ability to compel the living to follow through on commitments to their last
wishes and uphold responsibilities to children and families. The spirits of the dead
were "the voices of tradition admonishing those who had strayed in some way
from the ancient ways."[3] Sometimes they sounded more like voices of resistance,
however, telling the living about how those who came before them also suffered
cruelties and indignities at the hands of English colonizers, and how their people
had persisted.

Thus, despite their physical absence, the dead lingered among the living. On
their part, their descendants maintained an active relationship with them, rather
than passively receiving their occasional messages. Mourning and observing other
culturally institutionalized sanctions, such as wearing blackened or sooted faces,
wailing, and refraining from mentioning the dead by name, were ways in which
they stayed closely intertwined with the dead after the funeral. According to *A Key*,
the living carried out these sacred duties for weeks, months, and sometimes even
a year. Although Williams did not comment on the Narragansetts' reasons for following these mourning traditions, one could suppose that they were linked to beliefs about the soul's passage to the land of the ancestors and about how the survivors could aid the spirit-traveler in the journey. Other than references to these
behaviors, *A Key* is silent about how the living might have continued to interact
closely with the dead and keep the ties of blood and interest very much alive.

The proximity of the burial ground to the wigwams provided a visible and constant reminder of those who had long since departed. Viewed from the settlement
area, the burial ground and the stream beyond it offered a powerful metaphor of
the mythical journey of the ancestors and of the enduring connections among different generations of Narragansetts. These images could not be permitted to fade
through time and forgetfulness. Like the memories they evoked, they had to be
maintained in tangible ways. Gravesites were part of this imprint. As sacred landmarks within Narragansett homelands, they drew together people separated by
time and tragedy but nonetheless linked by blood and kinship.

Cultural traditions of the Narragansetts and other southern New England Native peoples tell of attachments to gravesites and of ceremonies of remembrance
conducted at these sacred places. Although *A Key* is silent, some other early accounts by New England authors contain references to the ways in which Native
people kept in touch with the dead. Edward Winslow of Plymouth mentioned that
the Wampanoags did this by digging small holes in the ground, which, like records
and chronicles, served to renew their memories of "many things of great antiquity."[4]
Later European Americans commented on the related practice of remembering
people and places by heaping up piles of brush or stones. Across southeastern New
England, and throughout most of the Atlantic seaboard, Algonkian-speaking

peoples were observed creating brush or stone piles by casting a stick or stone each time they passed places where they encountered spirits of ancestors.[5] For example, several written accounts refer to a monumental stone pile in Norwich, Connecticut, at a place where some local historians believe Miantonomi was executed and buried in a solitary grave, far from his communal cemetery, in September 1643.[6] For many years, Narragansetts would visit the site on the anniversary of the sachem's death, "in spite of almost continual hostility which existed between them and the Mohegans."[7] On these occasions and at other times, they would pay respect to the venerated ancestor by offering lamentations and "throwing new stones upon the heap," which they consecrated "with mournful cries and frantic gestures."[8]

How the practice of heaping stones commemoratively one by one began is not known for certain. Some early history writers said that Native people told them it was an ancient custom practiced by their fathers. Others added that their grandfathers and great-grandfathers did it too. Yet some Native informants were simply "unable or unwilling to answer" questions on the subject. Finding the answers of Native experts unsatisfactory, and their silences even more troubling, the inquisitive looked elsewhere for explanations. In 1798 Timothy Dwight commented that a large pile of stones over "the grave of one of the aborigines" that he saw en route from Great Barrington to Stockbridge, Massachusetts, had been formed by gradual accumulation, much in the same way that other nations, especially the ancient Israelites, raised monuments for the dead. Although he admitted that the biblical accounts were ambiguous about whether the practice expressed respect for the dead or abhorrence of the person buried, he suspected that among Native Americans it was "an expression of peculiar reverence, and an act of obedience to the dictates of their religion."[9] To most European Americans accustomed to the monotonous and labor-intensive task of field clearing in New England, piling stones may have been a familiar, everyday practice, not a behavior typically associated with ritual. Moreover, the stone heaps, which they sometimes referred to as "sacrifice rocks," neither resembled altars nor exhibited traces of the blood and carcasses of sacrificial victims.[10] If they were commemorative monuments, as some Natives claimed, the heaps certainly did not look like those built by Europeans and did not impose meaning in the form of sculpture or inscription. Instead, they required participation. Through simple ceremonial acts, the living made contact with ancestors, much as the stones they heaped on the pile touched and mixed with those placed there by earlier generations of Narragansetts.[11] In the ongoing creation of these monuments, the living kept in touch with the dead and honored them by impressing on the monuments their own meanings, histories, and memories.[12]

Native peoples in southern New England maintained their ties to the dead in other ways as well. In the early part of the twentieth century, a Mashpee informant reported to Frank Speck, who worked with New England and other Eastern

Algonkian peoples, that "the ancient Indians were always telling of meeting spirits on their journeys." These encounters were so common that the paths of the living became congested with ghosts who required propitiation before they could be induced to clear the way. The Mashpee attributed the practice of depositing some item of property, food, or alcoholic libations at sites where people encountered spirits of departed ancestors to these early roadside meetings.[13] This tradition, associated with brush memorials known as "taverns," continued among the Mashpee Wampanoags at least until the 1920s or 1930s.

Even today the Narragansetts speak of ceremonies of "continuance" being conducted at burial places.[14] Conanicut Island, said to be named for Canonicus, is a place of extensive communal burial grounds within the ancestral homeland centered around the Wickford Harbor and North Kingstown area. The island has a long history of use for burial and other ceremonies, dating to more than three thousand years ago, in which the living rekindle ties to the dead.[15] Evidence of secondary burial at the West Ferry cemetery reveals communal celebrations in which the living conducted final rites for the deceased, lamented their passing, and extolled their many virtues but also reaffirmed an existing relationship with the community of ancestors, which on the occasion of reburial included the deceased. Several small pits containing flecks of charcoal and sherds of steatite vessels located near the remains of a secondary burial suggest rites that may have accompanied the ceremony or were related to a later act of memorialization.[16]

According to conventional wisdom, seventeenth-century Narragansett Indians buried their dead and lighted ceremonial fires at gravesites on the island until the late 1650s.[17] Their involvement with these burial places is believed to have ended abruptly as a consequence of land "sales" in which their sachems agreed to relinquish their claims to Conanicut Island and remove all Native people living there. These land transactions occurred after earlier arrangements made by Canonicus and Miantonomi, giving the English use rights to the island's meadows and grasses, soured because of misunderstandings, abuses, and some unexplained intrigues. The later generation of Narragansett sachems, among them Scuttop and Quequaquenuit, two of Canonicus's grandsons, and Cojonoquant, Miantonomi's brother, renegotiated the terms of the "sale." As explained by Roger Williams in a letter of August 1658, among the concessions that the Narragansetts wanted from the English in return for certain rights to the land were contributions "to their Niccommoes or Devilish Feast."[18] The terms that were eventually agreed upon in these deeds suggest that by about 1660, at the very latest, Native people were gone from Conanicut Island or were about to leave.[19]

Despite the promises made by the sachems, it is not clear that the Narragansetts vacated the island. The records are silent until 1679, when the residents of Jamestown voted to prohibit wigwams within the town. Apparently, the ordinance failed to achieve its desired results, however, because Native people built a watch-tower chimney on the island in 1705 that served as a forerunner to the Beavertail lighthouse. Although the cultural affiliation of those mentioned in the records was not identified, one might reasonably guess that Narragansetts counted among them. Perhaps some were skilled stonemasons who, along with others, had remained on the island or continued to visit as their ancestors had done every summer for time out of mind. The Narragansetts today admit they never forgot the importance of Conanicut Island and its ancestral burial places and visited them regularly, though quietly and inconspicuously.[20] During these visits they would pay respect to ancestors who were buried there and reassert their claims to a place they believed was rightfully still theirs, regardless of how the words inscribed on the deeds were interpreted by others.

Archaeological evidence from RI-1000 also suggests that the Narragansetts maintained a continuing relationship with the dead and returned to their gravesites on more than one occasion. The sacred space was used as a burial ground for a relatively brief period (roughly twenty years) between the 1660s and 1670s, based on the known manufacturing dates of many of the European goods found in the graves. Narragansetts living when the burial ground was in use would have known who was buried there and exactly where they were interred. Their near descendants would also have known this, as well as their children and perhaps those who came after them. Even without the telltale signs of raw earth, a desiccated skin coat on a nearby tree, or even a memorial stone pile, they should have known who, when, and where. These were the chronicles of their lineage, passed on from generation to generation, give or take a few details in their subsequent retellings.

Within this exceptionally ordered cemetery, the majority of the graves were oriented in the same direction and evenly spaced, and they exhibited the same general shape and dimensions. In a single case, however, one grave overlapped another. From an archaeological (and geological) perspective, superimposition establishes a relative chronology for two events. Using this reasoning, Burial 27, which overlapped Burial 28, would have been dug sometime after Burial 28. Burial 27 was almost a perfect rectangle and aligned east–west, rather than conforming to the southwest–northeast axis of the other graves. It was also unusual in one other respect: it was empty. No skeletal remains were found, not even a trace. The only thing found in the fill was a tiny fragment of white earthenware, identified as creamware, dating to about 1750–1775.

Although the grave held neither a body nor grave goods, the careful, even expert excavation (to a depth of about 16 inches [40 centimeters]) with neatly squared corners suggested that "Burial 27" was dug as a grave. At the bottom was buried dark brown sandy loam, unlike the mottled soil found in the fill. The darker soil seemed to represent a prepared surface of plowed soil, homogeneous in color and with only a few pebbles. The "grave" did not intrude into the one lying beneath it (Burial 28); instead, it simply bottomed out. Seemingly planned and executed with a deliberate end in mind, the mission was then aborted.

One might expect that Narragansett descendants would have known this was the site of an ancestral burial ground. However, so much time had passed since the others were buried here—at least a century, or maybe more, based on the *terminus post quem* ("the date after which") implied by the earthenware sherd in the grave fill—that it would perhaps be unreasonable to expect that the living would know the precise location of individual graves. They had traditions and memories but not perfect recall, especially when so much had happened in the intervening period. The land on which the burial ground was situated had long since passed from their hands. In the eighteenth century, many of those who called themselves Narragansetts lived on the reservation in Charlestown; others, in almost every Rhode Island town. Although they could no longer move freely across their ancestral homelands, as they had before English colonization, they were not completely immobile. Narragansetts moved onto and off the reservation frequently, and from one town to another.[21] However, their movements were not like the communal outings of the past, when they all got together to set traps for deer or to break up a new planting field. Now a move involved fewer people, maybe several families or just an elderly relative, and with less structured scheduling. Yet they drew on the old ways, the patterns and places, among them the practice of visiting sacred sites to fulfill ritual obligations.[22]

Town records show that in the late eighteenth century, departure certificates, as well as removal orders, were issued for North Kingstown to persons identified as "Indian."[23] On the occasions that Narragansetts returned to the RI-1000 burial ground, they would have seen a plowed field instead of graves. In spite of the changes, they still would have remembered. Perhaps that one time, they took the chance of burying one of their own on this hallowed spot. What motivated them to do this can only be guessed, as can the reason why they did not follow through with their plan. It would not be unreasonable to suppose that the incentive for both was a belief in sacred traditions. A vision, some other warning, or even visible traces of the underlying grave would have provided sufficient justification for them to stop, lest they disturb the grave of an ancestor.[24]

Whatever the outcome, they had returned then, as other Narragansetts had in the past, to remember departed ancestors. Archaeological evidence suggests that on at least one other occasion they had visited the RI-1000 burial ground, not only to pay their respects but also to engage in ceremonies that seem to combine elements of memory, property, and lineage. Two of the RI-1000 graves had evidence of intrusive pits excavated after the original interment had been made. One such pit intruded into Burial 38. The archaeological stratigraphy suggests that it had been excavated into the grave fill and the surrounding soil matrix and that it was subsequently refilled. The refilling was incomplete, because the excavated depression eventually collected washed-in silts. These were later covered by additional soils, which filled the hole. A cluster of stones was placed at the center of the refilled pit.

At the bottom of the intrusive pit was a stone pipe, which had been placed on top of the cranium of the individual in Burial 38. Its position was unlike that of any other pipe found in the grave. The intrusive pit also contained charcoal, a burned wooden plank, and pieces of a Native-made ceramic vessel. Except for its larger size, the pot was typical of the other Native-made ceramic vessels found in the RI-1000 graves.[25] Curiously, the other grave with an intrusive feature, Burial 18, was situated just to the northeast of Burial 38. Like the feature in Burial 38, it appeared in profile to have distinct soil zones, characteristic of time lags between episodes of filling, and contained fragments of charcoal and ceramic sherds from a Native-made vessel.

Although these two intrusive features seem to represent similar yet different events, they may be connected. The shared attributes—the charcoal, the ceramics, and the closeness of the sites—would suggest that they were related in some way. In fact, the sherds might even have been from the same pot, because pieces from the separate features can be refitted. Oddly, and inexplicably, only undecorated body sherds were recovered from the intrusive pit in Burial 18, whereas decorated sherds, and rim as well as vessel body parts, were found in the other intrusive feature, along with an effigy castellation from a second pot. That the observed archaeological patterns were simply the product of random events would seem highly unlikely. Acts of grave robbing, for example, would seem improbable, especially in the case of Burial 38, where the extent of the intrusive pit was clearly demarcated and the contents of the grave hardly suggested careless defilement. Instead, the articulated skeleton and the rich and varied assortment of grave goods implied an otherwise undisturbed burial. The ancestral remains in Burial 18, however, were only partially articulated, especially in the region of the cranium and upper torso, which could have been a consequence of the later excavation. However, improper violation of the young woman's grave would be questionable, given the presence of grave goods comparable to those found with other females at the same life stage.

The archaeology of Burials 18 and 38 indicates a sequence of events that occurred after the original interment. However, reading the stratigraphy of these two graves may be easier than reconstructing the precise meanings of the specific actions undertaken. Why these two graves in the burial ground were selected as the sites of postinterment ceremonies is not altogether clear. The absence of any deliberately placed offering in the intrusive pit dug into Burial 18 might imply

a case of mistaken identity, perhaps a miscalculation about the location of an ancestor's grave. Alternatively, the other pit, the one in Burial 38, suggests no such
error in judgment, but instead the return of an object, perhaps a personal possession withheld from the grave at the time of burial. Ostensibly here was a case similar to the one described in the Silver Pipe legend, told by New England's Native
peoples for more than two hundred years, about the consequences of reneging on
promises such as following through on burial wishes.[26] According to the legend,
as told by Zerviah Gould Mitchell, a basket maker and publisher descended from
seventeenth-century Wampanoag sachems, to Hezekiah Butterworth in 1892, King
James had given a silver pipe to Massasoit, her legendary ancestor. The sachem
then gave the prized gift from his "white brother over the sea" to one of his warriors, but contrary to the warrior's last wishes, the pipe was not placed in his grave,
at least not initially. Because of the value of the object, his wife kept it instead of
burying it with her husband.

> One evening she went to the place where she had hidden the royal present, resolving
> to smoke from the pipe alone, and to hide it again. She put out her hand to take the
> pipe, but it moved away from her. Again, but it moved away, and again and again, but a
> dead hand was moving. Then she bitterly repented of her disobedience, and promised
> to bury the pipe if she were able. At this resolution, the pipe lay still, and she opened
> the grave, [and] fulfilled the warrior's command.[27]

That the pipe was "returned" to the grave of a habitual pipe smoker cannot be
denied, as shown in the wear facets evident on the teeth of the individual in Burial 38. However, whether this particular pipe was the warrior's is more difficult to
ascertain. Judging from the contents of his grave, he indeed had other pipes, but
none were like this. Expertly carved from fine-grained steatite, this large pipe (its
flat-based stem is 5 inches [12.7 centimeters] long) had an urnlike bowl with a
D-shaped cross section. Its raised collar was ornamented with drilled dots, and
its bowl was encircled with a deep, incised line at the point of its greatest flare.
A series of short incisions decorated the bowl's single flattened side. Presumably
made by a Narragansett artisan, based on its comparison to unfinished pipes of
similar form and material and metal tools suitable for working soft stone found
together in graves of a nearby burial area, the pipe was the only one of its kind
at RI-1000.[28]

This was no ordinary pipe. It was reminiscent of the "great pipes" mentioned
by Williams in *A Key*, which served as vehicles for intertribal communication and
ritual expression.[29] Thus, it evokes the kind of object that might have once moved
between people who were mutually entangled in an array of rights and obligations. It could be thought of as an "inalienable object," imbued with affective qualities that defined identity in a historical sense. Placing an object such as this—one

considered to be "proof" of a group's identity and immortality—in a grave of a communal burial ground may be viewed as a possible solution to the problems of social fragmentation, cultural decay, loss, and even death that the Narragansetts faced as a people beginning in the late seventeenth century.[30] Committed to the ground in ritual acts recalling earlier communal ceremonies of reburial, complete with charcoal and broken ceramics, the pipe was removed from circulation and put in safekeeping, perhaps with the intention of reclaiming it someday.

Archaeological evidence from RI-1000 provides further tangible testimony to the Narragansetts' involvement with ancestral burial places that went unnoticed by Williams. The intrusive pits, pieces of charcoal, broken ceramics, and remnants of possible stone piles indicate ways in which they kept in touch with the dead after generations had passed. These ceremonial acts become even more poignant when one considers that they continued to be conducted after the Narragansetts had been exiled from their ancestral homelands and their localities of long-standing sacredness. As if "guided by wonderful accurate tradition," they, like other Native peoples, returned to the places "where the bones of their tribe were anciently deposited; and there passed some time in silent lamentation over the ashes of their forefathers."[31] On some of these occasions, their lamentations might have included ceremonies of remembrance like those suggested by the archaeological evidence from RI-1000, in which they reaffirmed their ties to the past and silently defied any who dismissed their cultural persistence.

However, Narragansett descendants' efforts to remain in direct contact with their ancestors, even decades after they had departed, were sometimes frustrated by European Americans who had different interests in their burial places. For many colonists, the graves of New England's Native Americans were objects of curiosity, sources of commodities, subjects of scientific study, and confirmation of myths of Indian extinction.[32] Their involvement with Native burial places, which briefly predates English settlement at Plymouth, suggests that opening Native graves could be considered the colonists' oldest profession. It began in November 1620, when a few Pilgrims discovered a grave near Provincetown on Cape Cod. Like others who came after them, they "mused [about] what it should be, and resolved [themselves] to dig it up."[33] They found things they had heard that Indians used, but also an assortment of iron tools and "a sailor's canvas cassock and a pair of cloth breeches," which seemed to catch them completely off guard. Even more startling were the remains of an adult, whose skull had "fine yellow hair still on it" and some "flesh unconsumed," and in a nearby bundle, those of a little child, whose legs and other parts were bound with strings and bracelets of delicate white beads.[34] Yet even before they speculated on the events that could have produced this scene, they covered over the corpse and gathered up "sundry of the prettiest things" to take away with them.

The report of the incident illuminates how these early English colonists attempted to account for what they had seen in this grave. Some guessed that the adult was an Indian (though none had ever been reported as having yellow hair); others proposed that he was a European, "a Christian of some special note," whom Native people buried as one of their own in honor or in triumph. Their speculations about the identity of the adult individual buried in this Cape Cod grave prefigure the role that burial places have played in writing histories of New England's Native peoples. Although this grave exhibits many of the complexities and contradictions often associated with European colonialism, it has come to symbolize the inevitable consequences of European contact. The adult, probably a sailor shipwrecked or possibly abandoned on the Massachusetts coast, stands for the scores of anonymous Europeans who, beginning in the sixteenth century, helped to bring about dramatic changes in Native peoples' lives. This sailor (like other Europeans) had brought with him iron tools but also vices, which the Native people readily absorbed. Among these were the diseases that initiated a process of population decline accompanied by massive social and economic turmoil that ultimately resulted in the disappearance of their "Indianness."

Nowhere in the colonists' self-serving narrative is there any mention of Native peoples' abilities to survive the onslaught of sustained exchanges with those from the other side of the Atlantic, let alone persist into the present. Nor is there any discussion of why this grave held objects and was covered with boards or what the significance of these might have been. Clearly "sundry like places" where the Pilgrims dug in the Wampanoag homelands of Cape Cod were graves, not caches of corn.[35] But with the exception of a palisaded "great burying ground," where the graves appeared more sumptuous and hallowed, they seemed to care little for those whose graves they disturbed in their reconnaissance. However, a volley of arrows aimed at them suggests that the Natives, whose stores and graves they had violated, felt much differently.[36]

Despite this close encounter, if not because of it, the colonists desecrated the grave of a Massachusett sachem's mother at Passonagessit only a year later.[37] In what has been described as a "beautifully simple and pathetic harangue," the dead woman's ghost urged her son to take revenge on those who had defaced her grave "in despitefull manner, disdaining our ancient antiquities, and honourable Customes" by removing "two great Beares skinnes" that had been placed on it.[38] Heeding her eloquent words, the sachem called up his warriors and launched a raid on Plymouth. Perhaps in anticipation of the Massachusetts' reaction because of their earlier experience on Cape Cod, the colonists fired their muskets to fend off the warriors and avoided a bloody confrontation.

These incidents set the stage for similar events in Narragansett country and other Native homelands throughout southern New England. In some reported instances, greed—rather than curiosity, hunger, or disdain for overt signs of "pagan" beliefs—was the reason for opening Native graves. From the perspective of early colonists who needed supplies of goods for trade, the Native peoples' custom of placing still usable and valuable commodities in graves of the dead did not make much sense. Grave robbing was a way to put these goods back into circulation. In fact, this may have been what Jan Gereardy, a Dutch trader, and his motley crew of accomplices "one Samuel, a hatter, and one Jones, a seaman and an Irishman" had in mind when they robbed the grave of the sachem Pessicus's sister in 1654.[39]

Gereardy's actions enraged the Narragansetts. Along with eighty warriors, the sachems tracked him to Warwick, where they met Roger Williams to discuss what he described as "that gastly and sticking vilanie agst them."[40] According to Williams's account of the incident, the sachems were unanimous in their anger and "were so bold as to talke often of Mens lives and of fighting with us."[41] At the very least, they demanded to take an English child hostage until the matter was redressed to their satisfaction. Williams dissuaded them with a promise of "attaching the Dutchmans Goods and Debts" to bring their charges of grave robbing against Gereardy before either a Dutch or English court.[42] The case, which eventually came before the General Court of Trials of the Colony of Providence, was dismissed because "non of the saide Sachims, Either by themselves or by theire Atturneyes or agents" appeared in court even though they had allegedly been notified of the date by Williams.[43]

The Narragansetts' absence paints them as irresponsible or, even worse, as insincere in their rage over the desecration of an ancestor's grave.[44] However, their failure to appear before the magistrates may have had more do with inadequacies in intercultural discourse and resultant misunderstandings about the nature of the transgression. For Roger Williams, who seemed to have been truly scandalized by the actions of Gereardy and his associates, grave robbing was a theft for which he could mediate a solution by offering the victims compensation for their losses. But for the Narragansetts, robbing the woman's grave and mangling her flesh were more than criminal acts to be settled by legal process in the colonists' courts. The Natives had much more to deal with than the accused offender: There was the matter of the dead woman's ghost, for whom there could be no simple or adequate financial settlement.

Although the verdict had been rendered in the Gereardy case, the commissioners met a few days later and decided to enact strict sanctions against persons accused of grave robbing, involving fines, physical punishment, or both.[45] Not long after these laws were enacted, another incident of opening and robbing a Native grave was reported in what is now Westerly, Rhode Island. There are no additional details to indicate whether the new law was applied. In fact, after the Westerly incident, grave robbing and similar acts of desecration regarding Narragansett graves in Rhode Island are not mentioned again until 1859, when three Narragansetts—Henry Hazard, John Noka, and Gideon Ammons—brought a suit against nine men who had opened and robbed a Charlestown grave. The grave, believed to be that of Ninigret's daughter, was one of many that had been the focus of inquiry by local antiquarians on "Indian Burial Hill." Written accounts of the incident vary and are filled with ambiguities.[46] Yet there is general agreement that in May 1859, a grave was excavated to ascertain the posture of the buried remains. At a depth of 4 feet (1.2 meters) below the ground, the men exposed three very large flat stones, which they removed so that they could continue with their digging. After they went down about another 4 feet, they discovered a large iron pot, estimated to hold 4–5 gallons (15–19 liters), "filled with other iron, copper, and brass vessels, [such] as skillets, numerous small kettles and sauce pans," and nearby "a brass kettle quite as capacious, as the pot, filled with glass bottles, pewter porringers and small kettles."[47] Lying beneath these offerings was a sign of the treasure they were hoping to find: a wooden sarcophagus made from a large log, whose contents were secured by fastened hinges and an iron chain and padlock.

Inside of the locked coffin, they indeed found a skeleton—that of a woman whose body had been "enshrouded in a robe of green silk and whose head was adorned with either a cap or bonnet of the same."[48] A silver chain extended from her head to the bottom of her moccasined toes. Her waist was surrounded by "a belt, covered with wampumpeage or Indian coin, made of sea shells, and resembling in form and size small glass beads" that was fastened with silver brooches.[49] Her neck and arms were encircled with more of the same kind of beads. She also wore a copper necklace, and silver buttons, presumably part of her silk dress, appeared to adorn her wrists. In addition to her personal ornaments, the grave held two coins, one "a copper English farthing" and the other "a French silver half livre" bearing the date 1650, and what were described as Dutch spoons, a fork, pipes, and thimbles, all made of metal. Among the various other items found were a hermetically sealed glass bottle believed to contain a "fluid resembling brandy" and last, but not least, stone pestles.[50]

The grave was dubbed the "Tut-ank-ahmen of Rhode Island" because of the richness of the offerings.[51] Believed to be the largest collection of artifacts ever uncovered in any Indian grave, the finds were described, displayed, and coveted as no others from New England had been before them. "Relics" went to the Rhode Island Historical Society, the Peabody Museum at Harvard, private collectors, and treasure hunters. Even a lock of "Princess Ninigret's" hair came to be someone else's possession. Amid the excitement over the discovery, and almost as a footnote to the team of nine's original quest, it was noted that the posture of the corpse was "an imitation of the English custom." The body had been placed in a coffin, presumably in an extended position, much in the manner of the dominant race, which—given all the European objects in the grave—would not have been surprising.[52]

Compared with the attention being lavished on the dead woman's grave and its contents, her living descendants, who had filed charges against the grave robbers, attracted little notice. Even as the Narragansetts were bringing their accusations against the grave robbers to the courts, other graves at Indian Burial Hill were opened.[53] Additionally, the legal process they initiated failed to achieve its desired result. The accused were arraigned and questioned before Joseph H. Griffin, justice of the peace, about their "crime and misdemeanor against the laws of the state of Rhode Island" and held to answer the charges against them before the Supreme Court at Kingston, Rhode Island.[54] Although numerous written accounts of the incident indicate that the men were "duly acquitted and exonerated from blame," Rhode Island judicial records show that the charges were never prosecuted.[55] The Narragansetts' defeat in this case must have been especially bitter. Decades earlier, some had petitioned the Rhode Island General Assembly to define more precisely the boundaries of the "vacant" lands ceded to the colony by Ninigret II in 1709, so that the "burying ground and graves of [their] ancient sachems and fathers" would be excluded from the quitclaim agreement and ensured some protection. Although the request was granted, the land on which Indian Burial Hill was situated, like that of other sacred burial places, eventually fell out of their possession. Kept as a woodlot by its new owners and later sold at auction, this place of communal burial was purchased by the state of Rhode Island in 1878, one year before the legislature voted to dissolve the Narragansett tribe.

As the grave of Ninigret's daughter and others at Indian Burial Hill in Charlestown were being opened and robbed of their contents in the spirit of scientific investigation, other Narragansett graves and commemorative stone piles that had accumulated over the generations also were being destroyed or had been already. In some instances, their destruction was accidental, the unexpected consequence of plowing or digging a cellar or a foundation.[56] Such chance encounters of ancestral sites within much-altered landscapes would reveal little about their original context and meaning and so would leave them to be perceived as partial and scattered phenomena—much as the Narragansetts themselves had been since the end of King Philip's War. Even the stones of Miantonomi's memorial, which had stood on Sachem's Plain for more than 150 years, were eventually dispersed. Most were incorporated into the foundation of a barn by the landowner, to whom this obscure pile was both a source of building material and a nuisance but never a shrine. The rest were scattered in clearing the land for farming. Two oak trees, which had stood tall and erect like sentinels on either side of the stone memorial, also disappeared, leaving no visible markers to designate the spot where Miantonomi was said to have "yielded to his foe."[57]

Figure 28. Miantonomo Monument. The photograph shows the monument erected in
Norwich, Connecticut, in 1841 to replace a stone memory pile salvaged for building a
barn foundation. "Miantonomo" is one of many different spellings for the name of the
Narragansett sachem "Miantonomi" that appears in written sources. (The Connecticut
Historical Society, Hartford, Connecticut)

On July 4, 1841, a few citizens of Norwich, Connecticut, erected a new monument to replace Miantonomi's vanished shrine. It also was a stone memorial, but
very different from the original. Rather than a pile of small stones, it was a single
block of granite, measuring 5 feet (1.5 meters) square at its base, which they placed
on a large stone pedestal and inscribed with the sachem's name and date of death.
The boulder memorial was unveiled in the presence of people from the neigh-
borhood, both young and old, who had gathered for a children's festival, but there
is no mention of whether any Narragansetts living in Norwich attended. Consecrated with prayers and libations of pure water from a fresh spring, where
Miantonomi had undoubtedly "slaked his thirst and cooled his heated brow in his
marches through the wilderness," the rock came to be known as the "Sachem's
monument."[58] Other places near where it stands came to have the same appellation, even the previously mentioned spring.[59] Yet as these references to Miantonomi were being inscribed onto the landscape, non-Native people continued

to argue not only over the date and location of his execution but also his place in their town chronicles.

At Indian Burial Hill, the state of Rhode Island contracted to have a plat 20 by 100 feet (6 by 30 meters) enclosed by a substantial iron-post-and-rail fence standing 5 feet (1.5 meters) high, to rescue it from obscurity but also to afford it some measure of protection. In conjunction with the design of the enclosure, the ground outside of the fenced area was graded. The remains of those whose graves had been uncovered were removed. Several "relics" were found in association with these burials, including pipes, wampum, pottery, bottles, copper and iron vessels, spoons, and beads, but they paled in comparison to those taken from the grave of Ninigret's daughter in 1859. One well-preserved individual was discovered in a "sitting attitude" in a grave that extended to 7 feet (2 meters) below the ground, so deep that the exhumation proved to be a formidable undertaking.[60] In other cases where the preservation was not as good, and the burial presumably not as recent, the task of opening a grave and removing the contents posed less difficulty. Except for occasional pieces of deep red "soft punk" (presumably cedar matting), the "rude coffins" had decayed, as had the corpses of the ancestors they had once held.

The marker placed at the burial site was engraved with the words:

> This tablet is erected, and this spot of ground enclosed by the State of Rhode Island, to mark the place which Indian tradition identified as the Royal burying ground of the Narragansett Tribe, and in recognition of the kindness and hospitality of this once powerful nation to the founders of this State.[61]

Like written signs erected at other historical sites, this marble tablet intruded both as an object and as a linguistic symbol.[62] It identified what European Americans in nineteenth-century Rhode Island considered worth remembering about this place. By identifying it as "the Royal burying ground of the Narragansett Tribe," the marker invited visitors to compare this burial ground and those whose remains it held with others. In the opinion of local history writers, Indian Burial Hill represented a former era of Narragansett greatness. Here were "ancient" tombs of "princely dimensions" that held "the remains of the kings, queens, members of the royal family, and chiefs of the Narragansett nation."[63] This was the burial ground of a once-powerful nation, now almost extinct, that had little in common with Narragansetts living in the nineteenth century and their current practices. Many European Americans believed that Narragansett traditions—like their blood—had undergone significant changes because of intermingling with Europeans and Africans and, therefore, had almost wholly disappeared.[64] Thus, the marker erected at Indian Burial Hill solicited, if not imposed, an understanding that attempted to overwrite that held by generations of Narragansetts, to whom

Figure 29. An Indian burial ground, Charlestown, Rhode Island (ca. 1881). The state of Rhode Island enclosed and marked this burial place of Narragansett ancestors in 1878. (Courtesy of the Rhode Island Historical Society)

the graves in this burial ground were those of long-departed ancestors still very much connected by blood and interest.

The protection envisioned by the general assembly in voting to enclose and mark the burial ground was not merely physical, since an iron-post-and-rail fence, even one 5 feet (1.5 meters) high, would not have posed an insurmountable barrier to intruders. Rather, the protection the legislators offered was to affirm the historical importance of this burial place. Yet it is unlikely that the Narragansetts needed to be reminded about the importance of this burial ground or to have it rescued from obscurity and forgetfulness. They knew of this burial place and even the names of those buried there. Their involvement with this sacred site had never terminated; it was continuing, as their various petitions and actions in the eighteenth and nineteenth centuries demonstrated.

Other Narragansett Indians would also be commemorated by European Americans in the nineteenth century. In 1883 Canonicus received a simple and inexpensive monument, not unlike the one that the citizens of Norwich had erected to Miantonomi decades earlier. Rhode Islanders remembered Canonicus not only because of his friendship to the early colonists but also because of an interest in Indian affairs that for some history-minded individuals grew out of "the late formal dissolution of the Narragansett tribe."[65] However, this interest in Indian affairs

Figure 30. Dedication of the Canonicus Monument. Erected in Providence's North Burial Ground in 1883, Canonicus's boulder memorial was the first of its kind to be raised to distinguished Narragansett sachems following detribalization. The rock, retrieved from under 8 feet (2.4 meters) of fill during the excavation of a sewer, was inscribed with the sachem's name and the bow and arrow he sometimes used as his mark. (Courtesy of the Rhode Island Historical Society)

did not extend to all Narragansett people. The candidates for memorialization, like the monuments themselves, all exhibited certain attributes. The monuments were boulders—uniform in size, shape, and raw material and, of course, mute; the Narragansetts to whom these memorials were raised had to be long dead and, in addition, distinguished. At the very least, they had to be like the Narragansett Indians about whom Roger Williams wrote in the pages of *A Key*. Those who were not, because they were not prominent, or were female or too old or too young, did not have boulder memorials erected to them. They remained as invisible and as silent to European Americans in the nineteenth century as they had been to Roger Williams in the seventeenth century.

Yet the Narragansetts neglected by Williams and later European Americans had not been forgotten by their descendants. They were ancestors with whom the living remained in touch. On various occasions they visited their graves to venerate them, not because the dead were persons of influence or were in anyway exceptional but because of a sense of connection. Despite their ordinary lives, and the struggles of generations of Narragansetts in the years after King Philip's War, ancestors were not unimportant. Although the lives of Narragansetts in the nineteenth century were different from those that had come before them, and some tribal members occasionally objected to and expressed bitterness about the pressures to marry non-Indians, mixed blood was still considered Narragansett and interest continued just the same. The complex social and cultural world the ancestors had long occupied and shared with the living had only become more diverse and inclusive.

Although the Narragansetts were "all more or less tinctured" because of intermarriage and commingling with Africans and Europeans (and other Natives), they had not disappeared.[66] Intermarriage and living away from the reservation carried disadvantages, in the eyes of many European Americans and some other Indians alike, but also conferred advantages, not least of which was economic survival. Both gave them strength, not unlike that which they had gathered by acquiring European material culture. In adopting these goods, they made trade-offs and had mixed feelings—attraction, strangeness, and bewilderment—but mostly they embraced them as their own. Rather than marking the Narragansetts as assimilated or merely eclectic, these seemingly irreconcilable practices, like the European objects they adopted, became tools of their resistance. Because intermarriage and living off the reservation undercut their claims to a cultural heritage and persistent community—or so some argued—the Narragansetts found it imperative not to forget their ancestors. Claims to them would, if anything, become more important. By reminding the Narragansetts of a connectedness and continuity even more powerful than blood, ancestors provided an antidote to questions being raised and conflicts being fought, sometimes within their own communities, over their identity and history as a tribe.

In the 1930s, *Narragansett Dawn*, the monthly magazine of Narragansett culture and history, published a series of short articles on ancestral graves. Some were excerpts taken from local newspapers reprinted for a Native audience; others were editorials or observations written by Narragansetts that made some reference to burial places. For example, one article taken from the *Evening Bulletin* of February 25, 1878, retold the story of the 1859 grave robbing at Indian Burial Hill in Charlestown, as did another from the local *Shannock News*. The latter clipping contained a story conveyed by an elderly Native woman, who reported that the burial ground was a "haunted spot" where she had encountered a ghost one dark night. It was "something ghostly and white, and that no power on earth would ever draw her to the spot again after nightfall."[67]

The ghost that appeared at the scene of the grave robbing frightened the woman, but it also reminded her of the injustices Narragansetts suffered at the hands of European Americans. Above all, the ghost story reinforced a strong, even emotional, identification with this sacred burial place to Narragansett people living in the 1930s.[68]

Pieces written by Narragansetts told of other graves. An editorial by Princess

Figure 31. Cover of *Narragansett Dawn*. The pages of this monthly magazine, founded and edited by Princess Red Wing, expressed the oral traditions and opinions of Narragansett Indians, hoping to open to all "the great unwritten book of the Narragansett."

Red Wing mentioned "old Indian grave yards tucked away off on the hillsides," where a visitor had to travel by foot rather than car to reach them.[69] These deserted burial grounds containing old gray stones could be found in other parts of Rhode Island and throughout lower Connecticut, in addition to the more frequently mentioned burial places of South County.[70] Another commentary, by T. D. Brown, commented on the "Discovery of Queen Esther's Grave."[71] "Queen Esther" was Esther Ninigret, the great-granddaughter of the seventeenth-century Niantic sachem Ninigret, who inherited the position of leadership of the Narragansetts in 1770.[72] Identified in records as a "squaw sachem," members of her lineage formally recognized her authority by placing a cloth covered with blue and white peage, or wampum, on her head in a public ceremony held in Charlestown.[73] According to the account in *Narragansett Dawn*, her grave was found 12 feet (3.6 meters) below the surface and covered with stone slabs. She had been dressed in silk and placed "in a large chest made of axe hewn logs," but when the log coffin was opened, her remains "fell to dust" before the eyes of the onlookers. The "arrowheads, spears and pottery, copper utensils and beads, that were taken out the grave" had not been located.

The description of "Queen Esther's grave" is not unlike that of the young woman's grave opened at Indian Burial Hill in 1859. The latter, identified by local historians as that of one of Ninigret's daughters, was discovered at a depth of about 8 feet (2.4 meters) below the ground and covered by large flat stones.[74] She also was dressed in silk, placed in a coffin fashioned from logs, and buried with a rich assortment of offerings that subsequently disappeared. It is possible that some details were lost in the retelling of the incident, as it is unlikely that Esther Ninigret, a woman who died around the time of the American Revolution, would have been buried with the sorts of things mentioned as having been found in her grave. Other Narragansett graves have been robbed that have not earned the public notoriety of the young woman's grave from Indian Burial Hill. Therefore, it is possible that Queen Esther's grave belongs to this latter category.

However, the article in *Narragansett Dawn* may be about more than lost history. Instead, it is a story whose durable and most memorable elements were probably combed from masses of detailed memories passed down through successive generations. Minus some specifics and obscure facts, the account embodied the conviction that it is wrong to disturb, let alone rob, a grave, "even an Indian's grave."[75] But unlike treasure stories, twentieth-century folk narratives of New England Native Americans telling about the consequences of robbing graves of their valuable possessions and Indians' unwillingness to compromise their codes of decency to acquire wealth, the article conveyed another, even more powerful message.[76] The author's comments about the disintegration of the woman's remains suggest that grave robbing was not only a means of acquiring material wealth illicitly but also one more attempt by non-Natives to deprive Narragansetts of their ancestors and their history. The metaphor underscored the critical importance of the steps being taken by the Narragnasetts in the 1930s toward reasserting their community's survival and regaining their sovereignty as an Indian tribe.

About a half century later, the graves at RI-1000 were discovered. Although North Kingstown had a few Narragansett residents more or less continuously since the end of the seventeenth century, most no longer lived in this homeland. In the intervening decades, they sometimes visited these ancestral graves, as the archaeological evidence suggests. Maintaining these sacred traditions was not always easy for them, however; if anything, it probably became more difficult. Harsh accusations of cultural amnesia continued, even after they had been legally dissolved as a tribe of Indians. In the late nineteenth and early twentieth centuries, stories were told of "the last of the Narragansetts," who were "more African than Indian" in terms of blood and "religious predilections."[77] And despite their successful actions in reclaiming some of their land and their tribal status in the 1970s and 1980s, many people in Rhode Island still dismissed their persistence.[78] Their interest in the ancestral graves at RI-1000 was questioned by many European Americans as being a novelty and, probably, a recent cause of some activists. For a long time, they insisted, Narragansetts were uninterested in the graves of their ancestors. Within the tribe, some voiced objections about involvement in the excavations because they believed that no one should disturb graves. Based on past experiences, the Narragansett Tribal Council's decision to proceed with the excavations and to be engaged in the data recovery itself was painful to explicate. Perhaps forgetting was a part of their remembering. Memories of ancestors' graves being desecrated, their flesh being mangled, offerings stolen, and stone piles thrown down, all had to be temporarily suppressed to come to terms with the chance to confront the silences and misrepresentations about their history, which had been reinforced by uncritical reliance on *A Key* as a primary source of evidence.

In August 1983, John Brown of the Narragansett tribe conducted another postinterment ceremony at the RI-1000 burial ground. He repatriated the steatite pipe that had been placed in the intrusive pit in Burial 38 for safekeeping in an earlier postinterment ceremony. Although the pipe was not removed until the rest of the burial was excavated and recorded, the account of the repatriation indicates that Brown responded cautiously. He consulted with Lloyd Wilcox, the Narragansett medicine man, who provided him with instructions about removing the pipe. On Wilcox's advice, Brown placed cedar bark, a sprig of spruce, and a small piece of purple quahog shell in the pit containing the pipe and sprinkled some liquid around it. After the burial was mapped and photographed for posterity, John Brown made several incantations and gestures, and then removed the pipe and returned it the Narragansett people. He said that he was "pleased by the pipe and disturbance [the intrusive pit]: it was part of a ceremony, it completes the picture."

The Narragansetts had reclaimed an object of cultural patrimony that had long ago been placed in the temporary custody of the ancestors buried at RI-1000. This was a pipe that these ancestors and others had smoked on many occasions. It served as a vehicle for communication between them and with those already in the community of ancestors. Thus, the pipe connected members of Narragansett communities, even as they were fragmented, displaced, and relocated from the places of their former homelands. In 1983 as before, the carved pipe served as a visible reminder of their history and their continuing cultural identity. Yet their

Figure 32. Molly Ross, widow of Toby Ross and a descendant of Ninigret I. She claimed to be "the last pure bred Narragansett" and died in 1866 at the age of 83. According to William B. Weeden, the photograph was taken at Westerly in 1863. (Courtesy of the Rhode Island Historical Society)

claims to the pipe have been questioned, scrutinized in the name of objectivity, and labeled as spurious and insincere.[79] In addition, the repatriation ceremony itself has been suspected of being invented rather than handed down or simply "traditional." These opinions should come as no surprise, given the responses to the Narragansetts' efforts to reclaim their heritage in the past. Perhaps it was in their best interest to orchestrate the pipe's repatriation in a way that evoked elements of continuity and antiquity. They were after all expected to retain and adhere to their cultural practices unchangingly, because too much flexibility would also invite intense criticism.[80] For the Narragansetts, and for other Native peoples in New England, memories of these sorts of conflicts are the means through which they preserve and share knowledge of how their ancestors survived, maintained and enriched traditions, and nurtured enduring identities in homeland after homeland.[81] They recall a much richer, more complicated, and indeed, longer story about their struggles to survive in the wake of colonialism than the one predicted from Williams's *A Key*.

EPILOGUE

Although veiled in silences, the graves of the individuals buried at RI-1000 were never actually forgotten. Strands of textual and archaeological evidence braided with community memories have revealed enduring attachments and continuing involvement on the part of Narragansett peoples that cannot be explained by sudden surges of ancestor worship. Instead, these graves tell of communal and generational relationships that were maintained despite the many uncertainties of colonialism. Their material patterns supply evidence of traditions that imply something other than a strictly random pattern of life by underscoring learned social knowledge and order carved within a changing and chaotic world. These were proper burials, suggesting that these individuals had not been rushed into oblivion at death or even after. Years and even decades later, their descendants still remembered and, as the archaeological evidence has indicated, sometimes kept in direct contact with them.

In a variety of ways, telling about the lives and deaths of these individuals illustrates the difficulties and complexities of cultural translation. As the new century begins, the challenge for archaeologists, and other researchers, is not only to understand the problems of translating past lives, which are surely multifaceted and incredibly intricate, but also to show that there is indeed a past that can be known. The knowable past is not just a matter of pious patriotism or cultural victimhood. It is the past that has always been there, and though aspects of it may be unsettling and perhaps will make some uncomfortable, it is worth knowing.

In the past decade or so, a growing number of archaeologists along with other scholars have studied the histories and identities of the diverse peoples affected by the global processes set in motion by colonialism. These investigations have called attention to the existence of different pasts. By substituting multiple, and conflicting, accounts for a single comprehensive one, they have offered views of culture contact and colonialism from different angles. Although there is a sense that the notion of multiple pasts is preferable to the illusion of consensus, it has its drawbacks.

In many respects, the emphasis on separate pasts has led to considerable confusion. With so many different possibilities, can all be right? If all are equally plausible, then what are the epistemological and practical implications? Is it conceivable that the recognition of multiple pasts, none "objectively" judged to be any better than the other, may unwittingly victimize the peoples whose histories researchers have attempted to reaffirm? Has it obscured important intersections in the lives and experiences of peoples of diverse cultural affiliations, social classes, genders, and ages in colonial situations? Moreover, have these investigations lost sight of the frustrations, struggles, and indeed, discontent among colonized peoples, both in the past and continuing today?

In facing the current challenges of cultural translation, it is also important to reconsider what has been assumed in the emphasis sometimes given to the construction of Native-centered, and more specifically, "Indian" histories. One approach proposes to retrieve some semblance of what was meaningful in Native peoples' lives by reading between the lines in texts written by the colonists; another argues for using a different script entirely in attempting to represent them more in their own terms. Both have been tried, but the results have not been unproblematic. A central claim of this study is that the reconstruction of the lives of Native peoples in colonial situations necessarily involves the use of different strands of evidence, rather than just a single strand. Each strand has its partialities, ambiguities, and complexities and thus poses problems of translation. Yet each pathway to understanding may intersect and overlap others in ways that may lead to unexpected insights about Native peoples' experiences in the context of colonial relations.

Additionally, these ideas about cultural translation also call into question some of the assumptions that have driven collaborative research between Native groups and archaeologists. Conventionally, archaeologists talk to Native peoples to obtain specific answers to particular questions. For example, why were no infants under the age of three buried in the communal cemetery? Did the pipe oddly placed in an intrusive pit have special meaning? Why was the orientation of a certain grave unlike the rest? Was there a pattern to how weavers arranged the shell and glass beads frequently found clustered together? Sometimes questions like these, even in the most alienating contexts, receive direct answers that may reveal earned cultural and social knowledge about tribal ways or illuminate artistic traditions. In other instances, responses may be less forthcoming, because a person speaking for and from a Native culture to an outsider may not always be willing or empowered to do so.

More often what is learned from collaborations with Native peoples comes from ongoing conversations that start and stop, only to resume again much later. These conversations may encompass all sorts of ideas, including thoughts about Native peoples' lives and struggles. At the time, some of the issues raised may seem to be tangential and, often enough, repetitive. Yet these conversations, even their occasional lulls, may prove to be informative in communicating how outsiders might come to different understandings. Thus they make the non-Native researcher pause, take a step back, and consider alternative possibilities not previously considered. So even imperfectly, these off-and-on-again conversations teach about Native peoples' history and, especially, about the injustices and conflicts that were and still are a part of their everyday lives.

The story of the people buried at RI-1000 is remarkable because it challenges many prevailing assumptions about the Narragansetts in the seventeenth century and long after. With all that happened and all that followed, the Narragansetts could not be done away with so easily. Even when English colonists and European Americans decided that erasure was a desirable solution, they persisted. Even in death, those buried in this ancestral cemetery continued to be connected to their descendants. Surely, the living may have had lapses, when they suspended direct contact with the ancestors' burial place, but only temporarily. Other circumstances may have intervened, did, and will most certainly continue to do so. So even now, while these long-deceased kin await reburial as they have since 1984 (one year after the completion of the excavations), their story continues, as they are very much a part of the Narragansetts' ongoing history. At the request of the tribe, these ancestral remains are being held in a temporary repository in Providence, each in an acid-free cardboard box, until they can be properly reinterred, presumably in the cemetery behind the Narragansett Indian Church on the reservation in Charlestown. No date has been set for the reburial ceremony, but neither has the repository become a place of grave remembrances.

INVENTORY OF OBJECTS FROM RI-1000

| | | | Artifacts | |
Age	Burial	Sex	Beads and Other Ornaments	Other Objects
3	10	?	Bracelet, glass	Apothecary jar, tin glazed
			Bracelet, shell	Bell fragments, brass
			Headband, shell with glass closure	Hoe, iron
				Spoon, latten, slipped stem
				Swivel (?), iron
3	11	?	Bracelet, glass and brass	Bottle, glass medicine
				Hoe, iron
				Spoon, latten
3	33	?	None	Spoon, latten seal top
3	34	?	Earring (?), shell	None
3	37	?	Belt or girdle, glass	Bells, brass (hawk's bells) (11)
			Bracelet, brass	Container fragments, brass
			Bracelet, brass incised	Container fragments, iron
			Bracelet, glass and shell	Misc. fragments, mica and brass
			Earring, shell	Spoon, brass
			Epaulet, glass	Spoon, latten, seal top
			Necklaces, glass and shell (3)	Spoons, latten, slipped stem (2)
			Pouch, glass	
4	13	?	None	None
4	21	?	Headband, brass	None
			Hoops, brass with shell (10)	

			Artifacts	
Age	Burial	Sex	Beads and Other Ornaments	Other Objects
4	36	?	Bracelet, shell Buttons, cast metal (5) Buttons, glass (5) Headband, shell	Ceramic, Native Scissors, iron Spoon, latten, seal top
4	42	?	None	Nails, wrought iron, rosehead (3) Saw blade, iron
7	24	?	Bracelet, glass and shell Misc. glass	Bells, brass (hawk's bells) (2)
7	41	?	Buttons, lead, Native (13)	Clip, brass
11	14	F?	Fragment, shell	None
13	30	F?	None	None
13	39	F?	None	Cup or box fragments, brass Knife handle, antler/bone Spoon, latten, seal top
14	19	F?	Glass Rings, brass, Jesuit "IHS I" (3) Ring, brass, Jesuit "L-heart IV"	Nodule, graphite Spoons, latten, short seal (2)
15	22	F?	Comb, brass Headband, brass and shell Necklace, glass, shell, and brass Ring, brass wire	Bottle, glass Nodule, graphite with animal effigy Object, brass with cordage Scissors, iron Spoon, latten Spoon, Native/English
15	40	F?	Bracelet, glass Bracelet, shell Necklace, glass and shell	Bottle, glass, medicine Cup, tin glazed
15	47	F?	Bracelet, glass	Bottles, glass (2)
15	49	F?	Shell	None
16	3	M	Comb fragments, carved bone Headband, shell	Axe, iron Button mold, stone Knives, iron blade, wooden handle (3) Spoon fragments, brass Spoon, brass
16	17	F	Hoops, brass (2) Ring, brass, signet Ring fragments, brass	Bottles, glass (3) Clips, brass (2) Hooks, iron (5) Kettle, iron lug with legs Mirror box, wooden Spoon, brass with animal effigy
17	26	F	None	None
20	18	F	Necklace, brass and glass Rings, brass, Jesuit "IHS I" (4) Ring, brass, Jesuit "double heart"	Apothecary jar, tin glazed Box fragments, brass

			Artifacts	
Age	Burial	Sex	Beads and Other Ornaments	Other Objects
			Ring, brass, Jesuit "L-heart"	
			Ring, brass, signet	
			Ring, brass, signet "asterisk"	
22	16	M	None	Container, iron
24	29	F	Necklace, glass and shell	Bottle, glass
				Spoon, latten, seal top
26	48	F	Necklace, brass	Clip, brass
				Disk? glass
				Nail fragments, iron
				Nail, iron, flathead
				Spoon, latten, slipped stem
28	15	M	Rings, brass, Jesuit "IHS I" (3)	Abrader, grooved
			Rings, brass, Jesuit "L-heart" (2)	Abrader/whetstone
			Rings, brass, Jesuit "L-heart-IV"	Adze, iron
				Ceramic, Native
				Cylinders, lead (4)
				Fragments, brass
				Hoe, iron
				Musket ball, lead
				Nodules, graphite (3)
				Pipe, European
				Rod, iron
				Spoon, brass
28	25	M	None	Knife, wooden handle
				Muxes, iron (approx. 10)
				Pipe, English
28	38	M	Headband, shell	Abrader, groundstone
				Adze/chisel, iron, reworked
				Claw hammer, iron
				Flint/gunflint
				Fragments, brass (cache?)
				Horseshoe fragment, iron
				Knife, iron blade, wooden handle
				Knife, iron blade and tang
				Nails, iron, rosehead (2)
				Pintle, iron
				Pipes, English (3)
				Rod fragment, iron, reworked
				Spike, iron
				Spoon, brass
				Swivel, iron
				Wedges, iron, reworked (3)
29	28	F	None	Ceramic, Native

			Artifacts	
			---	---
Age	Burial	Sex	Beads and Other Ornaments	Other Objects
				Nodules, graphite
				Kettle, brass
33	2	M	Buckle, brass, double	Nail, iron, rosehead
			Headband, brass	Nails, iron (5)
			Ring, brass, signet	Pipe, English
			Ring, brass, "set"	Spoon, latten, seal top
33	35	F	None	Hooks, iron (5)
38	43	F	None	None
39	44	M	None	Kettle, brass
				Knife, wooden handle
				Wedge, iron
42	51	F	None	Bails, iron (2)
				Hoe, iron
				Kettles, brass (2)
				Knife, iron, antler/bone handle
				Pan, brass
				Pestle, stone
				Rods, iron, reworked (2)
				Spoon, latten, slipped stem
43	8	M	None	Fragments, brass
				Fragments/strips, iron
				Pipe, English (2)
				Scissors, iron
43	9	F	None	Awl or mux, iron
				Spoon, brass
43	12	F	None	Disk, glass with metal
43	45	F	None	None
43	46	F	None	None
43	50	M	None	Pipe, clay, Native
				Pipe, English
48	20	M	None	None
48	52	M	None	Container, iron
53	23	F	None	None
57	31	F	None	Hoe, iron
58	32	F	None	Awl tip, iron
				Hoe, iron
				Pestle, stone

Forty-six graves are listed in the inventory. One additional grave, Burial 27, appeared to be intact but contained no human remains and associated artifacts. Nine other graves (Burials 1, 4, 5, 6, 7, 53, 54, 55, and 56) were either wholly or partially disturbed by bulldozing and are not included in the inventory. Burials 2, 3, and 49 also exhibited some damage as a result of the bulldozing but possessed enough integrity to be included in the study. The ages listed in the inventory are mean ages or best estimates.

ADOLESCENTS' AND
ADULT WOMEN'S OBJECTS

		Artifacts	
Age	Burial	Beads and Other Ornaments	Other Objects
14	19	Glass	Nodule, graphite
		Rings, brass	Spoons (2)
15	22	Comb, brass	Bottle
		Headband, brass and shell	Nodule, graphite with animal effigy
		Necklace, glass, shell, and brass	Object, brass with cordage
		Ring, brass	Scissors
			Spoons (2)
15	40	Bracelet, glass	Bottle
		Bracelet, shell	Cup, tin glazed
		Necklace, glass and shell	
15	47	Bracelet, glass	Bottles (2)
15	49	Shell	None
16	17	Hoops, brass (2)	Bottles (3)
		Ring, brass	Clips (2)
		Ring fragments, brass	Hooks (5)
			Kettle
			Mirror box
			Spoon, brass with animal effigy
17	26	None	None
20	18	Necklace, brass and glass	Apothecary jar, tin glazed
		Rings, brass (8)	Box, brass

		Artifacts	
Age	Burial	Beads and Other Ornaments	Other Objects
24	29	Necklace, glass and shell	Bottle
			Spoon
26	48	Necklace, brass	Clip
			Disk?
			Spoon
			[Nail and nail fragments]
29	28	None	Ceramic, Native
			Nodules, graphite
			Kettle
14	19	Glass	Nodule, graphite
		Rings, brass	Spoons (2)
33	35	None	Hooks (5)
38	43	None	None
42	51	None	Bails (2)
			Hoe
			Kettles (2)
			Knife, iron, antler bone handle
			Pan
			Pestle
			Rods (2)
			Spoon
43	9	None	Awl or mux
			Spoon
43	12	None	Disk
43	45	None	None
43	46	None	None
53	23	None	None
57	31	None	Hoe
58	32	None	Awl tip
			Hoe
			Pestle

ADULT WOMEN'S AND MEN'S OBJECTS

Women

Age	Burial	Personal Ornament	Kettle	Hook	Hoe	Pestle	Awl/ Mux	Knife	Spoon	Abrader	Adze/ Wedge	Pipe	Other
29	28		X										X
33	35			X									
42	51		X		X	X		X	X				X
43	9						X		X				
43	12												X
57	31				X								
58	32				X	X	X						

Men

Age	Burial	Personal Ornament	Kettle	Hook	Hoe	Pestle	Awl/ Mux	Knife	Spoon	Abrader	Adze/ Wedge	Pipe	Other
22	16												X
28	15	X			X			X	X	X		X	X
28	25						X	X				X	
28	38	X						X	X	X		X	X
33	2	X							X			X	X
39	44		X					X			X		
43	8											X	X
43	50											X	
48	52												X

PLAN OF RI-1000

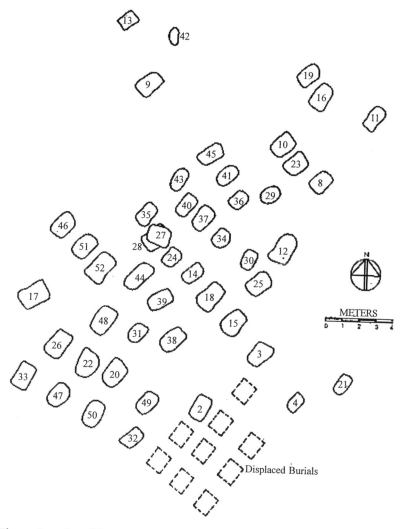

Displaced Burials

Electronic version of figure 2, p. 115, in Paul A. Robinson, Marc A. Kelly, and Patricia E. Rubertone, "Preliminary Biocultural Interpretations from a Seventeenth-Century Narragansett Indian Cemetery in Rhode Island," in *Cultures in Contact*, ed. William W. Fitzhugh (Washington, D.C.: Smithsonian Institution Press, 1985)

NOTES

Introduction

1. John J. Teunissen and Evelyn J. Hinz, "Introduction," in Roger Williams, *A Key Into the Language of America*, ed. John J. Teunissen and Evelyn J. Hinz (Detroit: Wayne State University Press, 1973), 29.

2. Carmel Schrire, *Digging through Darkness: Chronicles of an Archaeologist* (Charlottesville and London: University Press of Virginia, 1995), 3.

3. See, for example, James Deetz, *In Small Things Forgotten: The Archaeology of Early American Life* (Garden City, N.Y.: Anchor Press, 1977); Kent G. Lightfoot, Antoinette Martinez, and Ann M. Schiff, "Daily Practices and Material Culture in Pluralistic Social Settings: An Archaeological Study of Culture Change and Persistence from Fort Ross, California," *American Antiquity* 63, no. 2 (1998): 199–222; Janet D. Spector, *What This Awl Means: Feminist Archaeology at a Wahpeton Dakota Village* (St. Paul: Minnesota Historical Society Press, 1993).

4. David William Cohen, *The Combing of History* (Chicago and London: University of Chicago Press, 1994); James Clifford, "Fort Ross Meditation," in *Routes: Travel and Translation in the Late Twentieth Century* (Cambridge, Mass., and London: Harvard University Press, 1997); Michael Kammen, *Mystic Chords of Memory: The Transformation of Tradition in American Culture* (New York: Vintage Books, 1993); Williams S. Simmons, *Spirit of the New England Tribes: Indian History and Folklore, 1620–1984* (Hanover and London: University Press of New England, 1986).

5. Roger Williams, *A Key Into the Language of America*, ed. Howard M. Chapin, 5th ed. (1643; Rhode Island and Providence Plantations Tercentenary Committee, 1936), 137.

All subsequent references to the text of *A Key* refer to this edition unless indicated otherwise.

6. For reviews of some early discoveries in Rhode Island, see Howard Chapin, "Indian Graves: A Survey of the Indian Graves That Have Been Discovered in Rhode Island," *Rhode Island Historical Society* [hereafter RIHS] *Collections* 20 (1927): 14–31; Lauren J. Cook, "The Rhode Island Burial Survey. Part 1: A Study in Documentary Site Location," Office of Public Archaeology Report of Investigations, no. 28. Center for Archaeological Studies, Boston University, 1985; Patricia E. Rubertone, "Grave Remembrances: Enduring Traditions among the Narragansett," *Connecticut History* 35, no. 1 (1994): 22–45. For some examples of Native American cemeteries in southern New England that have been excavated or restudied by professional archaeologists, see Elise M. Brenner, "Strategies for Autonomy: An Analysis of Ethnic Mobility in Seventeenth-Century New England" (Ph.D. dissertation, University of Massachusetts, 1984); Susan G. Gibson, ed., *Burr's Hill: A Seventeenth-Century Wampanoag Burial Ground in Warren, Rhode Island,* Studies in Anthropology and Material Culture, vol. 2 (Providence: Haffenreffer Museum of Anthropology, Brown University, 1980); William S. Simmons, *Cautantowwit's House: An Indian Burial Ground on the Island of Conanicut in Narragansett Bay* (Providence, R.I.: Brown University Press, 1970).

1. Making a Life

1. Glenn W. LaFantasie, "A Day in the Life of Roger Williams," *Rhode Island History* 46, no. 3 (1987): 95.

2. A thumbprint of Roger Williams impressed into sealing wax is printed in *RIHS Collections* 14, no. 3 (1921): 65–67. An alleged portrait (Figure 1) was found to be a remodeling of the features of Benjamin Franklin (*RIHS Proceedings,* 1907–1908 [Providence: Printed for the Society, 1908], 44).

3. James D. Knowles, *Memoir of Roger Williams, the Founder of the State of Rhode Island* (Boston: Lincoln, Edmands, 1834), xi.

4. Although some early accounts of Williams's life indicate that he was born in 1599 (Knowles, *Memoir of Roger Williams,* 23), most modern scholars believe that the more accurate estimate is sometime between 1603 and 1605. Samuel H. Brockunier, *The Irrepressible Democrat, Roger Williams* (New York: Ronald Press, 1940), 4; Glenn W. LaFantasie, ed., *The Correspondence of Roger Williams,* 2 vols. (Hanover, N.H., and London: Published for the Rhode Island Historical Society by Brown University Press/University Press of New England, 1988), 1:xciii, 8, 11 fn. 9; Ola E. Winslow, *Master Roger Williams* (New York: Macmillan, 1957), 14–15.

5. Ola Winslow attempts to reconstruct Williams's boyhood by gauging what he might have seen, heard, or otherwise experienced growing up in London during the early seventeenth century. Much of what she says is based not on fact but on conjecture; *Master Roger Williams,* 9–34.

6. Brockunier, *Irrepressible Democrat,* 15; Ola Winslow, *Master Roger Williams,* 51–52.

7. Brockunier, *Irrepressible Democrat,* 15.

8. Brockunier, *Irrepressible Democrat*, 23; Edmund S. Morgan, *Roger Williams: The Church and the State* (New York: Harcourt, Brace and World, 1967).

9. See LaFantasie, *Correspondence of Roger Williams*, 1:1–8; Sydney V. James, "The Worlds of Roger Williams," *Rhode Island History* 37, no. 4 (1978): 99–109.

10. Ola Winslow, *Master Roger Williams*, 95.

11. LaFantasie, *Correspondence of Roger Williams*, 2:750.

12. The treatise, title unknown, is no longer extant; Williams, *A Key*, ed. Teunissen and Hinz, "Introduction," 16. According to LaFantasie, Gov. John Winthrop of Massachusetts Bay summarized and rebutted its main points in a lengthy letter to John Endicott; *Correspondence of Roger Williams*, 1:15.

13. Perry Miller, "Roger Williams: An Essay in Interpretation," in *The Complete Writings of Roger Williams*, ed. Perry Miller (New York: Russell and Russell, 1963), 7:7–8; see also LaFantasie, *Correspondence of Roger Williams*, 1:15. Lawrence C. Wroth ("Roger Williams," Marshall Woods lecture, October 26, 1936, Brown University papers, vol. 14 [Providence, R.I., 1937], 23–25) has argued that Williams's criticism of the impropriety of a European sovereign's right of appropriation over lands of Native peoples in the name of Christianity raised a fundamental human rights problem having "implications for innumerable other issues that arose from the contact between the races."

14. LaFantasie, *Correspondence of Roger Williams*, 1:129.

15. See LaFantasie, *Correspondence of Roger Williams*, 1:12–23, for a discussion of the events leading to Williams's banishment; in *Memoir of Roger Williams*, 64–81, Knowles also provides a detailed account of the proceedings leading to his banishment and the charges against him.

16. In a theological sense, the label "Seeker" is applied to individuals striving for spiritual perfection but unconvinced of the validity of a second baptism. Although there is no evidence to suggest that Williams actually joined a sect known as the "English Seekers," some "in the seventeenth century and beyond found the label to be a convenient way of classifying the unclassifiable"; see Edwin S. Gaustad, *Liberty of Conscience: Roger Williams in America* (Grand Rapids, Mich.: William B. Eerdmans, 1991), 98.

17. His reception, assured through negotiations with Narragansett Bay sachems, probably occurred after the general court sentenced him to banishment, according to LaFantasie, *Correspondence of Roger Williams*, 1:22, fn. 45.

18. See LaFantasie, *Correspondence of Roger Williams*, 1:55–56, fn. 3; Brockunier, *Irrepressible Democrat*, 90.

19. Alfred A. Cave, *The Pequot War* (Amherst: University of Massachusetts Press, 1996), 66; Francis Jennings, *The Invasion of America: Indians, Colonialism, and the Cant of Conquest* (New York and London: W. W. Norton, 1975), 213–214.

20. LaFantasie, "A Day in the Life," 95–111.

21. Brockunier, *Irrepressible Democrat*, 139–152; Gaustad, *Liberty of Conscience*, 59–87.

22. Mary Williams had given birth to a son in September 1638, a daughter in July 1640, and another son in February 1642. Her first two children were daughters. When Roger Williams left for England in 1643, she was pregnant with their sixth child.

23. James, "Worlds of Roger Williams," 103; LaFantasie, *Correspondence of Roger Williams*, 1:141–144.

24. Among these challenges were a patent obtained by William Coddington of Portsmouth for Aquidneck Island, attempts to annex Pawtuxet by interests in Massachusetts, and efforts by Connecticut to extend its borders further into Rhode Island.

25. Williams's sale to Richard Smith included his trading house together "with two Iron guns or murderers, there Lyeing as alsoe my fields & fenscing aboute the s'd House, is alsoe the use of the litle Island for goates which the old Sachem, deceased, Lent me for that use"; James A. Arnold, *The Records of the Proprietors of the Narragansett, Otherwise Called the Fones Record* (Providence: Narragansett Historical Publications, 1894), 93–94.

26. Brockunier, *Irrepressible Democrat*, 200–216; Gaustad, *Liberty of Conscience*, 133–142.

27. Gaustad, *Liberty of Conscience*, 175–188.

28. Ola Winslow, *Master Roger Williams*, 279–280.

29. Brockunier, *Irrepressible Democrat*, 276.

30. See Ola Winslow, *Master Roger Williams*, 280–281; cf. Jill Lepore, *The Name of War: King Philip's War and the Origins of American Identity* (New York: Knopf, 1998), for differing accounts of King Philip's War.

31. James Vose, *Notes on the Transaction of Roger Williams and Others, in Selling Indians into Slavery* (Providence: Rhode Island Historical Society Publications, 1894); William Gammell, *Life of Roger Williams, Founder of the State of Rhode Island* (Boston: Gould, Kendall and Lincoln, 1846), 194. *RIHS Proceedings, 1892–1893* ([1893] 234–238), contains specific information on the provisions established by the committee charged with the disposition of Indian war captives in Rhode Island.

32. Wroth, "Roger Williams," 28.

33. Knowles, *Memoir of Roger Williams*, 348.

34. LaFantasie, *Correspondence of Roger Williams*, 2:777.

35. Benjamin Cushing Harris, "Roger Williams' Funeral," *RIHS Collections* 27, no. 2 (1934): 54. See also Howard M. Chapin, *Report on the Burial Place of Roger Williams*, for a reference to Roger Williams's funeral (Providence: RIHS, 1918), 6.

36. Knowles, *Memoir of Roger Williams*, 354–355.

2. Eulogizing a Hero

1. Howard M. Chapin, *A List of Roger Williams' Writings* (Providence: Preston and Rounds, 1918), 27–28.

2. Zachariah Allen, "Memorial to Roger Williams" (paper read to the RIHS, May 18, 1860, Providence, R.I.).

3. LaFantasie, *Correspondence of Roger Williams*, 1:xlix; Miller, "An Essay in Interpretation," 7:10.

4. Cotton Mather, *Magnalia Christi Americana; or, The Ecclesiastical History of New England*, 7 vols. (London: Printed for Thomas Parkhurst, 1702).

5. William E. Foster, "Early Attempts at Rhode Island History," *RIHS Collections* 7 (1885): 10–11.

6. Williams's ties to the Baptist movement were tenuous. He briefly joined a Baptist congregation in 1639 but soon became dissatisfied with the movement.

7. Gaustad, *Liberty of Conscience,* 203.

8. Stephen Hopkins, "Historical Account of the Planning and Growth of Providence," *RIHS Collections* 7 (1885): 47, cited in LaFantasie, *Correspondence of Roger Williams,* 1:li, fn. 18.

9. Foster, "Early Attempts at Rhode Island History," 11.

10. The bulk of Williams's papers had been preserved in the town clerk's office among the records of the town of Providence. These records were in vast disarray, with most of the documents stuffed into cloth sacks or bound in volumes that showed signs of wear and tear. In 1796 a committee examined the records and recommended that they be transcribed and indexed. Loose papers, including many written by or pertaining to Williams, were left untouched. Many of Williams's documents remained in private hands, mixed among family papers; LaFantasie, *Correspondence of Roger Williams,* 1:liv.

11. Kammen, *Mystic Chords of Memory,* 62.

12. The society solicited information on the following subjects: "1. Topographical sketches of the [Rhode Island] towns and villages, including an account of their soil, agriculture, manufacturing, commerce, natural curiosities and statistics. 2. Sketches of the history of the settlement and rise of such towns and villages, and of the introduction and progress of commerce, manufactures and the arts, in them. 3. Biographical notices of original settlers, revolutionary patriots, and other distinguished men who have resided in this State. 4. Original letters, and documents, and papers illustrating any of these subjects, particularly those which show the private habits, manners, and pursuits of our ancestors, or those connected with the general history of this State. 5. Sermons, orations, occasional discourses and addresses, books, pamphlets, almanacs and newspapers printed in this State, and manuscripts, especially those written by persons born or residing in this State. 6. Accounts of the Indian tribes which formerly inhabited any part of this State, their numbers and condition when first visited by whites, their general character and peculiar customs and manners, their wars and treaties and their original grants to our ancestors. 7. The Indian names of the towns, rivers, islands, bays and other remarkable places within this State, and the traditional import of these names. 8. Besides these, the society will receive donations of any other books, pamphlets, manuscripts and printed documents, with which any gentlemen may please to favor them." "Charter and Constitution," *RIHS Collections* 1 (1827): 7–8.

13. William R. Staples, "An Account of the Rhode Island Historical Society," *American Quarterly Register* 11, no. 4 (1839): 362–363.

14. Zachariah Allen, Papers of Zachariah Allen, series 6, box 7, MSS 254, RIHS Manuscript Collections, Providence.

15. In 1842 Thomas W. Dorr, treasurer of the society, and William G. Goddard, one of its trustees, held opposing opinions on the question of extending voting privileges to disenfranchised factory workers. Dorr was the leader of the suffragists; Goddard supported the landholding voters. Because of their differences on this issue, Goddard refused to attend meetings of the society. Dorr, who was making a bid for the Rhode Island governorship, was accused of neglecting his duties as treasurer of the society. Paula M. Brennan, "A History of the Library of the Rhode Island Historical Society of Providence, RI" (master's thesis, Catholic University of America, 1959), 9.

16. Knowles, *Memoir of Roger Williams;* Donald Skaggs, "Roger Williams: His Image in the American Mind" (Ph.D. dissertation, University of Southern California, 1972), 63.

17. Job Durfee, *Whatcheer, Roger Williams in Banishment. A Poem* (Providence: Cranston and Hammond, 1832), 5.

18. The second biography on Roger Williams, written by Romeo Elton, appeared in 1853: *Life of Roger Williams, the Earliest Legislator and True Champion for a Full and Absolute Liberty of Conscience* (Providence: G. H. Whitney, 1853).

19. Knowles, *Memoir of Roger Williams,* ix.

20. Edward W. Coyle, "From Sinner to Saint: A Study of the Critical Reputation of Roger Williams with an Annotated Bibliography of Writings about Him" (Ph.D. dissertation, University of Massachusetts, 1974), 61–62.

21. See Warren I. Susman, "History and the American Intellectual: Uses of a Usable Past," *American Quarterly* 2, no. 2 (1964): 243–263, for discussions of history as a romantic art.

22. George Bancroft, *A History of the United States, from the Discovery of the American Continent to the Present Day,* 10 vols. (Boston: Little, Brown, 1834–1874), vol. 1.

23. From "Testimony as to the Site of the Grave of Roger Williams," memorandum read by Usher Parsons at a RIHS meeting, October 6, 1857; Minutes of the RIHS, records 1845–1861, 2:237, RIHS Archives, vol. 24.

24. Cf. Sidney S. Rider, "Notes on the Grave of Roger Williams," *Book Notes* 24, no. 8 (1907): 59–64. Rider contests assertions that the grave opened at this locality was that of Roger Williams.

25. Allen Papers, 351.

26. Allen, "Memorial to Roger Williams."

27. Allen Papers, 351.

28. Allen, "Memorial to Roger Williams."

29. *Fourteen Weeks Course in Chemistry,* by J. Dorman Steele, printed in 1868, told the story of "Who Ate Roger Williams?" to illustrate the circulation of matter in nature.

30. In 1857 the Providence Association of Mechanics and Manufacturers appropriated the proceeds of a lecture series amounting to one hundred dollars toward the cost of a monument to Roger Williams. The association appointed a committee to raise additional funds through subscriptions, which apparently were not forthcoming.

31. Roger Williams Monument Association, "Record of the Proceedings of the Board of Managers of the Roger Williams Monument Association," June 29, 1860, Roger Williams Monument Association Records, 1860–1960, MSS 692, RIHS Manuscript Collections.

32. RIHS, "Opinion as to the Possibility of Securing the Application of Two Funds, Created for the Purpose of Erecting a Memorial to Roger Williams, to the Erection of a Bronze Statue of Roger Williams on the Platform Upon the South Steps of the State House or Elsewhere on the State House Grounds," Roger Williams Monument Association Records, 1860–1960, MSS 692, RIHS Manuscript Collections.

33. LaFantasie, *Correspondence of Roger Williams,* 1:lxi.

34. LaFantasie, *Correspondence of Roger Williams,* 1:lxi.

35. Publications of the Narragansett Club, 1st ser., 6 vols. (Providence, R.I., 1866–1874).

36. Henry B. Anthony, *The Rhode Island Statues in the Capitol: Remarks of Hon. Henry B. Anthony, on the Presentation of the Statue of Maj. Gen. Greene, January 20, 1870, and the Presentation of the Statue of Roger Williams, January 9, 1972, by the State of Rhode Island to the Congress of the United States* (Washington, D.C.: F. & J. Rives and C. A. Bailey, 1[8]72).

37. "Ceremonies at the Unveiling of the Monument to Roger Williams" (1877), Roger Williams Monument Association Records, 1860–1960, MSS 692, p. 11, RIHS Manuscript Collections.

38. Robert Freeman and Vivienne Lasky, *Hidden Treasures, Public Sculpture in Providence* (Providence: Published for the Rhode Island Publications Society by the Rhode Island Bicentennial Foundation, 1980), 63.

39. Kammen, *Mystic Chords of Memory*, 196. For discussions of the crisis of Puritanism in the late nineteenth century, see Kammen, *Mystic Chords of Memory*; Susman, "History and the American Intellectual"; and Warren I. Susman, *Culture as History: The Transformation of American Society in the Twentieth Century* (New York: Pantheon Books, 1984).

40. Charles Francis Adams, *Massachusetts: Its Historians and Its History; An Object Lesson* (Boston: Houghton, Mifflin, 1893).

41. *RIHS Proceedings, 1893–1894*, n.s. (1894), 2:24–29.

42. *RIHS Proceedings, 1872–1873* (1873), 37–38; *RIHS Proceedings, 1901–1902* (1903), 44.

43. Freeman and Lasky, *Hidden Treasures, Public Sculpture in Providence*, 27; *RIHS Publications*, n.s., vol. 6, no. 3 (1898): 165; Elizabeth Warren, "Roger Williams Landmarks, Memorabilia, Writings, Memorials, Selected References" (July 1968), typescript, RIHS.

44. *RIHS Publications*, n.s., vol. 6, no. 4 (1899): 236–237; *RIHS Proceedings, 1906–1907* (1909), 24.

45. *RIHS Publications*, n.s., vol. 7, no. 1 (1899): 18–20.

46. For discussions of Puritanism in the 1920s, see Kammen, *Mystic Chords of Memory*; Susman, "History and the American Intellectual" and *Culture as History*; and Frederick Hoffman, *Marginal Manners* (Evanston, Ill.: n.p., 1962), cited in Susman, *Culture as History*, 170–171.

47. Vernon L. Parrington, *Main Currents in American Thought; an Interpretation of American Literature from the Beginnings to 1920* (New York: Harcourt, Brace, 1927–1930).

48. RIHS, "Roger Williams' Tablet in the Hall of Fame," *RIHS Collections* 14, no. 3 (1921): 65.

49. *Hand-Book of the Hall of Fame*, no. 1 (New York: Publications of the Hall of Fame, 1920), 8.

50. Statement on the design of the Williams sculpture in the Hall of Fame is taken from Coyle, "From Sinner to Saint," 145.

51. Chapin, "Introduction," in Williams, *A Key Into the Language*.

52. Miller, "An Essay in Interpretation," 7:9.

53. Warren, "Roger Williams Landmarks."

54. John W. Haley, "The Grave of Roger Williams," *The Old Stone Bank*, History of Rhode Island (Providence: Providence Institute for Savings, 1944), 4:60.

55. Roger Williams Monument Association Records, 1860–1960, MSS 692, RIHS Manuscript Collections.

56. Brockunier, *Irrepressible Democrat*.

57. Samuel H. Brockunier, "Roger Williams and the Democratic Faith" (address delivered in the exercises at the dedication of the Roger Williams monument, Prospect Terrace, Congdon Street, Providence, R.I., June 29, 1939, held by the Rhode Island Roger Williams Memorial Association), Roger Williams Monument Association Records, 1860–1960, MSS 692, RIHS Manuscript Collections.

58. Perry Miller, "An Essay in Interpretation," 10.

59. Perry Miller, "An Essay in Interpretation," 10.

60. Ola Winslow, *Master Roger Williams*, 290.

61. Ola Winslow, *Master Roger Williams*, 291.

62. The reference to the statue of Williams in the memorial on Prospect Terrace as "the serene grey giant" comes from James, "Worlds of Roger Williams," 108.

63. Patricia E. Rubertone and Joan Gallagher, *Archaeological Site Examination: A Case Study in Urban Archaeology, Roger Williams National Memorial, Rhode Island,* Cultural Resources Management Study, no. 4 (Washington, D.C.: Cultural Resources Management Division, North Atlantic Regional Office, National Park Service, U.S. Department of the Interior, 1981); see also Patricia E. Rubertone, "An Approach to Archaeology of the City: The Roger Williams National Memorial Project" and "Urban Land Use and Artifact Deposition: An Archaeological Study of the Change in Providence, Rhode Island," in *Archaeology of Urban America: The Search for Pattern and Process,* ed. Roy S. Dickens Jr. (New York: Academic Press, 1982), 19–39, 117–140.

64. As of 1972, more than three hundred publications had been written about Roger Williams (Coyle, "From Sinner to Saint"). Since that time, other works have been published, including a two-volume set of Williams's letters (LaFantasie, *Correspondence of Roger Williams*). The latter stands as the most definitive work on Williams published to date.

65. Ola Winslow, *Master Roger Williams*, 2.

3. Acclaiming a Canon

1. Williams's publications include *A Key Into the Language of America* (London: Printed by Gregory Dexter, 1643), *Mr. Cottons Letter Lately Printed, Examined and Answered* (London, 1644), *The Bloudy Tenent of Persecution* (London, 1644), *Queries of Highest Consideration* (London, 1644), *Christenings Make Not Christians* (1645), *The Bloudy Tenent Yet More Bloudy* (London: Printed for Giles Calvert, 1652), *The Hireling Ministry None of Christs* (London: Printed by Giles Calvert, 1652), *The Examiner Defended* (1652), *Experiments of Spiritual Life and Health* (London, 1652), and *George Fox Digg'd out of His Burrowes* (Boston: Printed by John Foster, 1676).

2. LaFantasie, *Correspondence of Roger Williams,* 1:159.

3. LaFantasie, *Correspondence of Roger Williams,* 1:14–16; Teunissen and Hinz, "Introduction," 16.

4. Brockunier, *Irrepressible Democrat,* and "Roger Williams and the Democratic Faith"; James Ernst, *Roger Williams: The New England Firebrand* (New York: Macmillan, 1931), 12; Gaustad, *Liberty of Conscience.*

5. Robert L. McCarron has classified Williams's published works into three stylistic types: controversial treatises, instructional works, and devotional tracts; "Some Considerations of Style and Rhetoric in the Writings of Roger Williams" (Ph.D. dissertation, Indiana University, 1980). The majority of Williams's published works are controversial treatises.

6. Alvar Núñez Cabeza de Vaca, *Relation of Alvar Nuñez Cabeça de Vaca,* trans. Buckingham Smith (1542; Albany, N.Y.: J. Munsell for H. C. Murphy, 1871); Bernardino de Sahagún, *Florentine Codex: General History of the Things in New Spain,* trans. Arthur J. O. Anderson and Charles E. Dibble, 12 vols. (1577; Santa Fe, N.M.: School of American Research and University of Utah, 1950–1982); and Gabriel Sagard, *Dictionnaire de la langue Huronne* (Paris: Denys Moreau, 1632).

7. James H. Trumbull describes *A Key* as containing 224 inclusive of the title leaf, whereas others indicate that it has 216 pages including the preface and table of contents ("Preface," in Roger Williams, *A Key Into the Language of America* [1643], ed. James H. Trumbull, Publications of the Narragansett Club, 6 vols., first ser., RIHS Manuscript Collections [Providence, 1866] 1:70). He states that "an error in the pagination makes the apparent number of pages less by eight, than the actual number."

8. Wroth ("Roger Williams") as well as Teunissen and Hinz ("Introduction") comment on, and offer specific examples of, the typographical errors contained in the original edition of *A Key.*

9. See LaFantasie, *Correspondence of Roger Williams,* 1:xxvii–xxviii, for a discussion of Williams's use of language.

10. The term "bloudy" in the title indicted the doctrine giving civil magistrates authority to persecute innocent people on religious grounds, but it also referred to the unnecessary bloodshed such actions might cause; Gaustad, *Liberty of Conscience,* 85.

11. Kathleen D. March, "Uncommon Civility: The Narragansett and Roger Williams." (Ph.D. dissertation, University of Iowa, 1985), 141.

12. March, "Uncommon Civility," 141–142; Teunissen and Hinz, "Introduction," 29.

13. Williams, *A Key Into the Language,* ed. Chapin, A2.

14. Williams, *A Key Into the Language,* ed. Chapin A2.

15. Williams, *A Key Into the Language,* ed. Chapin, A2.

16. Opinions differ concerning this treatise. Teunissen and Hinz ("Introduction," 20) suggest that it was published in 1645 as *Christenings Make Not Christians* (Providence: S. S. Rider, 1881).

17. See McCarron, *Style and Rhetoric in the Writings of Roger Williams;* Teunissen and Hinz, "Introduction"; John J. Teunissen and Evelyn J. Hinz, "Roger Williams, Thomas More, and the Narragansett Utopia," *Early American Literature* 11 (1976–1977): 281–295; and Joan C. Searles, "The Worlds of Roger Williams," (Ph.D. dissertation, Pennsylvania State University, 1971) for discussions of *A Key* from a literary standpoint.

18. Williams, *A Key Into the Language,* ed. Chapin, A4.

19. As I understand it, licensing was supposed to protect the press, rather than the author. Copyright laws protecting authors did not exist in England until 1710; see Phillip Gaskell, *A New Introduction to Bibliography* (Winchester, Eng.: St. Paul's Bibliographies; New Castle, Del.: Knoll Press, 1995), 183–184.

20. See W. W. Greg (*Some Aspects and Problems of London Publishing between 1550 and 1660*, Lyell Lectures, Oxford University, Trinity Term, 1955 [Oxford: Clarendon Press, 1956]) for a discussion of licensing under the provisions of an Order of the Lords and Commons, June 14, 1643. It should be noted, however, that despite such official decrees about entering copies of books into the register of the Stationers' Company before publication, not all printers complied.

21. Brockunier, *Irrepressible Democrat*, 146, fn. 18; see James Ernst ("Roger Williams and the English Revolution," *RIHS Collections* 24 [1931]: 1–58) for further discussion of opinions held by English civil and religious leaders about *A Key* and its effects on Williams's reputation as a missionary.

22. Ernst (*Roger Williams, New England Firebrand*, 50) states that Thomas Thoroughgood (or Thorowgood) quoted from and copiously paraphrased *A Key* in his pamphlet *Jews in America* (Thomasin Collection, E-600 [London: British Museum, May 6, 1651], 5, 81), in which he argued that the American Indians were Jews. His conclusions were challenged in a pamphlet written by Hamon L'Estrange that very year (*Americans no Jews*, Thomasin Collection, E-643 [London: British Museum, October 5, 1651]). L'Estrange drew on *A Key* and other works to disprove Thoroughgood's conclusions. According to Ernst, his pamphlet is "full of uninformed nonsense set out with much pedantry."

23. William Wood, *New England's Prospect*, ed. Alden T. Vaughan (1634; Amherst: University of Massachusetts Press, 1977), 110.

24. John Winthrop, cited in Trumbull, "Editor's Preface," 73; Cotton Mather, cited in Trumbull, "Editor's Preface," 70.

25. Teunissen and Hinz ("Introduction," 24–25) suggest that the Massachusetts Historical Society left out some sections of *A Key* to illustrate the persistent biases of the descendants of the first Puritans of Massachusetts. See also Coyle, "From Sinner to Saint," 34.

26. Roger Williams, *A Key Into the Language of America*, *RIHS Collections* 1 (1643; Providence: John Miller, 1827).

27. The society's 1827 edition of *A Key* was printed largely from an original obtained from the Bodleian Library.

28. RIHS, "Report in Reference to *A Key to the American Language* by the Publication Committee," n.d., Correspondence and Reports, vol. 1 (July 1822–September 1838), RIHS Archives, vol. 59.

29. RIHS, "Report of the Board of Trustees, July 21, 1829," Records (Minutes), 1822–1844, vol. 1, RIHS Archives, vol. 23.

30. William Staples to Henry R. Schoolcraft, April 29, 1828, Correspondence and Reports, vol. 1 (July 1822–September 1838), RIHS Archives, vol. 59.

31. Schoolcraft to the RIHS, August 10, 1828, Correspondence and Reports, vol. 1.

32. Sidney S. Rider, *Elisha Reynolds Potter, Late Judge of the Supreme Court of Rhode Island, An Address Delivered before the Rhode Island Historical Society, July 11, 1882* (Pawtucket: Press of the Chronicle Printing, 1905), 6–7.

33. Elisha R. Potter, "The Early History of Narragansett," *RIHS Collections* 3 (1835): 9.

34. LaFantasie, *Correspondence of Roger Williams*, 2:723.

35. Potter, "Early History of the Narragansett," 9.

36. Rider, *Elisha Reynolds Potter,* 6–7.

37. Williams, *A Key Into the Language,* ed. Chapin, 5. See, for example, Wilkins Updike, *History of the Episcopal Church, in Narragansett, Rhode Island; including a History of Other Episcopal Churches in the State; With an Appendix, Containing a Reprint of a Work Now Extremely Rare Entitled, "America Dissected," by Rev. Mac Sparran, D.D., with Notes Containing Genealogical and Biographical Accounts of Distinguished Men, Families, etc.* (New York: Henry M. Onderdonk, 1847), xi.

38. John De Forest, *History of the Indians of Connecticut from the Earliest Known Period to 1850* (Hartford, Conn.: Wm. Jas. Hamenly, 1853).

39. Russell G. Handsman and Neil Asher Silberman, "Critical Perspectives on the Archaeological Alienation of Palestinian and Algonkian Indian Histories" (paper presented at the annual meeting of the Society for Historical Archaeology, Richmond, Va., January 1991).

40. De Forest, *History of the Indians of Connecticut,* vi.

41. De Forest questioned projections that suggested that the Narragansetts could furnish 3,000 or even 5,000 fighting men. He dismissed them as the product of the colonists' heightened fears and anxieties about the strength of the hostile Narragansetts on the eve of King Philip's War. A far more reasonable estimate of the number of warriors would not have exceeded 2,000. See De Forest (*History of the Indians of Connecticut,* 63–64) for discussion.

42. De Forest, *History of the Indians of Connecticut,* 63–64.

43. See Simmons, *Spirit of the New England Tribes,* 152.

44. De Forest, *History of the Indians of Connecticut,* 300.

45. De Forest, *History of the Indians of Connecticut,* 300.

46. De Forest, *History of the Indians of Connecticut,* 300.

47. Paul R. Campbell and Glenn W. LaFantasie ("Scattered to the Winds of Heaven—Narragansett Indians 1676–1880," *Rhode Island History* 37 [1978]: 66) trace the outline of the narrative; but see also Colin G. Calloway, ed., *After King Philip's War: Presence and Persistence in Indian New England* (Hanover, N.H., and London: Dartmouth College, published by University Press of New England, 1997).

48. See, for example, Ruth Wallis Herndon and Ella Wilcox Sekatau, "Right to a Name: the Narragansett People and Rhode Island Officials in the Revolutionary Era," *Ethnohistory* 44, no. 3 (1997): 433–462.

49. Besides Potter ("Early History of Narragansett") and De Forest (*History of the Indians of Connecticut*), the only other early history writer to draw on *A Key* in describing the Narragansetts was John Callender, "An Historical Discourse on the Civil and Religious Affairs of Rhode Island," *RIHS Collections* 4 (1739; Providence: Knowles, Vose, 1838).

50. Campbell and LaFantasie, "Scattered to the Winds of Heaven," 76.

51. Rhode Island, Commissioner on the Narragansett Tribe of Indians, *Report of the Commissioner on the Narragansett Tribe of Indians, Made to the General Assembly at its January Session, A.D. 1858* (Providence: Anthony Knowles, 1858), 3.

52. Rueben A. Guild noted that "a merchant of Providence, distinguished for his zeal in collecting books pertaining to the early history of America, has five copies of the origi-

nal 'Key,' all finely bound and in excellent condition." Publications of the Narragansett Club, 6 vols., first ser. (Providence, 1866) 1:56.

53. "Literary Intelligence," n.d., News Clippings of the Narragansett Club, Narragansett Club Records, MSS 578, box 2, folder 7, RIHS Manuscript Collections.

54. Narragansett Club, Proceedings of the Narragansett Club, September 20, 1865, Narragansett Club Records, MSS 578, box 2, folder 5, RIHS Manuscript Collections.

55. Narragansett Club, Narragansett Club Circular, Narragansett Club Records, MSS 578, box 2, RIHS Manuscript Collections.

56. The volume also contained *A Letter of Mr. John Cotton's,* written to Williams to justify his banishment and printed in London in 1643, and Williams's reply. Known as *Mr. Cotton's Letter Lately Printed, Examined and Answered,* the letter was printed in London in 1644.

57. Trumbull, "Editor's Preface," 69.

58. Narragansett Club, Narragansett Club Account Book (1866–1875), Newspaper Clippings and Miscellaneous Records, Narragansett Club Records, MSS 578, box 2, RIHS Manuscript Collections.

59. RIHS, Records, 1862–1880, 3:47–48, RIHS Archives, vol. 26.

60. John Dunton, *John Dunton's Letters from New England. With Notes and an Appendix by W. H. Whitmore* (Boston: Published for the Prince Society, 1867).

61. Peter Murray Hill, *Two Augustan Booksellers: John Dunton and Edmund Curll,* 2d. Library Series, no. 3 (Lawrence: University of Kansas Libraries, 1958), 10.

62. "Critical Notices," *North American Review* (April 1868): 673–690.

63. Dunton, *Letters from New England,* 152–153.

64. Williams, *A Key Into the Language,* ed. Chapin, 13.

65. Whitmore, "Introduction," in Dunton, *Letters from New England.*

66. Whitmore, "Introduction."

67. Whitmore, "Introduction."

68. "Critical Notices," *North American Review,* 677. News clipping of the Narragansett Club, Narragansett Club Records, MSS 578, box 2, folder 7, RIHS Manuscript Collections.

69. Rhode Island, Committee of Investigation on the Narragansett Tribe of Indians, *Report of the Committee of Investigation; A Historical Sketch and Evidence Taken, Made to the House of Representative at its January Session, 1880* (Providence: E. L. Freeman, 1880), 9.

70. Rhode Island, Committee of Investigation, *Report.*

71. Samuel G. Arnold, *History of the State of Rhode Island and Providence Plantations,* 2 vols. (New York and London: D. Appleton, 1874), 2:418.

72. Arnold, *History of the State of Rhode Island,* 2:420.

73. Arnold, *History of the State of Rhode Island,* 1:72–87, 2:420.

74. Frederic Denison, *Westerly and Its Witnesses* (Providence, R.I.: J. A. Reid and R. A. Reid, 1878), 27.

75. Denison, *Westerly and Its Witnesses,* 27.

76. Denison, *Westerly and Its Witnesses,* 27.

77. Rhode Island, Committee of Investigation, *Report,* App. A, 10.

78. For discussions of the importance of Native Americans' attachment to place, see Karen

Blu, *Senses of Place*, ed. Steven Feld and Keith Basso (Sante Fe, N. Mex.: School of American Research Press, 1997), 197–227; Herndon and Sekatau, "Right to a Name"; Jean M. O'Brien, *Dispossession by Degrees: Indian Land and Identity in Natick Massachusetts, 1650–1790* (New York: Cambridge University Press, 1997), 144–161; the quote is from Denison, *Westerly and Its Witnesses*, 27, 29–30.

79. Rhode Island, Committee of Investigation, *Report,* App. A, 14.

80. Rhode Island, Committee of Investigation, *Report,* App. A, 22; but see also Denison, *Westerly and Its Witnesses*, 30.

81. U.S. Department of the Interior, Bureau of Indian Affairs, *General Conclusions, Recommendations and Summary of Evidence for the Proposed Finding for Federal Acknowledgment of the Narragansett Indian Tribe, Pursuant to 25CFR83*, July 29, 1982, Washington, D.C.

82. Rhode Island, Commission on the Affairs of the Narragansett Indians, *Third Annual Report of the Commission on the Affairs of the Narragansett Indians Made to the General Assembly*, January Session, 1883 (Providence: E. L. Freeman, 1883), 7.

83. Rhode Island, Commission on the Affairs of the Narragansett, *Third Annual Report*, 7.

84. Rhode Island, Commission on the Affairs of the Narragansett, *Third Annual Report*, 7.

85. Rhode Island, Commission on the Affairs of the Narragansett Indians, *Fourth Annual Report of the Commission on the Affairs of the Narragansett Indians Made to the General Assembly, January Session, 1884* (Providence: E. L. Freeman, 1884), App. C, 14, 15, and 25.

86. The Reverend Frederic Denison, for example, amassed a sizable collection of Native artifacts from excavations he conducted at various sites in Rhode Island (and possibly from donations as well). In a letter to Stephen Randall dated June 7, 1867, he expressed an interest in giving his "Indian art cabinet" of 190 items—at the time the largest in the state of Rhode Island—to the Roger Williams Monument Association so that it could be "deposited in a suitable alcove within the monument," where it would serve as a "memorial to the Ancient 'What Cheer' that greeted the noble founder of the State" (Roger Williams Monument Association Records, 1860–1960, MSS 692, RIHS Manuscript Collections). In 1878, Denison's cabinet comprised more than 300 objects gathered from sites between New London, Conn., and Newport, R.I. The number of Native artifacts he collected "in prosecuting his historical studies" may have been considerably larger, because he donated 500 pieces to Brown University and 150 to Yale College (Denison, *Westerly and Its Witnesses*, 33).

87. Henry C. Dorr, "Narragansetts," *RIHS Collections* 7 (1885): 138.

88. Dorr, "Narragansetts," 139.

89. Dorr, "Narragansetts," 139.

90. Sidney S. Rider questioned the historical accuracy of statements contained in Dorr's account of the Narragansetts, stating, "There is scarcely a paper ever printed here so utterly rotten in the fundamental statements in it as this by Mr. Dorr" ("Preliminary Note" to "The Character of the Narragansetts As Set Forth by Roger Williams in His Key to the Language of the Natives," *The Lands of Rhode Island as They Were Known to Caunounicus and Miantunnomu When Roger Williams Came in 1636: An Indian Map of the Principal Locations Known to the Nahigansets, and Elaborate Historical Notes*, ed. Sidney S. Rider [Providence: S. S. Rider, 1904], 42).

91. Rider, "Preliminary Note," 2–44.

92. Sidney S. Rider, *Book Notes* 3, no. 9 (August 15, 1885): 58.

93. Thomas W. Bicknell, *The History of the State of Rhode Island and Providence Plantations*, 1 (New York: American Historical Society, 1920), 1:72.

94. Bicknell, *History of the State of Rhode Island*, 1:72.

95. Ann McMullen, "What's Wrong with This Picture? Context, Conversion, Survival, and the Development of Regional Native Cultures and Pan Indianism in Southeastern New England," *Enduring Traditions*, ed. Laurie Weinstein (Westport, Conn.: Bergin and Garvey, 1994), 138.

96. McMullen, "What's Wrong with This Picture?" 140.

97. Bicknell, *History of the State of Rhode Island*, 81.

98. In the first issue of *Narragansett Dawn*, the editor announced that the magazine would publish twelve lessons in Narragansett, one each month, in order to alter the public perception that nothing remained of the Narragansett tongue; Princess Red Wing, ed., *Narragansett Dawn* 1, no. 1 (May 1935): 2–3.

99. Herndon and Sekatau, "Right to a Name," 445–446.

100. Glenn W. LaFantasie and Paul R. Campbell, *Land Controversies and the Narragansett Indians, 1880–1938* (Providence, R.I.: s.n., 1978), 11, 68–69, 72.

101. Chapin was the librarian of the RIHS from 1912 to the time of his death in 1940. During his tenure, he devoted himself to the society and made extensive use of its collections to produce works that have been invaluable to later scholars. Among his publications relating to Roger Williams are *A List of Roger Williams' Writings* (Providence: Preston and Rounds, 1918); an edited volume, *Letters and Papers of Roger Williams 1629–1682* (Boston: Massachusetts Historical Society, 1924), and *The Trading Post of Roger Williams, with Those of John Wilcox and Richard Smith* (Providence: RIHS, E. A. Johnson, 1933). He also wrote the introduction to the 1936 edition of *A Key*. See also "Bibliography of Howard M. Chapin," Howard Millar Chapin Records, MSS 344, RIHS Manuscript Collections; Howard M. Chapin, *Sachems of the Narragansetts* (Providence: RIHS, Roger Williams Press, E. A. Johnson, 1931).

102. William G. Roekler, "Roelker's Personal History of the Society" (1952), 1; RIHS Archives, box 9.

103. Chapin, *Sachems of the Narragansetts*, 103.

104. Herndon and Sekatau, "Right to a Name," 443.

105. Colin G. Calloway, "New England Algonkians in the American Revolution," in *Algonkians of New England: Past and Present*, annual proceedings of the Dublin Seminar for New England Folklife, June 29–30, 1991 (Boston: Boston University, 1993), 51–62.

106. The Narragansetts retribalized as a nonprofit corporation under Rhode Island law in 1934. Membership was open only to persons who could trace descent from individuals who were members of the tribe at the time of the 1880 detribalization; William Simmons, *The Narragansett* (New York: Chelsea House Publishers, 1989), 78. This action, along with participation in pan-Indian associations in the 1920s, were the initial steps taken toward recovering some ancestral lands in the 1970s and petitioning for federal recognition in the 1980s.

107. James Clifford, *The Predicament of Culture: Twentieth-Century Ethnography, Literature, and Art* (Cambridge, Mass., and London: Harvard University Press, 1988), 341.

108. Chapin, "Introduction."

109. See, for example, Simmons, *Cautantowwit's House.*

110. William A. Turnbaugh, "Assessing the Significance of European Goods in Seventeenth-Century Narragansett Society," *Ethnohistory and Archaeology: Approaches to Postcontact Change in the Americas,* ed. J. Daniel Rogers and Samuel M. Wilson (New York and London: Plenum Press, 1993), 133–160; but see also Elise M. Brenner, "Sociopolitical Implications of Mortuary Ritual Remains in Seventeenth-Century Native Southern New England," in *The Recovery of Meaning: Historical Archaeology in the Eastern United States,* ed. Mark P. Leone and Parker B. Potter Jr. (Washington, D.C.: Smithsonian Institution Press, 1988), 147–181.

111. David J. Bernstein, "Prehistoric Seasonality Studies in Coastal Southern New England," *American Anthropologist* 92, no. 2 (1991): 126.

112. Bernstein, "Prehistoric Seasonality," 127, has commented that prehistoric settlement was "more complex, variable over time, and probably not uniform throughout southern New England." Likewise, Lynn Ceci ("Method and Theory in Coastal New York Archaeology: Paradigms of Settlement Pattern," *North American Archaeologist* 3, no. 1 [1982]: 5–36) has argued that occupation of the coast was sparse and infrequent in the late prehistoric period and only became more regular in response to contact (and trade) with Europeans. More recently, Kathleen J. Bragdon (*Native People of Southern New England, 1500–1620* [Norman and London: University of Oklahoma Press, 1996]) has proposed a tripartite model to account for settlement diversity in estuarine, riverine, and upland areas of southern New England.

113. Russell G. Handsman and Trudy Lamb Richmond ("Confronting Colonialism: The Mahican and Schaghticoke Peoples and Us," in *Making Alternative Histories: The Practices of Archaeology and History in Non-Western Settings,* ed. Peter R. Schmidt and Thomas C. Patterson [Santa Fe, Ariz.: School of American Research, 1996], 99) suggest that the emphasis on residential mobility often obscures enduring traditions of settlement and land use among New England's Native peoples.

114. See, for example, William Cronon, *Changes in the Land* (New York: Hill and Wang, 1983).

115. Bruce Trigger, *A History of Archaeological Thought* (New York: Cambridge University Press, 1989), 125; but see also Patricia E. Rubertone, "Matters of Inclusion: Historical Archaeology and Native Americans," in *Current Perspectives on Global Historical Archaeology,* ed. Charles E. Orser, *World Archaeology Bulletin* 7 (1996): 77–86.

4. Casting *A Key*

1. Williams, *A Key Into the Language,* ed. Chapin.

2. George Stocking Jr., "Maclay, Kubray, Malinowski: Archetypes from the Dreamtime of Anthropology," *Colonial Situations: Essays on the Contextualization of Ethnographic Knowledge,* ed. George Stocking Jr., History of Anthropology (Madison: University of

Wisconsin Press, 1991), 7:9–10; for a discussion of Williams as a primitivist, see also Teunissen and Hinz, "Introduction," 121–122.

3. John R. Stilgoe, *Common Landscape of America, 1580–1845* (New Haven, Conn.: Yale University Press, 1982), 10.

4. Roger Williams, June 22, 1670; LaFantasie, *Correspondence of Roger Williams,* 2:610.

5. Ola Winslow, *Master Roger Williams,* 143.

6. Ola Winslow, *Master Roger Williams,* 175.

7. Anne Keary, "Retelling the History of the Settlement of Providence: Speech, Writing, and Cultural Interactions on Narragansett Bay," *New England Quarterly* 64, no. 2 (June 1996): 253.

8. LaFantasie, *Correspondence of Roger Williams,* 2:611.

9. W. H. R. Rivers, "'Report on Anthropological Research Outside America,' Report upon the Present Condition and Future Needs of the Science of Anthropology," ed. W. H. R. Rivers, A. E. Jenks, and S. G. Morley (Washington, D.C.: n.p., 1913), in Stocking, "Maclay, Kubray, Malinowski," 10.

10. See Nicholas Thomas, *Out of Time: History and Evolution in Anthropological Discourse,* 2d ed. (Ann Arbor: University of Michigan Press, 1996).

11. See Lawrence Wroth, *The Voyages of Giovanni da Verrazzano, 1524–1528* (New Haven: Yale University Press, 1970).

12. See Christopher L. Miller and George R. Hamell, "A New Perspective on Indian–White Contact: Cultural Symbols and Colonial Trade," *Journal of American History* 73, no. 2 (1986): 311–328.

13. See T. J. Brasser, "Early Indian–European Contacts," in *Northeast,* ed. Bruce G. Trigger, vol. 15 of *Handbook of North American Indians,* ed. William Sturtevant (Washington, D.C.: Smithsonian Institution Press, 1978), 78–88; Neil Salisbury, *Manitou and Providence: Indians, Europeans, and the Making of New England, 1500–1643* (New York and Oxford: Oxford University Press, 1982).

14. For an account of the provisions brought by the Plymouth colonists in 1620, see Azel Ames, *The Mayflower and Her Log. July 15, 1620–May 6, 1621. Chiefly from Original Sources* (Boston and New York: Houghton Mifflin, Riverside Press, 1907).

15. Cf. Paul A. Robinson, "The Struggle Within: The Indian Debate in Seventeenth Century Narragansett Country" (Ph.D. dissertation, State University of New York, Binghamton, 1990), and Salisbury, *Manitou and Providence,* for different interpretations of this event.

16. David Cressy, *Coming Over: Migration and Communication between England and New England in the Seventeenth Century* (New York: Cambridge University Press, 1987), 68.

17. Estimates of the number of English colonists in New England in 1640 range from about 9,000 (Donald W. Meinig, *Atlantic America 1492–1800,* vol. 1 of *The Shaping of America: A Geographical Perspective on Five Hundred Years of History* [New Haven, Conn., and London: Yale University Press, 1986], 90) to 13,500 (Cressy, *Coming Over,* 70).

18. Cressy, *Coming Over,* 70.

19. Sherburne F. Cook, "The Significance of Disease in the Extinction of the New England Indians," *Human Biology* 45, no. 3 (1973): 487. The term *plague* has been used in

reference to the first recorded epidemic (1616–1619) among the Native people of New England. However, its clinical diagnosis remains uncertain. Although it may have been the bubonic plague, other possibilities have been proposed including yellow fever, typhus, trichinosis, chicken pox, and typhoid fever. Symptoms described in written accounts, especially references to a jaundiced appearance of the afflicted, led Arthur E. Spiess and Bruce D. Spiess ("New England Pandemic of 1616–1622: Cause and Archaeological Implication," *Man in the Northeast* 34 [1987]: 71–83) to suggest infectious hepatitis as the probable cause. Timothy L. Bratton ("The Identity of the New England Indian Epidemic of 1616–1619," *Bulletin of the History of Medicine* 62, no. 3 [1988]: 351–388) has argued in favor of smallpox, although most who have commented on the early post-Contact epidemics of New England Indians indicate that the 1616–1619 disease was not smallpox (e.g., Cronon, *Changes in the Land;* Alfred W. Crosby, *The Columbian Exchange: Biological and Cultural Consequences of 1492* [Westport, Conn.: Greenwood Press, 1972], and *Ecological Imperialism: The Biological Expansion of Europe, 900–1900* [Cambridge and New York: Cambridge University Press, 1986]; Dean R. Snow and Kim M. Lanphear, "European Contact and Indian Depopulation in the Northeast: The Timing of the First Epidemics," *Ethnohistory* 35, no. 1 [1988]: 15–33).

20. Bernard I. Cohen, ed., *Cotton Mather and American Science and Medicine: With Studies and Documents Concerning the Introduction of Inoculation or Variolation* (New York: Arno Press, 1980); Thomas Thacher, *A Brief Rule to Guide the Common-People of New England How to Order Themselves and Theirs in the Small Pocks, or Measles* (1677; Baltimore: John Hopkins Press, 1937); Ola E. Winslow, *A Destroying Angel: The Conquest of Smallpox in Colonial Boston* (Boston: Houghton Mifflin, 1974) all provide excellent discussions of the history of smallpox among the early English colonists.

21. Although the 1616–1619 epidemic did not cross Narragansett Bay, Henry F. Dobyns (*Their Numbers Become Thinned: Native American Population Dynamics in Eastern North America* [Knoxville: University of Tennessee Press, 1983]) suggests that sixteenth-century pandemics spread into New England. In support of his argument, Dobyns cites a letter written by Roger Williams to John Winthrop in 1638. In the letter, Williams states that the Narragansetts told him of a series of earthquakes that occurred around 1568, 1574, 1584, and 1592 (LaFantasie, *Correspondence of Roger Williams*, 1:160). Each was followed within a few years by an epidemic. There is no corroborative evidence for either the earthquakes or the epidemics.

22. See James Mooney (*The Aboriginal Population of America North of Mexico*, Smithsonian Miscellaneous Collections, vol. 8, no. 7 [Washington, D.C.: Smithsonian Institution, 1928], 1–40) for the more conservative estimate of 4,000 and Salisbury (*Manitou and Providence*, 29) for the higher estimate of 35,000–40,000. Salisbury (*Manitou and Providence*, 26, 29) estimates pre-epidemic Narragansett population at 35,000–40,000 by multiplying Daniel Gookin's estimate of 5,000 Narragansett men by a factor of 7.5 (average number of persons per family) on the assumption that the number of men and the number of families were about the same (Gookin, "Historical collections of the Indians in New England," Massachusetts Historical Society Collections, 1st series, 1 [1792], 147–148). Salisbury (*Manitou and Providence*, 26, 29–30) notes that Gookin defined

the Narragansetts as including all of the people living on (1) the shores of Narragansett Bay, except for the Pokanoket village of Sowams near Bristol; (2) the Blackstone drainage; (3) Block Island; and (4) the eastern end of Long Island.

23. Sherburne F. Cook, *The Indian Population of New England in the Seventeenth Century* (Berkeley and Los Angeles: University of California Press, 1976); Crosby, *Ecological Imperialism*; Dobyns, *Their Numbers Become Thinned*; and Snow and Lanphear, "European Contact and Indian Depopulation."

24. Williams indicates that visitation of the sick was common, "unlesse it be infectious diseases, and then all forsake them aud flie, that I have often seene a poore House left alone in the wild Woods, all being fled, the living not able to bury the dead: so terrible is the apprehension of an infectious disease, that not only persons, but the Houses and the whole Towne takes flight"; *A Key Into the Language,* ed. Chapin, 196.

25. Alfred W. Crosby, "Virgin Soil Epidemics as a Factor in the Aboriginal Depopulation in America," *William and Mary Quarterly*, 3d ser., 33, no. 2 (1976): 294.

26. Cook, "Indian Population of New England," 496.

27. Cf. Cronon, *Changes in the Land*.

28. Historian Francis Jennings (*Invasion of America*, 207–208) has gone as far as to suggest that the smallpox epidemic may have provided sufficient motivation for murdering John Oldham, an English trader, whose bloody execution off the shores of Block Island in 1636 is cited as an official cause of the Pequot War. Believing that smallpox had been sent deliberately by the English, the Narragansett may have held Oldham personally responsible as its official carrier, because the epidemic broke out soon after he had made the first recorded overland journey by an Englishman to the upper reaches of the Connecticut River and had lodged at Native villages all along the way.

29. In November 1634, the Narragansetts had tried to persuade Oldham to set up a trading post on Dutch Island in Narragansett Bay (Jennings, *Invasion of America*, 107). Their interest in having Oldham live among them makes it somewhat dubious that they would have had a hand in his murder.

30. For discussions of the Pequot War, and especially the role of the Narragansetts, see Jennings, *Invasion of America*, 259; LaFantasie, *Correspondence of Roger Williams*, 1:187, n. 10; Patrick M. Malone, *The Skulking Way of War: Technology and Tactics among the New England Indians* (Baltimore and London: Johns Hopkins University Press, 1991); Cave, *Pequot War.*

31. Lion Gardiner, "Leift Lion Gardiner His Relation of the Pequot Wares," in *Appendix to the History of the Wars of New England with the Eastern Indians*, ed. Samuel Penhallow (Cincinnati: William Dodge, 1859), 26.

32. Gardiner, "Leift Lion Gardiner," 26.

33. Salisbury, *Manitou and Providence*, 232; Cave, *Pequot War*, 165; David Murray, *Forked Tongues: Speech, Writing, and Representation in North American Indian Texts* (Bloomington and Indianapolis: Indiana University Press, 1991), 44.

34. Cronon, *Changes in the Land*, 163.

35. Williams, *A Key Into The Language*, ed. Chapin, 38, 45, 159–167.

36. Malone, *Skulking Way of Wars.*

37. See Clifford, *Predicament of Culture,* for a discussion of the Mashpee's cultural survival.

38. William S. Simmons, "Cultural Bias in the New England Puritans' Perception of Indians," *William and Mary Quarterly,* 3d ser., 38, no. 1 (1981): 68.

39. Curtis M. Hinsley, *The Smithsonian and the American Indian: Making a Moral Anthropology in Victorian America* (Washington, D.C.: Smithsonian Institution Press, 1981), 191–192.

40. Gaustad, *Liberty of Conscience,* 159.

41. LaFantasie, *Correspondence of Roger Williams,* 1:58.

42. LaFantasie, *Correspondence of Roger Williams,* 1:xxxiii.

43. Ola Winslow, *Master Roger Williams,* 26–27, for a discussion of Williams's early life and factors that might have influenced his decision to participate in the colonization of New England.

44. See Richard Hakluyt, *The Principall Navigations, Voiages and Discoveries of the English Nation* (London: George Bishop and Ralph Newberrie, 1589); John Smith published several accounts of New England, including *A Description of New England* (London: Printed by Humphrey Lownes, for Robert Clerke, 1616); *New England's Trials* (London: Printed by William Jones, 1620 and 1622); and *The Generall Historie of Virginia, New England, and the Summer Isles* (London: Printed by I. D. and I. H. for Michael Sparkes, 1624).

45. Francis Higginson, *New-Englands Plantation; or, A Short and True Description of the Commodities and Discommodities of that Countrey. / Written by a reverend divine now there resident.* (London: Printed by T. C. and R. C. for Michael Sparkes, 1630; Washington, D.C.: P. Force, 1835).

46. Karen O. Kupperman, ed., *Captain John Smith: A Select Edition of His Writings* (Chapel Hill and London: Published for the Institute of Early American History and Culture, Williamsburg, Va., by the University of North Carolina Press, 1988), 8.

47. Cressy, *Coming Over,* 12.

48. Higginson, *New-Englands Plantation,* 12.

49. Higginson, *New-Englands Plantation,* 13.

50. Williams's letters provide some insight into his reading tastes. His own book collection was limited, but he borrowed books, manuscripts, and reports from John Winthrop Jr., who is known to have had one of the best imported libraries in seventeenth-century New England. By 1640 Winthrop's library contained more than a thousand volumes, including works on religion, history, philosophy, law, science, grammar, and travel; see Samuel Eliot Morison, *The Puritan Pronaos: Studies in the Intellectual Life of New England in the Seventeenth Century* (New York: New York University Press, and London: Oxford University Press, 1936), 130–132. See George R. Potter, "Roger Williams and John Milton," *RIHS Collections* 13, no. 4 (1920): 113–129, for a listing of books "surely owned, surely read, and probably or possibly read by" Williams.

51. Wood, *New England's Prospect;* Thomas Morton, "New English Canaan, or New Canaan Containing an Abstract of New England" (Amsterdam: Printed for J. F. Stam, 1637), in *Tracts and Other Papers Relating Principally to the Origin, Settlement, and Progress of the Colonies in North America,* vol. 2 (Washington, D.C.: n.p., 1838).

52. Alden T. Vaughan, "Introduction," in Wood, *New England's Prospect,* 8.

53. Wroth implies that Williams may have assisted Wood in compiling the short vocabu-

lary of Native terms contained in *New England's Prospect* ("Roger Williams," 120). If so, then this lends credence to the suggestion that Williams envisioned *A Key* as different from other accounts of New England Indians.

54. Richard White, *The Middle Ground: Indians, Empires, and Republics in the Great Lakes Region, 1650–1815* (Cambridge and New York: Cambridge University Press, 1991).

55. John Canup, *Out of the Wilderness: The Emergence of an American Identity in Colonial New England* (Middletown, Conn.: Wesleyan University Press, 1990), 105–125; Kupperman, *Captain John Smith;* Daniel B. Shea, "Our Professed Old Adversary": Thomas Morton and the Naming of New England," *Early American Literature* 23 (1988): 52–69; Michael Zuckerman, "Pilgrims in the Wilderness: Community, Modernity, and the Maypole at Merry Mount," *New England Quarterly* 50, no. 1 (1977): 255–277.

56. In a letter written to John Winthrop on July 15, 1637, Williams stated, "'Tis true there is no feare of God before their eye, and all the Cords that ever bound the Barbarous to Foreiners were made of Selfe and Covetuousnes. Yet if I mistake not I observe in Miantunnomu some sparkes of true Friendship. Could it be deeply imprinted in to him that the English never intended to despoile him of the Countrey I probably Conjecture his friendship would appeare in attending of us with 500 men (in Case) agst any forreigne Enemies." LaFantasie, *Correspondence of Roger Williams,* 1:101.

57. In a letter written to John Winthrop dated November 10, 1637 (LaFantasie, *Correspondence of Roger Williams,* 1:132), Williams reported an incident in which he questioned three young Native women—two Pequots and one possible Niantic—who had run away from English households. The oldest of the three told Williams that she had been physically abused because "a fellow lay with her . . . but for her part she refused." The questioning of these women is the only evidence that I have found either in *A Key* or in Williams's letters to document, let alone suggest, an exchange with Native women.

58. Roger Williams, *The Bloody Tenent Yet More Bloody,* Publications of the Narragansett Club, ed. Samuel L. Caldwell (1652; Providence, 1870), 4:372–373.

59. Williams (*A Key Into the Language,* ed. Chapin, 20) indicates, "I had once travailed to an Island of the wildest in our parts . . . and little could speak to them to their understanding especially because of the change of their Dialect, or manner of Speech from our neighbours."

60. Trumbull, "Editor's Preface."

61. See Williams's comments on learning and teaching foreign languages (LaFantasie, *Correspondence of Roger Williams,* 2:393, 395 fn.).

62. LaFantasie, *Correspondence of Roger Williams,* 2:751.

63. The Narragansett sachems suspected Benedict Arnold—who was fluent in local Algonkian dialects and frequently asked by the commissioners of the United Colonies to act as interpreter and messenger in their transactions with the Indians of Narragansett Bay—of altering their meaning in his translations. LaFantasie, *Correspondence of Roger Williams,* 1:253 n.

64. Teunissen and Hinz, "Introduction," 33. Williams seems to have had a good ear for lan-

guages and much preferred learning (and teaching) foreign languages using a conversational method. LaFantasie, *Correspondence of Roger Williams,* 2:393, 395 fn.

65. See Williams's letter to Gov. John Winthrop of July 10, 1637. LaFantasie, *Correspondence of Roger Williams,* 1:96.

66. Williams, *A Key Into the Language,* ed. Chapin, 136.

67. Williams, *A Key Into the Language,* ed. Chapin,159.

68. See, for example, Williams to John Winthrop Jr., August 19, 1669 (LaFantasie, *Correspondence of Roger Williams,* 2:591–592); and Williams to the Assembly of Commissioners, November 17, 1677? (LaFantasie, *Correspondence of Roger Williams,* 2:752).

69. See Bernard Bailyn, *The New England Merchants in the Seventeenth Century* (Cambridge, Mass., and London, England: Harvard University Press, 1982) and LaFantasie, "A Day in the Life," 95–111, for discussions of Williams as a trader.

70. Williams, *A Key Into the Language,* ed. Chapin 168.

71. Williams, *A Key Into the Language,* ed. Chapin, 160–166.

72. LaFantasie, *Correspondence of Roger Williams,* 1:146.

73. See, for example, comments by Anthony Pagden *(European Encounters with the New World* [New Haven, Conn., and London: Yale University Press, 1982], 158) on the possible misinformation conveyed due to language barriers and the failure to understand Native cultural practices.

74. Williams, *A Key Into the Language,* ed. Chapin, 130–132.

75. In a letter to Gov. John Winthrop dated February 28, 1637/38, Williams commented that "I find what I could never heare before, that they have plenty of Gods or divine powers: the Sunne, Moone, Fire, Water, Snow, Earth, the Deere, the Beare, etc. are divine powers. I brought home lately from the Nanhiggonsicks the names of 38 of their Gods all they could remember and had I not with feare and caution withdrew they would have fallen worship O God." (LaFantasie, *Correspondence of Roger Williams,* 1:146).

76. LaFantasie, *Correspondence of Roger Williams,* 1:xxxiv.

77. Wroth, "Roger Williams," 27.

78. LaFantasie, *Correspondence of Roger Williams,* 1:163.

79. LaFantasie, *Correspondence of Roger Williams,* 2:400.

80. James, "Worlds of Roger Williams," 104–105.

81. James Axtell, *The European and the Indian: Essays in the Ethnohistory of Colonial North America* (New York: Oxford University Press, 1981), 170.

82. LaFantasie, *Correspondence of Roger Williams,* 1:26, 140, 145, and 155.

83. James Axtell, *The Invasion Within* (New York: Oxford University Press, 1985): 325; Simmons, "Cultural Bias," 69.

84. Axtell, *Invasion Within,* 325.

85. What barrier, if any, Williams's note taking imposed on his exchanges with Native people is unknown. His surviving letters indicate that he lacked an ample supply of paper and made use of whatever he had on hand, often writing on scraps of paper or reusing blank spaces on letters sent to him (LaFantasie, *Correspondence of Roger Williams,* 1:181 fn., 313 fn., 317 fn., 324 fn.; 2:429 fn., 714, and 729). From this, it would

seem that his recording may not have been as obtrusive as it might have been had he been furnished with an adequate supply of notebooks and other paraphernalia; cf. Murray (*Forked Tongues*, 136) for a discussion of Frank Hamilton Cushing's note taking at Zuni. Although much has been said about the degree to which European writing impressed Native North American peoples, and how they at times entertained the possibility that the written word was more authoritative than orality, it is important to think about transcription not just in an abstract or ideological sense, but also in terms of what effect the act of note taking might have had in the context of verbal communication between Williams and the Narragansetts.

5. Unlocking *A Key*'s Silences

1. Williams, *A Key Into the Language*, ed. Chapin, A2.
2. March, "Uncommon Civility."
3. Perry Miller, *Roger Williams: His Contributions to the American Tradition* (Indianapolis and New York: Bobbs-Merrill, 1953), 53.
4. See McCarron, "Style and Rhetoric in the Writings of Roger Williams," and Searles, "Worlds of Roger Williams," regarding the use of stylistic conventions in *A Key*. Both Murray (*Forked Tongues*) and Pagden (*Encounters with the New World*) have commented on stylistic conventions, including the first-person voice ("I") and dialogues, to create authority in the representation of the "other" in colonialist literature.
5. The gap in Williams's correspondence, both by him and to him, is from March 8, 1640/41, to June 25, 1645 (LaFantasie, *Correspondence of Roger Williams*, 1:218).
6. See James, "Worlds of Roger Williams," 99–109; LaFantasie, *Correspondence of Roger Williams*, 1:xxv; Perry Miller, "An Essay in Interpretation"; and Wroth, "Roger Williams," for comments on Williams's letters.
7. Williams, *A Key Into the Language*, ed. Chapin, A3.
8. Williams, *A Key Into the Language*, ed. Chapin, A3.
9. In two of his later tracts, *The Bloudy Tenent of Persecution* (1644) and *Christenings Make Not Christians* (1645), written within several years of *A Key*, Williams expressed his criticism of applying the term *heathen* to Indians. He believed that the term should not be restricted to unconverted people, like Indians, but could easily be applied to Christians who had not attained spiritual fulfillment and yet attempted to impose conversion on Native peoples. See Canup, *Out of the Wilderness*, 83–84.
10. Robert F. Berkhoffer Jr., *The White Man's Indian: Images of the American Indian from Columbus to Present* (New York: Vintage Books, 1979), 15–16; Anthony Pagden, *The Fall of Natural Man: The American Indian and the Origins of Comparative Ethnology* (Cambridge: Cambridge University Press, 1982); Simmons, "Cultural Bias," 56–72.
11. Williams, *A Key Into the Language*, ed. Chapin, A3.
12. Williams, *A Key Into the Language*, ed. Chapin, A3.
13. Williams, *A Key Into the Language*, ed. Chapin, A4.
14. Williams, *A Key Into the Language*, ed. Chapin, A4. See Michael T. Ryan ("Assimilating New Worlds in the Sixteenth and Seventeenth Centuries," *Comparative Studies in So-*

ciety and History 23, no. 4 [1981]: 519–538) for a discussion of the intellectual conquest of "new worlds" in the sixteenth and seventeenth centuries, though not of Williams specifically.

15. Williams, *A Key Into the Language*, ed. Chapin, A4; by the time he wrote, Williams and other Europeans defined *Tartaria* as the lands of eastern Europe and Asia occupied by tribal peoples they called "Tartars."

16. Williams, *A Key Into the Language,* ed. Chapin, A4.

17. See Canup (*Out of the Wilderness,* 64–73) for a discussion of the significance of the Jewish origins theory. Williams's opinion of Jewish origins for Native Americans seems to have changed over time. In a letter written to Thomas Thorowgood, dated December 20, 1635, he articulated his reasons for suspecting this pedigree (LaFantasie, *Correspondence of Roger Williams,* 1:30). Although Thorowgood quoted and paraphrased freely from *A Key* in his book, *Jews in America* (1651), Williams's confidence in the Jewish origins theory seems to have waned a bit by the time of its writing (Ernst, "Roger Williams and the English Revolution," 50). Williams appears to be even less certain of the hypothetical Jewish origins of Native Americans in an allusion to the matter in a letter to John Winthrop Jr., dated ca. February 15, 1654[55] (LaFantasie, *Correspondence of Roger Williams,* 2:429).

18. Williams, *A Key Into the Language*, ed. Chapin, A4.

19. Teunissen and Hinz, in Williams, *A Key Into the Language,* ed. Teunissen and Hinz, 284 fn.; see Michael A. Volmar, "Maugua the Bear in Northeastern Indian Mythology and Archaeology," *Bulletin of the Massachusetts Archaeological Society* 57, no. 2 (1996): 37–45, for a discussion of bears in Northeastern mythology.

20. Williams, *A Key Into the Language*, ed. Chapin, A5.

21. Williams, *A Key Into the Language*, ed. Chapin, 132–134.

22. Williams, *A Key Into the Language*, ed. Chapin, 135.

23. Williams, *A Key Into the Language*, ed. Chapin, A4.

24. Williams, *A Key Into the Language*, ed. Chapin, 68.

25. Williams, *A Key Into the Language*, ed. Chapin, 95.

26. Williams, *A Key Into the Language*, ed. Chapin, 31.

27. Williams, *A Key Into the Language*, ed. Chapin, 46.

28. Williams, *A Key Into the Language*, ed. Chapin, 47.

29. Williams, *A Key Into the Language*, ed. Chapin, 47.

30. Bragdon (*Native People of Southern New England,* 125), for example, uses the term *locale* instead of *homeland*. Her definition, emphasizing "cyclicity and repetitiveness of subsistence activities" in contributing to the creation of meaningful space, draws largely on the work of Anthony Giddens (*Central Problems in Social Theory: Structure and Contradiction in Social Analysis* [Berkeley and Los Angeles: University of California Press, 1990]), Erving Goffman (*Presentation of Self in Everyday Life* [New York: Doubleday, 1959]), and Maurice Merleau-Ponty (*Phenomenology of Perception* [London: Routledge and Kegan Paul, 1962]).

31. The description of southern New England Native homelands is derived from Russell G. Handsman, "The Weantinock Indian Homeland Was Not a 'Desert'," *Arti-*

facts 18, no. 2 (1990): 3–7; and Handsman and Lamb Richmond, "Confronting Colonialism," 97.

32. Williams, *A Key Into the Language,* ed. Chapin, 47.

33. Williams, *A Key Into the Language,* ed. Chapin, 28–29.

34. Williams, *A Key Into the Language,* ed. Chapin, 29, 148; Bragdon, *Native People of Southern New England,* 157.

35. William S. Simmons and George F. Aubin, "Narragansett Kinship," *Man in the Northeast* 9 (1975): 29.

36. See, for example, Helen C. Roundtree, "Powhatan Indian Women: The People Captain John Smith Barely Saw," *Ethnohistory* 45, no. 1 (1998): 1–2, for a similar assessment of Englishmen like Smith, William Strachey, and Henry Spelman, who observed the Powhatan. In addition, several articles have commented on the pervasive gender-linked bias in English sources, especially in regard to Native women's leadership roles in seventeenth-century New England (e.g., Trudie Lamb Richmond, "Native Women as Leaders in Algonkian Society," *Artifacts* 16, nos. 3–4 (1988): 7–10; Ann Marie Plane, "Putting a Face on Colonization: Factionalism and Gender Politics in the Life of Awashunkes, the 'Squaw Sachem' of Saconet," in *Northeastern Indian Lives, 1632–1816,* ed. Robert Grumet (Amherst: University of Massachusetts, 1996): 140–165.

37. The question of descent among the Native peoples of southern New England has been the subject of much speculation. Simmons and Aubin ("Narragansett Kinship") imply that the Narragansett were matrilineal, although their findings are not conclusive. William Burton and Richard Lowenthal ("The First of the Mohegans," *American Ethnologist* 1, no. 4 [1974]: 595) state that lineal (that is, patrilineal) descent is of little consequence in determining qualifications for chieftancy among ruling families; however, they present genealogical evidence that strongly suggests that descent through females was important in assuming leadership positions. Others (e.g., Lorraine E. Williams, "A Study of Seventeenth-Century Culture Contact in the Long Island Sound Area" [Ph.D. dissertation, New York University, 1972]; Eric S. Johnson, "Some by Flatteries and Others by Threatenings" [Ph.D. dissertation, University of Massachusetts, 1993]) imply that kinship organization across southern New England underwent changes in the seventeenth century. Bragdon (*Native People of Southern New England,* 156–168) provides a good review of the arguments on the subject along with insights derived from the anthropological literature.

38. Williams, *A Key Into the Language,* ed. Chapin, 99.

39. Williams, *A Key Into the Language,* ed. Chapin, 100.

40. Bragdon, *Native People of Southern New England,* 158.

41. Karla Poewe, *Matrilineal Ideology: Male–Female Dynamics in Luapula, Zambia* (New York: Academic Press, 1981).

42. For terms and description of "longer houses," see Williams, *A Key Into the Language,* ed. Chapin, 32.

43. For terms and description of "little round houses," see Williams, *A Key Into the Language,* ed. Chapin, 31.

44. See, for example, Williams's letters dated October 26, 1637, and November 10, 1637, in which he refers to Winthrop's Reprieve, an Indian servant of Gov. John Winthrop, who was given permission to travel from Boston to Rhode Island, where he lodged for two nights with Williams in Providence, before going to Block Island to visit with "friends." Thus, even though bound by indentureship, he returned to what was apparently his homeland and, as conveyed by Williams, wished "that he might now take his last fare well of his friends, to whom you [Winthrop] would rather pleased to give leave to visit him at Boston, for you can not believe how hard it is for him to escape much evil and especially uncleanenes while he is with them" (LaFantasie, *Correspondence of Roger Williams,* 1:127). Sometime during this furlough, Ninigret accused Reprieve of being a spy for Winthrop and threatened to kill him, forcing him to leave the place "where he desired to stay longest" (LaFantasie, *Correspondence of Roger Williams,* 1:132).

45. Williams, *A Key Into the Language,* ed. Chapin, 127–128.

46. Williams, *A Key Into the Language,* ed. Chapin, 177–178.

47. Brooks Holifield, "Peace, Conflict, and Ritual in Puritan Congregations," *Journal of Interdisciplinary History* 23, no. 3 (1993): 560–563; Morgan, *Roger Williams: The Church and State,* 35, 39, 104–106. See also Williams, *A Key Into the Language,* ed. Chapin, 129.

48. Williams, *A Key Into the Language,* ed. Chapin, 127.

49. Williams, *A Key Into the Language,* ed. Chapin, 128–129. For terms and descriptions of *"their* Coyne," see Williams, *A Key,* 152–155. According to his account, six small white beads (*wauômpeg*) or three black were the equivalent of an English penny in the context of intercultural trade in early 1640s.

50. Williams, *A Key Into the Language,* ed. Chapin, 128–129.

51. Williams, *A Key Into the Language,* ed. Chapin, 180; LaFantasie, *Correspondence of Roger Williams,* 1:160–161. The spring of 1638 was marked by severe weather, including an earthquake, violent storms, and severe cold. These conditions may have necessitated a late spring planting (Eva L. Butler, "Algonkian Culture and the Use of Maize in Southern New England," *Archaeological Society of Connecticut Bulletin* 22 [1948]: 14).

52. Williams, *A Key Into the Language,* ed. Chapin, 180.

53. LaFantasie, *Correspondence of Roger Williams,* 1:110, 113.

54. Williams, *A Key Into the Language,* ed. Chapin, 127.

55. Williams, *A Key Into the Language,* ed. Chapin, 67. In a story told to Ezra Stiles around 1730, a Narragansett shaman expressed reasons for calling upon Cheepi, the god often blamed for illness and misfortune, in seeking relief from a drought:

> Some 40 or 50 years ago there was a great Drought and the Indians of Narragansett held a great Powaw for sundry Days. One Babcock or Stanton at length, being well known to the Indians, went among them and rebuked them as serving and worshipping the devil: an old Powaw Indian readily owned and justified it—saying all the Corn would die without rain and Chepi the Evil Power witheld that—now said he, If I was to beat you, who would you pray to? to me, or to your Father Ten miles off? you would pray to me to leave off and not beat you any more: so we pray to the Devil to leave off affecting us with Evil.

See Simmons, *Spirit of the New England Tribes,* 121. Although the shaman's reasons for invoking Cheepi were in response to an inquiry about the Christian god, Cheepi was the spirit who could appear to the living, sometimes imparting extraordinary powers but also bringing tragedy and suffering. Cautantowwit, their principal deity, was remote from everyday life and thus did not appear to the living in dreams or visions: Constance A. Crosby, "From Myth to History, or Why King Philip's Ghost Walks Abroad," in *The Recovery of Meaning: Historical Archaeology in the Eastern United States,* ed. Mark P. Leone and Parker B. Potter Jr. (Washington, D.C.: Smithsonian Institution Press, 1988), 183–210.

56. Williams, *A Key Into the Language,* ed. Chapin,127.

57. Williams, *A Key Into the Language,* ed. Chapin, 198.

58. Bruce Trigger, "Maintaining Economic Equality in Opposition to Complexity: an Iroquoian Case Study," in *The Evolution of Political Systems: Socio-Politics in Small-Scale Sedentary Societies,* ed. Steadman Upham (Cambridge: Cambridge University Press, 1990), 136; but see also Pierre Clastres, *Society against the State* (New York: Zone Books, 1989).

59. Ann Marie Plane ("Childbirth Practices among Native American Women of New England and Canada, 1600–1800," *Medicine and Healing,* annual proceedings of the Dublin Seminar for New England Folklife, vol. 15 [Boston: Boston University, 1990], 15) suggests that Native American women in New England may have given birth in small houses or "huts" set apart from others in the community. Women's separation may have extended beyond the act of childbirth. Williams (*A Key Into the Language,* ed. Chapin, 147), for example, recorded that men sequestered themselves from their wives "after conception, until after the child is weaned, which with some is long after a yeare old." An analogous situation occurred at the time of a woman's menstrual period, when "their women and maids live apart four, five, or six dayes and no *Male* may come into that house." (Williams, *A Key Into the Language,* ed. Chapin, 31–32).

60. Williams, *A Key Into the Language,* ed. Chapin, 146.

61. Williams, *A Key Into the Language,* ed. Chapin, 130.

62. In a letter to Gov. John Winthrop, dated February 28, 1637/38, Williams mentioned that he saw Miantonomi's "father-in-law [stepfather], Canounicus his brother (whome I saw neere death with above a thoughsand men mourning and praying about him)" (LaFantasie, *Correspondence of Roger Williams,* 1:145). These solemn visits were curtailed only when the dying person was suspected of having an infectious disease, then "all forsake them aud flie" (Williams, *A Key Into the Language,* ed. Chapin, 196).

63. Williams, *A Key Into the Language,* ed. Chapin, 201.

64. Williams, *A Key Into the Language,* ed. Chapin, 203.

65. Williams, *A Key Into the Language,* ed. Chapin, 203.

66. Williams, *A Key Into the Language,* ed. Chapin, 203–204.

67. Williams, *A Key Into the Language,* ed. Chapin, 29.

68. Williams, *A Key Into the Language,* ed. Chapin, 201.

69. Williams, *A Key Into the Language,* ed. Chapin, 43.

70. Williams, *A Key Into the Language,* ed. Chapin, 123.

71. Williams, *A Key Into the Language,* ed. Chapin, 43.

72. Williams, *A Key Into the Language,* ed. Chapin, 202. No statements in *A Key* identify the mourning house. Presumably, the immediate kin stayed in the house where the per-

son died to be consoled by other family members and friends. However, Williams (*A Key Into the Language,* ed. Chapin, 4) noted that "after the death of a Husband or Wife, they often break up a house, and live here and there a while with Freinds, to allay their excessive Sorrowes." He did not specify how soon after the death of a spouse this occurred.

73. Williams, *A Key Into the Language,* ed. Chapin, 202.

74. Williams, *A Key Into the Language,* ed. Chapin, 203.

75. I have drawn on James Clifford's discussion of the work of the French anthropologist Marcel Griaule to problematize Williams's account of Narragansett funerals (*Predicament of Culture,* 68–71).

6. Undertaking Narragansett Graves

1. Samples of bone and artifacts were first brought to the Public Archaeology Laboratory (PAL) of Brown University. The PAL archaeologists advised the individual to contact Paul Robinson, the state archaeologist at the Rhode Island Historical Preservation Commission.

2. Paul Robinson, Marc Kelley, and Patricia E. Rubertone, "Preliminary Biocultural Interpretations from a Seventeenth Century Narragansett Indian Cemetery," in *Cultures in Contact: The European Impact on Native Cultural Institutions in Eastern North America, A.D. 1000–1800,* ed. William Fitzhugh (Washington, D.C.: Smithsonian Institution Press, 1985), 113.

3. "Summary of Activities and Recommendations for Protection of the Lischio Site, RI-1000," Manuscript on File, Rhode Island Heritage and Preservation Commission, Providence.

4. Among the involved parties were the landowner; Ella Wilcox Sekatau, Narragansett tribal coordinator; Edwin Connelly, Rhode Island cemeteries director; various town officials from North Kingstown; a representative for the Rhode Island Department of Transportation (RIDOT); and Paul Robinson and Edward Sanderson of the Rhode Island Historical Preservation Commission. The RIDOT was represented because the bulldozed area was close to the Route 4 extension right-of-way. It was later determined that the highway's impact zone was located to the west of the site (Rhode Island Historical Preservation Commission files, n.d.).

5. Paul A. Robinson and Gail Gustafson, "A Partially Disturbed Seventeenth Century Indian Burial Ground in Rhode Island: Recovery, Preliminary Analysis, and Protection," *Archaeological Society of Connecticut Bulletin* 45 (1983): 41. Their projection was based on a comparison with the Narragansett cemetery on Conanicut Island, excavated by William Simmons in the 1960s, that was less than one-half acre (2,000 square meters) and contained fifty-eight historic-period burials. A survey of the surrounding area in 1988 and 1989 revealed that this burial ground (known as West Ferry) was part of a much larger, long-term-use cemetery (Kevin McBride, "Phase I and II Archaeological Investigations, West Ferry Site [RI 84], Jamestown Elementary School, Jamestown, Rhode Island," Public Archaeology Survey Team [Storrs, Conn.: 1989]).

6. The contents of several others were only partially affected.

7. According to Rhode Island law at that time, a landowner was obliged to notify the state and the public about accidental disturbances to cemeteries. If the remains were not claimed by the next of kin within three weeks, then they could be removed and reinterred elsewhere. Although it was assumed that the graves were Narragansett, and therefore belonged to the Narragansett Indians, there was no legal precedent on which to stake these claims in the early 1980s. As Robinson ("Struggle Within," 22–23) indicates, the legal precedent for such claims only came in 1986 with the Louisiana Supreme Court decision in the case of *Charrier v. Bell* concerning the "Tunica Treasure"; see Jeffrey Brain, with contributions by T. M. Hamilton et al., "Tunica Treasure," papers of the Peabody Museum (Cambridge, Mass.: Peabody Museum of Archaeology and Ethnology, Harvard University; Salem, Mass.: Peabody Museum of Salem, 1979)

8. See discussion in Robinson and Gustafson, "Partially Disturbed Seventeenth Century Indian Burial Ground."

9. The U.S. Department of Interior, Bureau of Indian Affairs, formally recognized the Narragansetts as an Indian tribe on April 11, 1983. The process of "detribalization" was completed in 1880. Final decisions concerning entitlement to the proceeds from the sale of tribal lands were made in August 1881.

10. For discussion of 1709 quitclaim agreement, see Campbell and LaFantasie, "Scattered to the Winds of Heaven," 71; Simmons, *Narragansett*, 53–54. Purchases of the "vacant" lands sold by the state of Rhode Island are listed in Elisha Potter, "Early History of Narragansett"; but see also Elisha R. Potter, *Several Purchases of the Lands West of Wickford, Sold by the Committee of the Colony for the Sale of Vacant Lands in 1709 as Shown on a Map by Hon. Elisha Reynolds Potter, 1838* (Providence: E. L. Freeman, 1937).

11. LaFantasie, *Correspondence of Roger Williams*, 2:578, fn. 2.

12. Howard M. Chapin, "Queen's Fort," *RIHS Collections* 24, no. 4. (1931): 141–156.

13. These place names and their associations with Narragansett sachems are taken from Sidney S. Rider, "Preliminary Note," *Lands of Rhode Island*. The precise geographical locations of the sachems' "villages" are unknown to archaeologists and historians.

14. E. Pierre Morenon, ed., *Archaeological Sites at an Ecotone: Route 4 Extension, East Greenwich and North Kingstown, Rhode Island*, 6 vols., Occasional Papers in Archaeology, no. 14 (Providence: Rhode Island College, Public Archaeology Program, 1986).

15. See Morenon, "Conclusions," *Archaeological Sites at an Ecotone*, 3:150–151; and L. Anthony Zalucha, "Charcoal Analysis of Sites RI 667 and RI 670, Route 4 Extension, North Kingstown, Rhode Island," in Morenon, *Archaeological Sites at an Ecotone*, 3:115–120.

16. E. Pierre Morenon, "Flotation and Sediment Analysis at RI 670 and RI 667: An Overview of the Results," in *Archaeological Sites at an Ecotone*, 3:69; but see Handsman and Lamb Richmond, "Confronting Colonialism"; Stephen Loring, "Boundary Maintenance, Mortuary Ceremonialism, and Resource Control in the Early Woodland: Three Cemetery Sites in Vermont," *Archaeology of Eastern North America* 3 (1985): 93–127.

17. See, for example, Bernstein, "Prehistoric Seasonality Studies," 110.

18. McBride, "Phase I and II Archaeological Investigations," 75; Simmons, *Cautantowwit's House,* 10–34.

19. Simmons, *Cautantowwit's House,* 11.

20. Williams, *A Key Into the Language,* ed. Chapin, A4.

21. Williams, *A Key Into the Language,* ed. Chapin, 95; Eric S. Sekatau and Ella W. Thomas Sekatau, "The Nahahiggansick Indians," in *Reflections of Charlestown, Rhode Island, 1876–1976,* Charlestown Bicentenniel Book Committee (Westerly, R.I.: Utter, 1976), 4.

22. Morenon, "Flotation and Sediment Analysis," 69–71.

23. The two carbon dates for the feature are 1570±80 and 2140±70 (John McDonough, "RI 667 Feature Descriptions," in Morenon, *Archaeological Sites at an Ecotone,* 5:191). Measuring about 10.5 by 10.5 feet (3 by 3 meters), the dimensions of this feature are remarkably close to those of the "hot-houses" described by Roger Williams, *A Key Into the Language,* ed. Chapin, 197. It was about 3 feet (1 meter) in depth. The complex stratigraphy indicated repeated use, perhaps sometimes as a hearth, at some point in the site's history.

24. Eva Butler, "Sweat-houses in the Southern New England Area," *Bulletin of the Massachusetts Archaeological Society* 7, no. 1 (1945): 11–15.

25. Williams, *A Key Into the Language,* ed. Chapin, 197.

26. Ninety lithic artifacts of quartz, quartzite, felsite, argellite, chert, sandstone, slate, and graphite were recovered from this feature, along with three pieces of shell, and some carbonized seeds and nutshell fragments (McDonough, "RI 667 Feature Descriptions," 191).

27. E. Pierre Morenon, "Understanding the Structure of a Seventeenth Century Narragansett Village at RI 667," in *Archaeological Sites at an Ecotone,* 3:145–147.

28. The effects of agricultural plowing on archaeological sites are well known. In general, plowing displaces the archaeological deposits and brings artifacts up to the surface, exposing them to the elements and to collectors. Sites repeatedly plowed (and collected) will gradually be depleted of most of their artifacts, especially the larger and perishable ones, and retain smaller items such as lithic debris and small sherds (see Michael B. Schiffer, *Formation Processes of the Archaeological Record* [Albuquerque: University of New Mexico Press, 1987], 129–132, for a brief overview). Because of plowing's effects on sites, archaeologists in New England typically remove the plowzone completely before proceeding with more controlled excavations.

29. The residential site was investigated as part of the Route 4 Extension project. As part of the data recovery program for this site, several large areas, 165 by 330 feet (50 by 100 meters), to the south and east were intensively tested. Small lithic and historic artifact scatters were located, which may represent other domestic sites. Therefore, it is possible that this residential site may have been part of a more extensive settlement (Morenon, "Conclusions," in *Archaeological Sites at an Ecotone,* 152).

30. E. Pierre Morenon, *Establishing the Context of RI 1000, A Narragansett Indian Burial Ground in North Kingstown, Rhode Island,* Occasional Papers in Archaeology, no. 21 (Providence: Rhode Island College, Department of Anthropology and Geography, Public Archaeology Program, 1984), 76. As part of a context study of RI-1000, a 1.6-

square-mile (4-square-kilometer) block of space centering on the burial ground was investigated. The area immediately north of the burial ground was examined more intensively, using closer interval testing, machine stripping, and remote sensing.

31. George R. Hamell, "Trading in Metaphors: The Magic of Beads," *Proceedings of the 1982 Glass Trade Bead Conference*, ed. C. F. Hayes III, Research Records 16 (Rochester, N.Y.: Rochester Museum and Science Center, 1983), 5–28, and "Mythical Realities and European Contact in the Northeast during the Sixteenth and Seventeenth Centuries," *Man in the Northeast* 33 (1987): 63–87.

32. Hamell, "Mythical Realities," 68 (for quotation).

33. Williams (*A Key Into the Language*, ed. Chapin, 122–126) loosely translates the term *manit* as "god." He indicates that the Narragansetts recognized many gods and attributed godlike attributes to different animals (especially rare ones) and inanimate things. These included "named" gods mentioned in *A Key* (e.g., those of the cardinal directions, houses, women, children). In addition, Williams writes that "there is a generall Custome amongst them, at the apprehension of any Excellency in Men, Women, Birds, Beasts, Fish, &c. to cry out *Manittoo*, that is, a God: and therefore when they talke amongst themselves of the *English* ships, and great buildings, of the plowing of their Fields, and especially of Bookes, and Letters, they will end thus: *Manittowock* They are Gods" (*A Key Into the Language*, ed. Chapin, 126). Although the whole Native landscape was alive with *manitos*, the more powerful ones were linked to certain domains where real human beings were more likely to encounter them.

34. Hamell, "Trading in Metaphors," 8.

35. Williams, *A Key Into the Language*, ed. Chapin, 203.

36. Dwight B. Heath, ed., *Mourt's Relation: A Journal of the Pilgrims at Plymouth* (1622; Chester, Conn.: Applewood Books, 1963), 21, 34; Morton, "New English Canaan," 18–19, 36; Frank Speck, "Native Tribes and Dialects of Connecticut: A Mohegan-Pequot Diary," *Forty-Third Annual Report of the Bureau of American Ethnology 1925–1926* (Washington, D.C.: U.S. Government Printing Office, 1928), 257–258.

37. Shovel scraping along transects extending from the area of disturbance conducted prior to the excavations revealed twenty-six burial stains within the known boundaries of the cemetery.

38. The graves ranged from 36 to 80 inches (91–203 centimeters) long, with an average length of 60 inches (152 centimeters), and from 17 to 63 inches (43–160 centimeters) wide, with an average width of 40 inches (101 centimeters). These measurements were taken from plan views at a depth of 4 inches (10 centimeters) below the surface of the each grave. When this was not possible, measurements were taken from grave profiles. These figures are remarkably similar to those recorded for the historic period Narragansett graves at West Ferry, where lengths ranged from 30 to 80 inches (76–203 centimeters), with a mean of 53.6 inches (136.14 centimeters); widths varied between 18 to 59 inches (46–150 centimeters), with an average of 40 inches (101 centimeters); Simmons, *Cautantowwit's House*, 64. Although the lengths and widths of the West Ferry graves were measured slightly above the skeleton, a comparison of measurements taken near the surface (i.e., 4 inches / 10 centimeters below the top of the grave) and at

the level of the skeleton for the RI-1000 graves suggests little variation between the two burial grounds.

39. The traditional tools used for digging graves are not known with any certainty. One anonymous commentator, referring to the funeral customs of Connecticut Indians, indicated that "their manner of burial was to dig holes in the ground with stakes which were made broad and sharpened at one end" (Frank Glynn, "A Foreword to 'Notes to Wawekas Hill, or Mohegan's Watchtower and Tombstone,'" *Archaeological Society of Connecticut Bulletin* 34 [1966]: 45).

40. Michael S. Nasseney, "An Epistemological Enquiry into Some Archaeological and Historical Interpretations of Seventeenth Century Native-American-European Relations," in *Archaeological Approaches to Cultural Identity*, ed. S. J. Shennan (London: Unwin Hyman, 1989), 88.

41. The topsoil layer that had been removed prior to the start of the excavation is estimated to have been less than 1 foot (30 centimeters) thick, based on what is known about the typical profile of the Bridgehampton silt loam on which the burial ground is located. This soil type has a surface layer about 8 inches (20 centimeters) thick, a subsoil 33 inches (84 centimeters) thick, and a substratum extending to depths of 60 inches (152 centimeters) or more (Rhode Island Soil Survey 1984: 6). The depths of the graves ranged from 7 to 14 inches (18–36 centimeters) below the burial ground's cleared surface.

42. Climate would have posed only limited seasonal restrictions to grave digging in southern New England. The frost-free season averages between 153 and 163 days; thus the ground would have been frozen solid for only a relatively short time following the first hard freeze of the late fall, during which grave-digging might have been affected or even curtailed. Pollen samples taken from the RI-1000 graves suggest, at least tentatively, that burials occurred during the summer and fall months, from June through October, and perhaps earlier in the spring, but not in the winter. See Gerald W. Kelso to Paul A. Robinson, March 26, 1984, Correspondence and Notes on Palynological Research Conducted at RI-1000, Rhode Island Historical Preservation Commission, Providence, 1984.

43. Lawrence Kaplan, "Report on the Fiber Analysis of Native-Made Textiles from RI-1000," Rhode Island Historical Preservation Commission, Providence, 1988.

44. Williams, *A Key Into the Language,* ed. Chapin, 90, 124; Constance Crosby ("From Myth to History," 191, 205, fn. 15) comments on the association between the living and the land of Cautantowwit that was mediated through the planting of corn and burial of the dead in the earth.

45. Lauren Cook, "The Rhode Island Burial Survey, Part 1," 54. See also Brenner, "Sociopolitical Implications of Mortuary Ritual Remains," 154–155.

46. Lauren Cook, "The Rhode Island Burial Survey, Part 2: The Data Base," Office of Public Archaeology, Report of Investigations no. 28, Center for Archaeological Studies, Boston University (report submitted to Rhode Island Historical Preservation Commission, 1985), 118–119. See also Turnbaugh, "Assessing the Significance," 118.

47. Burr Harrison and Alan Leveillee, "Phase I Archaeological Survey, North Kingstown

Retail Development, Wal-Mart Project Area, Rhode Island," draft report (Pawtucket, R.I.: Public Archaeology Laboratory, 1994), 1:23.

7. Retelling Narragansett Lives

1. Rubertone, "Grave Remembrances," 28; but see Robert S. Grumet, *Northeastern Indian Lives, 1632–1816* (Amherst: University of Massachusetts, 1996) for biographical accounts of Native Americans, many of whom are well-known historical figures who represented their culture and times.

2. Cf. Turnbaugh, "Assessing the Significance."

3. Disarticulated remains of at least nine other individuals were recovered from the disturbed portion of the burial ground. Assuming that these also were single interments, the cemetery would have held about fifty-six graves.

4. For example, multiple burials were recorded at Burr's Hill (Gibson, *Burr's Hill*, 2:13) and at West Ferry (Simmons, *Cautantowwit's House*, 83–84).

5. Robinson, Kelley, and Rubertone, "Preliminary Biocultural Interpretations," 122.

6. Simmons, *Cautantowwit's House*, 60.

7. Hamell, "Trading in Metaphors," 6.

8. Robinson, "Struggle Within," 224–225.

9. Simmons (*Cautantowwit's House*, 54) and Hamell ("Trading in Metaphors") have commented on the linguistic and conceptual link between metallic quality of spoons (and mirrors) and the soul.

10. Archaeological evidence for burying brass kettles upside down and over other grave goods has been found at West Ferry (Simmons, *Cautantowwit's House*). See also Laurier Turgeon, "Tale of the Kettle: Odyssey of an Intercultural Object," *Ethnohistory* 44, no. 1 (1997): 14, for a discussion of the practice among Micmac groups in New France.

11. Robinson, Kelley, and Rubertone, "Preliminary Biocultural Interpretations," 122.

12. See Williams, *A Key Into the Language*, ed. Chapin, 164–165.

13. There is, however, a 1686 inventory of Roger Williams's son, Robert, also believed to be a merchant who traded with Indians. His inventory included such items as "a broken parcel of silk, glass beads, jew's harps, buttons, four thousand pins, five Bermuda baskets, knives, scissors, knitting needles, silk crepe, and twenty-five gallons [95 liters] of rum" (LaFantasie, *Correspondence of Roger Williams*, 2:690, fn. 8).

14. Patricia E. Rubertone and Robert K. Fitts, "Historical Archaeology at Cocumscussoc: A Pilot Study for Local Preservation Planning," report submitted to the Rhode Island Historical Preservation Commission, Providence, 1990; Patricia E. Rubertone and Charlotte Taylor, "Historical Archaeology at Cocumscossoc: Report on the 1991 Excavations," report submitted to the Rhode Island Historical Preservation Commission, Providence, 1992.

15. Linda Welters, "Textiles from New England Indian Burial Sites," papers from the 1991 International Conference and Exhibition of the American Association of Textile Chemists and Colorists (Charlotte, N.C., October 8–11, 1991); Narragansett Bay Survey, "Conservation and Analysis of European Textiles from RI-1000: Report to the

Rhode Island Historical Preservation Commission," Rhode Island Historical Preservation Commission, Providence, 1985.

16. See Turnbaugh, "Assessing the Significance," for a discussion of smoking equipment among the Narragansett.

17. See LaFantasie, *Correspondence of Roger Williams*, 1:289. Likewise, Williams also said that he resisted selling anything that might be construed as having a "civilizing" effect on Native people, stating: "I therefore neither brought nor shall sell them Loose Coats nor Breeches," (LaFantasie, *Correspondence of Roger Williams*, 2:392–393). However, he indicated that Richard Smith and his son sold alcohol to the Indians regularly, and he hurled similar accusations against the Quakers (LaFantasie, *Correspondence of Roger Williams*, 1:266, fn. 20; 2:591, 655, 675). As partners in the Atherton Company, a group of land speculators from Massachusetts and Connecticut intent upon the acquisition of Narragansett country, they may have engaged in what has been described as "the fraudulent purchase technique" of obtaining deeds to prime acreage by seducing their clients with alcohol (Jennings, *Invasion of America*, 279).

18. Lion Gardiner, "Leift Lion Gardiner," 26.

19. Eugene Farrell, Dennis Piechota, and Paul Whitmore, "Chemical and Metallurgical Report on Metal Artifacts from RI-1000," Rhode Island Historical Preservation Commission, Providence, 1978.

20. See William Turnbaugh, "Material Culture of RI-1000, A Mid-Seventeenth Century Narragansett Indian Burial Site in North Kingstown, Rhode Island" (Kingston: University of Rhode Island, 1984), 64.

21. See Turnbaugh, "Material Culture of RI-1000," for a description of the artifacts.

22. See Wroth, *Voyages of Giovanni da Verrazzano, 1524–1528* (New Haven, Conn.: Yale University Press, 1970), 138, for a translation of Verrazzano's account of initial exchanges with the peoples of Narragansett Bay. It has been suggested that glass beads ceased to be important as trading stock, from 1630 at least through the time of King Philip's War, because they are seldom, if ever, itemized in trade accounts during this period (James W. Bradley, "Blue Crystals and Other Trinkets: Glass Beads from the Sixteenth and Early Seventeenth Century New England," *Proceedings of the 1982 Glass Trade Bead Conference*, ed. C. F. Hayes III, Research Records 16 [Rochester, N.Y.: Rochester Museum and Science Center, 1983], 36). Although the reasons for their decline in popularity as a trade item are not entirely clear, historical sources suggest that, at least for a time, Native people preferred other types of merchandise.

23. The quantities of glass beads by principal color were: blue (1,603), yellow (1,136), white (1,130), green (552), black (289), red (32), burgundy (52), turquoise (68), and indeterminate (68). These counts are based on beads recovered from individual graves; beads from miscellaneous lots collected as part of the 1982 investigations are not included. Adding the beads from these proveniences does not alter the ranking of the dominant colors in the glass bead assemblage (see Turnbaugh, "Material Culture of RI-1000," 32).

24. Marjorie B. Cohn to Paul A. Robinson, November 28, 1983, Correspondence Files for RI-1000, Rhode Island Historical Preservation and Heritage Commission, Providence;

for a further discussion of the engraved image, see Hugh Amory, "The Trout and the Milk: An Ethnobibliographic Talk," *Harvard Library Bulletin*, n.s., vol. 8, no. 1 (spring 1997): 50–65.

25. See also Hamell, "Trading in Metaphors," 23.

26. Clifford, *Predicament of Culture*, 341–343.

27. Williams, *A Key Into the Language*, ed. Chapin, 38–39; 40.

28. Age at death was assessed using criteria including dental eruption, crown and root formation, dental attrition, epiphysial closure, and pubic symphisis metamorphosis. Osteon counts were done for twenty adults (Marc A. Kelley, untitled manuscript, Rhode Island Historical Preservation and Heritage Commission, Providence; Marc A. Kelley, Paul S. Sledzik, and Sean P. Murphy, "Health, Demographics, and Physical Constitution in Seventeenth-Century Rhode Island Indians," *Man in the Northeast* 34 [1987]: 2). The age estimations represented here are mean ages (or best estimates).

29. The sex of each individual was estimated using morphological features of the pelvis, skull, and long bones. See Kelley, unititled manuscript, for the list of the specific criteria employed in making these determinations.

30. Barry O'Connell, "Introduction," in *On Our Own Ground: The Complete Writings of William Apess, A Pequot*, ed. Barry O'Connell (Amherst: University of Massachusetts Press, 1992), xxvi; but see also Kevin McBride, "The Historical Archaeology of the Mashantucket Pequots, 1637–1900: A Preliminary Analysis," in *The Pequots in Southern New England: The Fall and Rise of an American Indian Nation*, ed. Laurence M. Hauptman and James D. Wherry (Norman: University of Oklahoma Press, 1990), 81–95; Jack Campisi, "The Reemergence of the Mashantucket Pequot Tribe, 1637–1975," in Hauptman and Wherry, *Pequots in Southern New England*, 96–116.

31. Robinson, Kelley, and Rubertone, "Preliminary Biocultural Interpretations," 116.

32. Sekatau and Sekatau, "Nahahiggansick Indians," 14.

33. Marc A. Kelley, "A Biocultural View of Health, Illness, and Demographic Patterns from a Seventeenth Century Narragansett Indian Cemetery" (paper presented at the annual meeting of the Northeastern Anthropological Association, Hartford, Conn., March 22, 1984).

34. George A. Clark, Marc A. Kelley, John M. Grange, and M. Cassandra Hill, "The Evolution of Mycobacterial Disease in Human Populations," *Current Anthropology* 28, no. 1 (1987): 49.

35. Simmons (*Spirit of the New England Tribes*, 55) states that the Plymouth-area Wampanoag speculated that their losses in the epidemic of 1617–1619 could have been avoided if they had performed the property destruction ritual in which the Narragansett honored the creator.

36. Williams, *A Key Into the Language*, ed. Chapin, 149–150. For a discussion of childbirth practices among Native American women in the colonial period, see Ann Marie Plane, "Childbirth Practices," 13–23.

37. Ezra Stiles, *Extracts from the Itineraries and Other Miscellanies of Ezra Stiles, D.D., LL.D.,*

1755–1794, ed. Franklin B. Dexter (New Haven, Conn.: Yale University, 1916), 145, cited in Simmons, *Spirit of the New England Tribes*, 152.

38. Harold Mars, interview with William Simmons, April 20 and June 30, 1983, Charlestown, R.I., quoted in Simmons, *Spirit of the New England Tribes*, 152–153.

39. Herndon and Sekatau, "Right to a Name," 447–448.

40. In "A Son of the Forest," Williams Apess, a Pequot who identified himself as biologically of mixed blood, describes being badly beaten by his grandmother when he was four years old (O'Connell, "Introduction," *On Our Own Ground,* 6). See also Barry O'Connell, "Once More Let Us Consider": William Apess in the Writing of New England Native American History," in *After King Philip's War: Presence and Persistence in Indian New England*, ed. Colin G. Calloway (Hanover, N.H., and London: Dartmouth College, published by University Press of New England, 1997), 162–177.

41. Plane, "Childbirth Practices," 153.

42. Cf. Simmons (*Spirit of the New England Tribes*, 126–127) for the Mohegan legend of "Papoose Rock." In this tale, a Montauk woman kills her infant because her Mohegan husband has left her and she cannot raise the child alone.

43. Williams, *A Key Into the Language,* ed. Chapin, 29.

44. See Alfred L. Kroeber ("Disposal of the Dead," *American Anthropologist* 29 (1927): 308–315] and Lewis R. Binford ("Mortuary Practices: Their Study and Their Potential," *Memoirs of the Society for American Archaeology* 25 [1971]: 6–29) for opposing views on emotion and sentiment in mortuary remains. Peter Metcalf and Richard Huntington (*Celebrations of Death: The Anthropology of Mortuary Ritual*, 2d ed. [1991; Cambridge and New York: Cambridge University Press, 1992], 2–5, 43–48) provide a discussion of the same for ethnographically known examples.

45. There are no specific references to naming ceremonies for young children among the Narragansetts. The practice has been noted for other Algonkian peoples such as the Montauks (Simmons, *Spirit of the New England Tribes*, 46–47) and the Delaware (Jay Miller, "Delaware Personhood," *Man in the Northeast* 42 [1991]: 19–21).

46. Names were not permanent. In addition to those that were adopted (and shed) at different stages in a life's course, individuals in Native American cultures sometimes changed their name in association with a momentous event or major accomplishment. According to Edward Winslow ("Good News from New England," in *Chronicles of the Pilgrim Fathers*, ed. John Masefield [1624; reprint, New York: E. P. Dutton, 1910], 267–357), "All their names are significant and variable; for when they come to the state of men and women, they alter them according to their deeds or dispositions."

47. See, for example, Nancy Scheper-Hughes, "Culture, Scarcity, and Maternal Thinking: Maternal Detachment and Infant Survival in a Brazilian Shantytown," *Ethos* 13, no. 4 (1985): 311–312.

48. See John O'Shea, *Mortuary Variability: An Archaeological Investigation* (New York: Academic Press, 1984).

49. Williams, *A Key Into the Language,* ed. Chapin, 118.

50. Lynn M. Pietak, "Body Symbolism and Cultural Aesthetics: The Use of Shell Beads and Ornaments by Delaware and Munsee Groups," *North American Archaeologist* 19, no. 2 (1998): 135–161.

51. Jay Miller, "Delaware Personhood," 19.

52. See Terrance Turner ("Social Body and Embodied Subject: Bodiliness, Subjectivity, and Sociality among the Kayapo," *Cultural Anthropology* 10, no. 2 [1995]: 143–170) for a discussion of representations of the body using material culture.

53. Turner, "Social Body," 158.

54. Robinson, "Struggle Within," 230–231.

55. See Scheper-Hughes ("Culture, Scarcity, and Maternal Thinking") and Dean R. Snow (The Iroquois [(Oxford: Basil Blackwell, 1994], 72).

56. Clark, Kelley, Grange, and Hill, "Evolution of Mycobacterial Disease," 49–50.

57. Scheper-Hughes ("Culture, Scarcity, and Maternal Thinking," 312) uses the phrase "watchful waiting" to describe an environment in which a mother is emotionally guarded and partially estranged from a child because of anticipated loss. Although these sentiments may not be transferable to seventeenth-century Narragansetts, the phrase seems to be an apt way to characterize the circumstances surrounding the lives of some Narragansett children.

58. Although located within the ancestral burial ground, both graves (Burial 42 and Burial 13) were situated at the northern periphery of the cemetery, forming what may have been a discrete burial cluster along with Burial 9.

59. Simmons, *Cautantowwit's House*, 62; see Snow (*Iroquois*, 72) for similar comments about Iroquois; and Jay Miller ("Delaware Personhood," 21) for the Delaware.

60. Williams, *A Key Into the Language*, ed. Chapin, 29.

61. According to Williams in *A Key*, the Narragansett term for this "little house" was *wetuomemése*. These structures are where Narragansett women and maids lived apart from the rest of the community for "four, five, or six dayes, in the time of their monethly sicknesse" (Williams, *A Key Into the Language*, ed. Chapin, 31–32).

62. Princess Red Wing, "History of the Indians Religion," *Narragansett Dawn* 1, no. 8 (December 1935): 197.

63. *Narragansett Dawn* 1, no. 1 (May 1935): 26.

64. *Narragansett Dawn* 1, no. 1 (May 1935): 27.

65. An assortment of other beads found near the young woman's upper body could be part of another necklace. They include an oblong bead with impressions and gold overlay; a tubular bead in brick red; another with a clear greenish center layered with brick red and stripes of blue and white; and a long cylindrical shell bead.

66. Some long, dark tubular beads, scattered between the young woman's disarticulated skull and postcranial skeleton, may have been part of another necklace.

67. Burial 49 was very disturbed and the bones were poorly preserved. Therefore, it is impossible to determine how the shells were arranged into a design or where they were placed on the body.

68. Turnbaugh, "Assessing the Significance," 150.

69. The "scar" of pregnancy and parturition, or preaurilcular sulcus, is a gouged-out arc

just anterior to the auricular area of the hip bone. It is formed during the later stages of pregnancy when the hormone relaxin is released to "relax" or loosen the ligaments tying the bony birth canal together in anticipation of the demands of childbirth (Mehmet Yasar Iscan and Kenneth A. R. Kennedy, eds., *Reconstruction of Life from the Skeleton* [New York: Liss, 1989], 290).

70. Donald J. Ortner and Walter G. J. Putschar (*Identification of Pathological Conditions in Human Skeletal Remains* [Washington, D.C.: Smithsonian Institution Press, 1981], 182) indicate that tertiary syphilitic bone lesions usually develop between two and ten years after infection but may occasionally occur earlier or much later.

71. The frequency of traverse lines estimated for Burial 26 was 14 on the femur, 9 on the tibia, and 12 on the humerus compared to the averages of 5.84, 3.13, and 6.0 for the females within the radiographed burial population ($n = 19$ between the ages of 15 and more than 50 years of age). For a discussion of synergistic interactions between infectious disease and nutrient availability, see Marc A. Kelley, "Infectious Disease," in Iscan and Kennedy, *Reconstruction of Life,* 191–200.

72. Williams (*A Key Into the Language,* ed. Chapin, 197) discusses the use of sweathouses in healing the "French disease" as the English sometimes called syphilis. According to Williams, "by sweating and some potions," they were able to cure this ailment effectively and speedily.

73. The risk of an infected mother transmitting the disease to the fetus during pregnancy is quite high. The result is fetal death followed by an abortion in the first half of the pregnancy, fetal death with the delivery of a premature or mature diseased stillborn fetus, or delivery of a living infected infant. Before effective treatment for the infected mother became available, the rate of mortality for congenital syphilis was quite high. See Ortner and Putschar, *Identification of Pathological Conditions,* 198.

74. Mark A. Kelley, T. G. Barrett, and S. D. Saunders, "Diet, Dental Disease, and Transition in Northeastern Native Americans," *Man in the Northeast* 33 (1987): 113–125.

75. Kelley, untitled manuscript; Kelley, Sledzik, and Murphy, "Health, Demographics, and Physical Constitution," 1–25.

76. Williams, *A Key Into the Language,* ed. Chapin, 146–148.

77. Williams, *A Key Into the Language,* ed. Chapin, 148.

78. Williams, *A Key Into the Language,* ed. Chapin, 150.

79. Simmons (*Spirit of the New England Tribes,* 273–276) reports a Mohegan story of Chahnameed, told to Frank Speck by Fidelia Fielding. In the story, the woman leaves her husband, Chahnameed, because of his neglect both of her and of Native traditions. Numerous instances of Native women (and men) separating and remarrying in order to strengthen political alliances are reported for the seventeenth century. See Howard Chapin, *Sachems of the Narragansetts* (Providence: RIHS, Roger Williams Press, E. A. Johnson, 1931); Robert S. Grumet, "Sunksquaws, Shamans, and Tradeswomen: Middle Atlantic Coastal Algonkian Women during the Seventeenth and Eighteenth Centuries," in *Women and Colonization,* ed. Mona Etienne and Eleanor Leacock (New York: Praeger, 1980), 43–62; Lamb Richmond, "Native Women as Leaders."

80. Williams, *A Key Into the Language,* ed. Chapin, 146–147; but see Ann Marie Plane, "The

Examination of Sarah Ahhaton: The Politics of 'Adultery' in an Indian Town of Seventeenth-Century Massachusetts," in *Algonkians of New England: Past and Present*, annual proceedings of the Dublin Seminar for New England Folklife (Boston: Boston University, 1991), 14–25.

81. Williams, *A Key Into the Language*, ed. Chapin, 148.

82. Williams, *A Key Into the Language*, ed. Chapin, 37.

83. For a discussion of birth regulation among Native women in the Southeast, see Patricia Galloway, "Where Have All the Menstrual Huts Gone? The Invisibility of Menstrual Seclusion in the Late Prehistoric Southeast," in *Women in Prehistory: North America and Mesoamerica*, ed. Cheryl Classen and Rosemary A. Joyce (Philadelphia: University of Pennsylvania Press, 1997), 47–62, and especially 55–56.

84. Burial 12, which held the remains of an adult woman past the age of forty, had only a glass disk with fragments of metal adhering to it (see appendixes). Some traces of brass and iron in the grave tentatively suggest the possibility of other objects. However, the grave was extremely shallow and situated on or near glacial till with evidence of severe and active rodent disturbance.

85. Turnbaugh, "Assessing the Significance," 150.

86. Williams, *A Key Into the Language*, ed. Chapin, 99.

87. Michael Volmar, "Effigy Pestles from Massachusetts," *Bulletin of the Massachusetts Archaeological Society* 55, no. 1 (1994): 15–23.

88. Turnbaugh, "Material Culture of RI-1000," 78, 149.

89. See, for example, Turgeon, "Tale of the Kettle," 14–15.

90. Burial 28 also contained a piece of graphite and a Native-made ceramic pot. The pot was small, measuring only about 3.6 inches (9.14 centimeters) in height and slightly larger at its orifice. It held about 24 ounces (720 milliliters). Portions of its interior and exterior surfaces were encrusted with carbonized residue. Compared with the other two Native-made pots from RI-1000, this one was poorly constructed. It had "a relatively flat bottom, slightly constricted neck, a narrow, round-lipped collar ringed on the exterior with outward-projecting lobes that appeared to have been appliquéd to the collar." In profile, the pot appeared somewhat lopsided, and the clay was tempered with poorly sorted medium-sized shell fragments. Its only decoration was a pair of horizontal lines encircling the vessel immediately below the lip and a single wide vertical line on each projecting lobe (Robert Goodby, "Style, Meaning, and History: A Contextual Study of Seventeenth Century Native American Ceramics from Southeastern New England" [Ph.D. dissertation, Brown University, 1994], 140).

91. See Williams (*A Key Into the Language*, ed. Chapin, 156); both Robinson ("Struggle Within," 175–176) and Turnbaugh ("Material Culture of RI-1000," 95) have interpreted "awllike" tools from RI-1000 as wampum drills or muxes. The dimensions of these awllike objects indicate that some were larger than others. The smaller ones were associated with women; larger and smaller examples occurred in the grave of an adult male (Burial 25).

92. Paul A. Robinson, "Lost Opportunities: Miantonomi and the English in Seventeenth-Century Narragansett Country," in *Northeastern Indian Lives, 1632–1816*, ed. Robert S. Grumet (Amherst: University of Massachusetts Press, 1996), 13–28.

93. Chapin, *Sachems of the Narragansetts*, 110.
94. Howard M. Chapin, *Illustrations of the Seals, Arms, and Flags of Rhode Island* (Providence: RIHS, 1913), 1. The heart motif appears on the seal of Gregory Dexter, who printed Roger Williams's *A Key Into the Language of America* in London in 1643 (*RIHS Collections* 12, no. 4. [1919]: 114). Dexter accompanied Williams on his return to New England in 1644 and became a leading figure in civil and religious affairs (Howard M. Chapin, "Gregory Dexter, Master Printer," *RIHS Collections* 12, no. 4 [1919]: 105–113). Seals of other early Rhode Island families that incorporate hearts into their design are illustrated in "Early Rhode Island Seals," *RIHS Collections* 15, no. 4 (1922): 101–108.
95. Chapin, *Seals, Arms, and Flags.*
96. Welters, "Textiles from New England Indian Burial Sites."
97. Williams, *A Key Into the Language*, ed. Chapin, 14, 45.
98. Although pipes were exclusive to males, the teeth of two older women buried at RI-1000 exhibited pipe wear facets. The statements about the occasions for smoking are taken from Williams, *A Key Into the Language*, ed. Chapin, 55, 197, 73.
99. Williams, *A Key Into the Language*, ed. Chapin, 14, 50.
100. Although females experienced more dental disease, men had their share of dental caries. In fact, gross caries made up a greater proportion of their total caries (Kelley, Barrett, and Saunders, "Diet, Dental Disease, and Transition, 117).
101. Williams, *A Key Into the Language*, ed. Chapin, 44.
102. At 5 feet 11 inches (1.8 meters), the individual identified as Burial 16 was taller than the average male in the burial population. Marc A. Kelley, who did the analysis of the human remains at RI-1000, tentatively labeled Burial 16 as having an endocrine disorder known as hypogonadism based on "feminine morphology" of the skull and the pelvis, which appeared to be male with a deformation of the pubis. Although the individual exhibited no dental caries and no enamel hypoplasias, the long bones showed a higher than average number of traverse or growth arrest lines, which might be evidence of nutritional deprivation. See Kelley, untitled manuscript; and Kelley, Sledzik, and Murphy, "Health, Demographics, and Physical Constitution," 1–25. For a description of hypogonadism, see Ortner and Putschar, *Identification of Pathological Conditions*, 306.
103. Turnbaugh, "Material Culture of RI-1000," 134–137.
104. Farrell, Piechota, and Whitmore, "Chemical and Metallurgical Report."
105. Several chroniclers, including Williams, mention a "Stone-Wall" or "Stone-Layer" John, a Narragansett who was a skilled blacksmith and mason. In a letter dated April 1, 1676, Williams refers to "one Nawham Mr. R. Smiths John Wall Maker an Ingenious Fellow and peasable" (LaFantasie, *Correspondence of Roger Williams*, 2:723. Stone-Wall John allegedly built the forge at the Narragansetts' palisaded village in the Great Swamp as well as the fortifications there and at Queen's Fort (Malone, *Skulking Way of War*, 99). Although he presumably escaped from the massacre unscathed, he was later killed in a surprise attack at Nipsachuck Swamp in the summer of 1676 led by Maj. John Talcott (LaFantasie, *Correspondence of Roger Williams*, 2:727 fn.; see also Charles H. Lincoln, ed. *Narratives of the Indian Wars 1675–1699* [New York: Charles Scribner's Sons,

1913], 59, 96). What became of his remains, or those of another Narragansett black-smith, skilled in repairing firearms, who was reported to have been killed at Great Swamp, cannot be ascertained from the written record. However, both the technical abilities evidenced in the archaeological record of Burial 38 and the time period with which this burial is associated raises the possibility that the individual in Burial 38 could have been Nawham.

106. See Simmons (*Spirit of the New England Tribes*, 110–112) for stories among southeastern New England Indians in which a single horseshoe is linked to shamanistic powers.

107. Kelley, untitled manuscript; see also Charles F. Merbs, "Trauma," in Iscan and Kennedy, *Reconstruction of Life*, 169–171.

8. Remembering the Dead

1. This is adapted from Wood, *"New England's Prospect,"* 111–112.

2. According to Roger Williams (*A Key Into the Language*, ed. Chapin, 130), the unworthy who were denied admittance to the land of spirits in the southwest were "Murtherers thieves and Lyers."

3. Constance Crosby, "From Myth to History," 199.

4. Edward Winslow, "Good News from New England," 325–353, quoted in Simmons, *Spirit of the New England Tribes*, 251.

5. Eva Butler, "The Brush or Stone Memorial Heaps of Southern New England," *Bulletin of the Archaeological Society of Connecticut* 19 (1946): 2–11; Stephen Jett, "Cairn and Brush Travel Shrines in the United States Northeast and Southeast," *Northeast Anthropology* 48 (1994): 61–67; Simmons, *Spirit of the New England Tribes*, 251–256.

6. Based on different readings of John Winthrop's accounts (see John Winthrop, *The History of New England from 1630 to 1649* [Boston: Phelps and Farnham, 1825–26]), which locate Miantonomi's murder someplace "between Hartford and Windsor" (cited in Chapin, *Sachems of the Narragansetts*, 49), historians have debated where Miantonomi was executed and buried. Trumbull and others (e.g., John De Forest, *History of the Indians of Connecticut*, 198) argue that Miantonomi was both executed and buried at "Sachem's Plain," located north of the present-day town of Greenville on the Shetucket River. Frances M. Caulkins, however, suggests that although Miantonomi may have been executed somewhere near Sachem's Plain, he was not buried there, but rather somewhere along the Podunk River (*History of Norwich Connecticut: From Its Possession by the Indians, to the Year 1866* [Hartford, Conn.: Frances Caulkins, 1866], 36–37).

7. De Forest, *History of the Indians of Connecticut*, 198.

8. De Forest, *History of the Indians of Connecticut*, 198.

9. Timothy Dwight, *Travels in New England and New York*, ed. Barbara Miller Solomon with the assistance of Patricia M. King (1823; Cambridge, Mass.: Belknap Press of Harvard University, 1969), 2:264. In his subsequent travels, he and his companions viewed another stone monument from the summit near New Milford, Conn., similar to the one near Stockbridge, except that it was more like an enclosure than "an obtuse cone." Dwight surmised that both monuments were erected "on high and solitary grounds,

remote from every Indian settlement, and that the persons buried were excluded from the customary burying places of their respective tribes, places considered, I believed, . . . as consecrated ground." He speculated that the chief buried at this location was guilty of having committed a gross crime. "This last fact makes the practice of forming monuments in this manner approximate still nearer to the custom of the Israelites, mentioned in my account of Stockbridge" (Dwight, *Travels*, 3:283).

10. Butler, "Brush or Stone Memorial Heaps," 9.

11. Simmons, *Spirit of the New England Tribes*, 256.

12. James Scott's (*Seeing Like a State: How Certain Schemes to Improve Human Conditions Have Failed* [New Haven, Conn., and London: Yale University, 1998], 355) discussion of the symbolic power of the Vietnam Memorial provided a useful analogy for interpreting the stone piles as commemorative monuments. Although very different in scale and design, time and context, both engage the visitor and elicit participation. Thus, both monuments would seem to achieve meaning in the same manner, i.e., by what people bring to them.

13. Simmons, *Spirit of the New England Tribes*, 254–255; but see also Constance A. Crosby, "The Algonkian Spiritual Landscape," in *Algonkians of New England: Past and Present*, annual proceedings of the Dublin Seminar for New England Folklife, 1991 (Boston: Boston University, 1993), 35–41.

14. McBride, "Phase I and II Archaeological Investigations," 61.

15. J. R. Cole, "Town of Jamestown," in *The History of Newport County, Rhode Island from the Year 1638 to the Year 1887 including the Settlement of Its Towns and Their Subsequent Progress*, ed. Richard M. Bayles (New York: L. E. Preston, 1888).

16. William Simmons (*Cautantowwit's House*, 30–32) describes two small, circular pits near the secondary burial pit (Burial G-1). The pit located to the west of Burial G-1, Burial (?) H-10, contained charcoal and burned steatite sherds from a single large vessel, but no traces of burned bone. Other sherds, a "rubbed pebble of hard graphite," a black porphyry drill, and two side-notched, slate projectile points were found nearby. The other pit (Burial [?] W-1) contained charcoal, sometimes in dense concentrations, and a complete steatite bowl buried upside down. A side-notched porphyry spearpoint was positioned near the vessel; small quartz pebbles lay nearby. Pieces of another large, but incomplete, steatite vessel were also recovered in the pit.

17. Varying amounts of charcoal were observed in association with almost all 195 burial features in an area adjacent to the West Ferry burial ground. They were located in a 1988 archaeological survey conducted in conjunction with the proposed expansion of the Jamestown Elementary School. The charcoal concentrations, which did not extend beyond a depth of 4 inches (10 centimeters) within the features, have been interpreted by John Brown of the Narragansett Tribe as residues of fires built on the tops of graves as part of the burial ceremony (McBride, "Phase I and II Archaeological Excavations," 66). See also Desiree Zymroz, "The Titicut Site: An Alternative Perspective of Native Experiences and Actions in Seventeenth Century Southern New England" (master's thesis, University of Massachusetts, 1997), 254, for similar evidence at the Titicut cemetery in Bridgewater, Mass.

18. In the letter, Williams indicated that the Narragansetts wanted "poyson to dispatch Onkas: That we should constantly send [out?] English Souldiers with theirs agnst Onkas: That we should constantly send up Contribucion to their Niccommoes or Devilish Feast" (LaFantasie, *Correspondence of Roger Williams,* 2:489).

19. Simmons, *Cautantowwit's House,* 39.

20. Paul A. Robinson, "One Island, Two Places: The Use of Archaeological, Documentary, and Oral Sources in the Making of Traditions in Jamestown, Rhode Island" (paper presented at the annual meeting of the American Society for Ethnohistory, Kalamazoo, Mich., November 2–5, 1995).

21. Herndon and Sekatau, "Right to a Name," 434–435.

22. Handsman and Lamb Richmond, "Confronting Colonialism"; Jean M. O'Brien, "'Divorced' from the Land: Resistance and Survival of Indian Women in Eighteenth-Century New England," in *After King Philip's War: Presence and Persistence in Indian New England,* ed. Colin G. Calloway (Hanover, N.H., and London: Dartmouth College, published by University Press of New England, 1997), 144–161.

23. Ruth Herndon, personal communication, September 18, 1998. Excerpts of town records from 1750 to 1800 indicate that among the departure certificates issued to North Kingstown for nonwhite people, two were to persons identified as "Indian." These were issued to Winsor Fry and Lucy Davis, leaving East Greenwich for North Kingstown on January 30, 1790. Removal orders (to North Kingstown) were issued to a number of persons identified as "Indian," who, by implication, were the responsibility of the town. Other nonwhite persons in the records could also have been Native American.

24. Simmons (*Spirit of the New England Tribes,* 163) reports of a legend told to Gladys Tantaquidgeon by her uncle that dates to around 1900. In the legend, her uncle tells of having the same dream for three days, in which he was walking "in the old Shantup burying ground along the banks of the river" where he saw "a stand of three white birches near a flat rock." Deciding that this was the place to dig, he asked a friend to join him on a certain night. They arrived at midnight and began to dig at the spot with the three birches and the flat rock. "We began digging and not a word was said. Just as my shovel hit what seemed to be board, a large black animal ran between me and my partner. We let out a yell and ran from the place leaving our shovels behind. After a few days, we went and got the shovels, but never tried digging at midnight again."

25. The sherds were from a thin-walled vessel (or vessels) with smoothed exterior and interior surfaces, and fine shell (or possibly grit) temper. The interior surfaces were carbonized. The decorative treatment was similar to that found on other pots recovered from graves in the RI-1000 burial ground (Robert Goodby, personal communication). See also Goodby, "Style, Meaning, and History."

26. Simmons, *Spirit of the New England Tribes,* 124; but see also Michael S. Nassaney, "Archaeology and Oral History in Tandem" (paper presented at the annual meeting of the American Society for Ethnohistory, Kalamazoo, Mich., November 2–5, 1995).

27. Hezekiah Butterworth, "The Silver Pipe," in *Exercises under the Auspices of the Thalia Club, Warren, R.I.* (Providence: Massasoit Monument Association, 1893), 16, cited in Simmons, *Spirit of the New England Tribes,* 124.

28. See William A. Turnbaugh, "Post-Contact Smoking Pipe Development: The Narragansett Example," *Proceedings of the 1989 Smoking Pipe Conference Selected Papers*, Research Records no. 22 (Rochester, N.Y.: Rochester Museum and Science Center, 1992), 113–124.

29. Williams (*A Key Into the Language,* ed. Chapin, 44–45) indicated that "sometimes they make such great *pipes*, both of *wood* and *stone*, that they are two foot [61 centimeters] long, with men or beasts carved so big or massie, that a man may be hurt mortally by one of them." See also Wood, *New England's Prospect*, 81.

30. See Nicholas Thomas, *Entangled Objects: Exchange, Material Culture, and Colonialism in the Pacific* (Cambridge, Mass., and London: Harvard University, 1991), 22–23; also Annette Weiner, "Inalienable Wealth," *American Ethnologist* 12, no. 2 (1985): 210–227.

31. Williams Apess, "A Son of the Forest," in *On Our Own Ground: The Complete Writings of William Apess, a Pequot,* ed. Barry O'Connell (Amherst: University of Massachusetts Press, 1992), 63.

32. Rubertone, "Grave Remembrances," 24–45.

33. Heath, *Mourt's Relation,* 27.

34. Heath, *Mourt's Relation,* 28.

35. Heath, *Mourt's Relation,* 28.

36. Heath, *Mourt's Relation,* 34–35.

37. Morton, "New English Canaan," 36. See also James Axtell, *The European and the Indian: Essays in the Ethnohistory of Colonial North America* (New York: Oxford University Press, 1981), 118.

38. Morton, "New English Canaan," 73, cited in Apess, "Son of the Forest," 63.

39. LaFantasie, *Correspondence of Roger Williams,* 2:425.

40. LaFantasie, *Correspondence of Roger Williams,* 2:425.

41. LaFantasie, *Correspondence of Roger Williams,* 2:425.

42. LaFantasie, *Correspondence of Roger Williams,* 2:425.

43. Howard M. Chapin, ed., *Rhode Island Court Records* (Providence: n.p., 1920), 1:10.

44. LaFantasie, *Correspondence of Roger Williams,* 2:430, fn.; see also Chapin, *Rhode Island Court Records,* 9–10.

45. John Russell Bartlett, ed., *Records of the Colony of Rhode Island and Providence Plantations* (Providence: A. C. Green and Brothers, 1856), 1:319–320.

46. Usher Parsons, "Indian Relics," *Historical Magazine* 7, no. 2 (1863): 41–44; Sidney S. Rider, "Aboriginal Remains in Rhode Island and the Exhumation of Weunquesh, Daughter of Ninigret, and Queen of the Niantics," *Book Notes* 29, no. 4 (1912): 25–32; Chapin, "Indian Graves," 14–32; William Franklin Tucker, *Historical Sketch of the Town of Charlestown in Rhode Island from 1636–1876* (Westerly, R.I.: G. B. and J. H. Utter, 1877).

47. Parsons, "Indian Relics," 43.

48. Chapin, "Indian Graves," 18.

49. Parsons, "Indian Relics," 44.

50. Parsons, "Indian Relics," 44.

51. Chapin, "Indian Graves," 17.

52. Chapin, "Indian Graves," 23.

53. Chapin, "Indian Graves," 23; Tucker, *Historical Sketch.*

54. J. R. Cole, *History of Washington and Kent Counties, Rhode Island* (New York: W. W. Preston, 1889), 645.

55. Rubertone, "Grave Remembrances," 31.

56. Chapin, "Indian Graves," 14–32; Lauren Cook, "Rhode Island Burial Survey. Part 1."

57. Caulkins, *History of Norwich, Connecticut,* 37–38.

58. Caulkins, *History of Norwich, Connecticut,* 38.

59. Caulkins, *History of Norwich, Connecticut,* 38.

60. Cole, *History of Washington and Kent Counties,* 646.

61. Cole, *History of Washington and Kent Counties,* 646.

62. David Lowenthal, *The Past Is a Foreign Country* (Cambridge and New York: Cambridge University Press, 1985), 268.

63. Denison, *Westerly and Its Witnesses,* 29.

64. Denison, *Westerly and Its Witnesses,* 29.

65. For discussion of the proposal to erect monuments to Indian sachems, see *RIHS Proceedings 1874–1875* (1875), 68. For a statement regarding the erection and dedication of the Canonicus Memorial, see "Canonicus Memorial, Services of Dedication" (Providence: Providence Press Company, 1883), 3, on file at the RIHS.

66. Rhode Island, Committee of Investigation on the Narragansett Tribe of Indians, *Report,* App. B, 42.

67. Anne Hoxie, "The Royal Indian Burial," *Narragansett Dawn* 2, no. 6 (October 1936): 5.

68. See, for example, Simmons, *Spirit of the New England Tribes.*

69. Princess Red Wing, "Editorial," *Narragansett Dawn,* 20.

70. Princess Red Wing, "Editorial," 20.

71. T. D. Brown, "Discovery of Queen Esther's Grave," *Narragansett Dawn* 1, no. 6 (October 1935): 122.

72. For genealogy of the Niantic sachems, see Chapin, *Sachems of the Narragansetts,* 111. Esther Ninigret's sachemship was apparently brief, as she died during the American Revolution. Her son, George Sachem, succeeded her as sachem. (Chapin, *Sachems of the Narragansetts,* 103).

73. Chapin, *Sachems of the Narragansett,* 102–103.

74. Dr. Usher Parsons first suggested that the remains were those of a daughter of Ninigret who died twenty years before the sachem himself. The assessment was based on the richness of her burial, which indicated a person "of exalted rank," and the location of her grave within the cemetery, which indicated to him that her death was the first in the family because it was "where the interments commenced." He stated that the second grave opened was that of an individual "over seventy years," whom he identified as Ninigret I, and that Ninigret's "other children married and lived to advanced age" (Parsons, "Indian Relics," 44). Sidney S. Rider later stated that the grave was that of Weunquesh, Ninigret's daughter, who died about 1690 (Chapin, "Indian Graves," 21; Rider, "Aboriginal Remains," 25–26).

75. Brown, "Discovery of Queen Esther's Grave," 122.

76. For discussion of treasure stories in New England Indian folklore, see Simmons, *Spirit of the New England Tribes,* 162–163; 171.

77. Nathan B. Lewis, "The Last of the Narragansetts," *Proceedings of the Worcester Society of Antiquity* 21 (1897): 45.

78. From 1892 into the 1930s, several Narragansetts pressed to have a 5-rod (82.5-foot/25-meter) strip of the Rhode Island shoreline from Westerly to Pawtucket reserved for "pitching [their] tents, and fishing." These shore claims were denied by the Rhode Island State Supreme Court, and subsequent attempts to pursue the matter with the Bureau of Indian Affairs failed. In 1975, the Narragansetts filed suit in federal court for the return of land lost at the time of detribalization. The case was settled out of court and the Narragansetts recovered 1,800 acres (720 hectares) of woodland and swamp in Charlestown. See Glenn W. LaFantasie and Paul R. Campbell. "Land Controversies"; Paul A. Robinson, "A Narragansett History from 1000 B.P. to the Present," in *Enduring Traditions,* ed. Laurie Weinstein (Westport, Conn., and London: Bergin and Garvey, 1994), 79–89.

79. Michael S. Nassaney, "Archaeological and Historical Interpretations of Seventeenth Century Native American–European Relations," *Archaeological Approaches to Cultural Identity,* ed. S. J. Shennan (London: Unwin Hyman, 1989), 82.

80. See, for example, James Clifford, "Identity in Mashpee," in *Predicament of Culture,* and Cohen, "Silences of the Living, Orations of the Dead," in *Combing of History.*

81. Handsman and Lamb Richmond, "Confronting Colonialism," 90.

INDEX